D0022269

Hospice and Palliative Care

WITHDRAWN
From Toronto Public Library

Hospice and Palliative Care

The Essential Guide, Second Edition

Stephen R. Connor

National Hospice and Palliative Care Organization

Routledge
Taylor & Francis Group
New York   London

Routledge
Taylor & Francis Group
270 Madison Avenue
New York, NY 10016

Routledge
Taylor & Francis Group
2 Park Square
Milton Park, Abingdon
Oxon OX14 4RN

© 2009 by Taylor & Francis Group, LLC
Routledge is an imprint of Taylor & Francis Group, an Informa business

Printed in the United States of America on acid-free paper
10 9 8 7 6 5 4 3 2

International Standard Book Number-13: 978-0-415-99356-2 (Softcover)

Except as permitted under U.S. Copyright Law, no part of this book may be reprinted, reproduced, trans-
mitted, or utilized in any form by any electronic, mechanical, or other means, now known or hereafter
invented, including photocopying, microfilming, and recording, or in any information storage or retrieval
system, without written permission from the publishers.

Trademark Notice: Product or corporate names may be trademarks or registered trademarks, and are
used only for identification and explanation without intent to infringe.

Library of Congress Cataloging-in-Publication Data

Connor, Stephen R.
   Hospice and palliative care : the essential guide / Stephen R. Connor. -- 2nd ed.
      p. ; cm.
   Rev. ed. of: Hospice / by Stephen R. Connor. c1998.
   Includes bibliographical references and index.
   ISBN 978-0-415-99356-2 (pbk. : alk. paper) 1. Hospice care. I. Connor, Stephen R.
   Hospice. II. Title.
   [DNLM: 1. Hospice Care. 2. Palliative Care. WB 310 C752h 2009]

R726.8.C686 2009
362.17′5--dc22   2008042221

Visit the Taylor & Francis Web site at
http://www.taylorandfrancis.com

and the Routledge Web site at
http://www.routledge.com

This book is dedicated to all the volunteers
and professionals around the world who toil
daily in caring for those at life's end.

Contents

Preface

This book describes the practice of hospice and palliative care in the United States and, to a lesser extent, around the world. In the past 35 years, the hospice movement has undergone major changes and has grown enormously. What was once a small rebellion against the way dying people were cared for has become a small health care industry. Hospices have improved the way people die. Still, the majority die in institutions, alone and in distress (SUPPORT Investigators, 1995).

There is a growing interest in the subject of care at the end of life. Society's aged population is growing larger than ever, owing to postwar demographic trends and advances in medical treatment. People want to live as long as possible, but expect life to be free from the indignities of advanced age. There should be quality of life in old age, but death is still avoided. The continuing social debate on assisted suicide is a reflection of the concern over how people die.

In spite of the impressive growth of hospice and palliative care, the great majority of people still do not understand how hospices work and are just beginning to understand what palliative care is generally. It is as if hospices are on the public's blind side. People do not seem to want to know what hospice does unless they need hospice services. Professionals are beginning to embrace hospice care, but still only refer when a patient is unambiguously near death.

Whether hospices succeed in changing the way death is handled throughout society is still uncertain. Public policy currently limits reimbursement for hospice care in such a way that many of those who could benefit never get referred, and more than half of those admitted are cared for for fewer than 20 days.

It will also be up to hospices themselves to go beyond their own limitations. If hospices prefer to remain comfortable with caring only for those patients who are easy to care for, their impact will be limited. Hospices must continue to work at improving access for people of color and those with limited resources for caring.

After an initial period of slow but steady growth following the creation of the Medicare Hospice Benefit in 1983, the number of hospices in the United States leveled off at about 2,000 in the mid-1990s. However, in the past 10 years, there has been an enormous growth in both the number of hospices and the number of people they serve. There has also been substantial growth in European palliative care since the fall of Soviet Communism (Saunders & Kastenbaum, 1997), in Africa as a result of the HIV pandemic, and in the world generally as it has become clearer that palliative care is an essential part of the overall continuum of health care in any country.

There is considerable need for those coming into hospice and palliative care work and for those who are interested in end-of-life care to have an up-to-date grasp of where the field is today. This book is intended to give the reader an overall grasp of how hospice care is practiced in the United States and, to a lesser extent, around the world, the challenges palliative care currently faces, and the direction the movement is taking.

For those interested in how hospice care is organized and delivered, the first 6 chapters cover everything from history, to team functioning, to symptom management and psychospiritual care, to community education. The next 4 chapters take an honest and in-depth look at the challenges facing the hospice and palliative care community. The final 4 chapters point to the strengths of the palliative and hospice care movement and how the end of life can become not just something to endure, but also a time for life completion and growth.

In the first part, chapter 1 serves as an introduction. Hospice and palliative care are defined, and a history of the movement is outlined. The 10 characteristics common to all hospices are described. The philosophical underpinnings of hospice and palliative care are discussed. An explanation of the needs of the whole patient is given in personal spheres, which include the physical, emotional, and spiritual needs of patients. An overview of the psychosocial issues facing dying patients is given. The standards that apply to hospice and palliative care are discussed. The chapter ends with a case that illustrates how effective hospice care can be.

In chapter 2, the role and work of each clinical team member are presented. The work of the administrative support team is also framed. This chapter explains how different types of team dynamics operate (from unidisciplinary to transdisciplinary). A case example is given. Chapter 3 addresses pain and symptom management. Dying is universally associated with distress. Palliative care makes it possible to face death by relieving these symptoms. Rather than discuss stages, it is helpful to examine the different trajectories the terminally ill patient faces. These trajectories may be associated with different disease types. Pain is the most feared symptom. How pain and other common symptoms are managed through palliative care principles is presented. The concept of quality of life is discussed, along with the controversy about how it is measured. Successful hospice care depends on caregivers' involvement in care delivery. How hospice staff educate patients and families is described. This chapter ends with a case illustration of good symptom management in a difficult case.

Chapter 4 concerns psychosocial and spiritual issues. The various stage theories and their limitations are discussed. Death occurs on a number of dimensions. The loss of social identity, psychological adjustment to impending death, and spiritual issues faced by the dying are explored. Dying may involve certain psychological tasks, which are examined. The International Work Group on Death, Dying, and Bereavement (1993) has formulated assumptions and principles for psychosocial care of dying persons and their families. These principles are reviewed here. The concept of acceptance of death is evaluated and presented in a case example.

Chapter 5 is on grief and bereavement. One of hospice's unique services is to provide bereavement support and counseling to families. The routine follow-up with hospice families is described, as is that provided to the community at large. Special considerations for grieving children are given. Included is an examination of how complicated grief reactions can be distinguished from normal grief reactions and an update on current research into predicting poor outcomes. My study on hospice's impact on the use of health care resources by widowers is included, as are the current issues in bereavement research and the debate over the effectiveness of bereavement interventions. The chapter concludes with cases illustrating treatment of complicated grief.

Many hospices have extensive community education programs to increase awareness of the needs of dying patients and their families. In chapter 6, this little-discussed aspect of hospice care is highlighted. In spite of efforts by hospices, the public remains unaware of the issues faced by terminally ill persons. This is due, at least in part, to a practiced avoidance of terminal illness by the public. Hospice has found a receptive audience in school systems that are eager to help children learn about and respond to death in healthier ways. Hospice has a role in helping the community to respond to disasters and traumatic deaths. The medical community is in continual need of education about the principles of palliative care. Finally, in this chapter the use of "common concern" support groups by hospice is discussed.

Chapter 7 begins the second part of the book and discusses the unique aspects of managing a hospice. It is a business, and it is a calling. The people who work in hospices are drawn there for a variety of reasons, some noble, some problematic. Running a hospice calls for more than just business skills. There is much emphasis on creating an organizational climate where staff and volunteers are supported and empowered. The role of volunteers in hospice care is explained. Standards of the National Hospice and Palliative Care Organization (2006b) are summarized, along with difficulties in hospice accreditation. The chapter ends with specific examples of problems seen in starting and running hospices.

Chapter 8 includes a brief history of how the U.S. health care system has dealt with dying patients, the development of the Hospice Medicare Benefit, and other forms of hospice coverage. Also discussed is the problem of determining prognosis in terminally ill people, including work on the development of clinical parameters for determining prognosis in nonmalignant terminal illness. Also examined is how entry into the mainstream of health care has resulted in certain problems of inflexibility for hospices and a tendency toward overestimation of hospice's ability to manage all aspects of the dying experience. The problem of measuring the quality of care given to dying patients is discussed, along with problems in conducting research in the hospice setting that has limited acceptance by the scientific community. This lack of acceptance extends to the physician community, which has viewed palliative care as unimportant. Recent efforts to reform the health care system and their impact on hospice are mentioned, along with a discussion of the impact of the growth of for-profit hospices.

Chapter 9 examines the extensive impact of denial and avoidance on the ability of hospice to achieve its mission. Some historical perspectives on denial in American culture are given. The limitations of stage theories of denial are given, and my research into the effects of psychosocial intervention on denial is discussed. How to effectively work with hospice and palliative care patients is illustrated through case examples.

Chapter 10 includes an examination of hospice and palliative care's position on assisted suicide. Explored are the motivations for suicide requests and situations involving unbearable suffering. How hospices and society have responded to these most difficult circumstances is presented. A discussion of efforts to legalize physician-assisted suicide and its impact on hospice and palliative care is given. A case illustrating these points is presented.

Chapter 11 looks at what is unique about hospice and palliative care. Hospice is a unique blend of services that aim to work in a truly collaborative fashion. The traditional hierarchical model with the physician as the central figure is replaced by one in which the patient is central and all services have relative significance depending on patient need. Palliative care, more than any other subspecialty, seeks to empower patients and families to meet their goals. There is an emphasis on deinstitutionalization of care and prevention of distress rather than reaction to inevitable problems. Certainly, provision of spiritual care, in-depth psychosocial support, and bereavement care are unique aspects of palliative care. The people who come to work in hospice and palliative care tend to be dedicated in ways unlike other providers. There is a tendency to go beyond expectations and to see work as an expression of a higher self. Hospice and palliative care emphasis on quality of life goes beyond the notion of providing discipline-specific services. It is a community of people who are dedicated to helping each family find its way through life's most difficult transition. Chapter 11 also includes a section on growth at the end of life and a summary of the work of Ira Byock, MD, on developmental landmarks and tasks for the end of life (e.g., Byock, 1997).

Chapter 12 looks at how hospice care is evaluated. In spite of the difficulties inherent in palliative care research, there have been a number of important studies of the effectiveness of hospice and palliative care that are reviewed. I discuss how hospices can evaluate themselves both internally and externally. Work on evaluating outcomes of hospice care is summarized. Finally, there is a look at quality improvement and clinical pathway development efforts.

Chapter 13 takes a look at hospice and palliative care around the world. Palliative care is rapidly spreading throughout the globe and is shown to be an essential part of the health care continuum of any health care system.

The final chapter, on the future of hospice and palliative care, is an exploration of the nature of palliative care, who its patients ought to be, and how it fits in the health care system. Questions addressed include the following: should hospice strive to become obsolete, or will there always be a need for specialized care for the dying? How has hospital-based palliative care helped to bring care for those with life-limiting illness into the mainstream of health care? Is hospice for terminally ill patients only or for all with life-threatening illnesses? Will physicians embrace palliative care as a respected science?

This book may be particularly useful to hospice and palliative care programs that are growing and bringing in new staff and volunteers. This text gives detailed information that can greatly help orient new hospice and palliative caregivers, not only to the necessary knowledge of hospice and palliative practice but also to many of the more subtle issues and aspects of palliative care that can take staff months or years to understand.

The text may also be useful to educators who are teaching about hospice and palliative care in an undergraduate or community college setting. There are sample questions and study activities to assist teachers in applying the text to coursework.

Palliative care is of growing importance to society as our culture struggles with how to provide compassionate end-of-life care to a growing segment of the population. Many different professionals can obtain an accurate understanding of hospice and palliative care through this book.

Throughout this book are case illustrations and stories that come from actual experiences in hospice. Names have been changed to preserve confidentiality.

Acknowledgments

This book would not have been possible without the support and encouragement of Hannelore Wass, one of the grande dames of the death and dying movement. In many respects, thanks is also due to the International Work Group on Death, Dying, and Bereavement, which has been a fertile ground for pushing the envelope of knowledge about the human encounter with death.

My wife Connie, and my children Patrick, Eric, and Keara, have been incredibly patient in allowing me to work at times they would rather have had my attention. I would also like to thank the following people, who helped with their critical review or inspiration at points along the way: Don Schumacher, Galen Miller, Judi Lund-Person, John Mastrojohn, Carol Spence, Allison Petrilla, Jon Radulovic, Phil DiSorbo, Jon Keyserling, Kathy Brandt, David Casarem, Joan Teno, Dale Larson, Marcia Lattanzi-Licht, Connie Holden, Larry Beresford, Ira Byock, Neil and Marie Yates, Chris Cody, Jorelia Adams, Paul Gerard, Inge Corless, Colin Murray Parkes, Gretchen Brown, Bill Worden, Phyllis Silverman, Denny Klass, Danai Papadatou, Bob Neimeyer, Carol Wogrin, Stephen Fleming, Betty Davies, Tom Attig, and everyone in the International Work Group on Death, Dying, and Bereavement. Also my colleagues with the Worldwide Palliative Care Alliance, especially David Praill and Cynthia Goh and the other board members Sharon Baxter, Mary Callaway, Liliana DeLima, Liz Gwyther, Joan Marsten, Daniela Mousiu, Faith Mwangi-Powell, Margaret O'Connor, Anil Paleri, Lucas Radbrach, and Roberto Wenk. Finally, Dana Bliss and all the great folks at Taylor & Francis.

CHAPTER 1

What Are Hospice and Palliative Care?

What is the meaning of the word *hospice* and the word *palliative*? Many believe a hospice is a place where people die. Others simply associate the word with death and feel uncomfortable. Those who have used hospice and palliative care think of them as caregiving in the finest tradition: care that is both competent and compassionate—care provided to people facing death by people unafraid to face death.

In truth, hospice and palliative care are all of the above and much more. The word *hospice* comes from the Latin word *hospitium*, meaning hospitality, and from the old French word *hospes*, or host. Webster's defines *hospice* as a shelter or lodging for travelers, children, or the destitute, often maintained by a monastic order. Today, it is a word used to describe a program of care for individuals and their families facing a life-limiting illness. The National Hospice and Palliative Care Organization (NHPCO, 2000) describes hospice and palliative care thus:

> Hospice provides support and care for persons in the last phases of an incurable disease so that they may live as fully and as comfortably as possible. Hospice recognizes that the dying process is a part of the normal process of living and focuses on enhancing the quality of remaining life. Hospice affirms life and neither hastens nor postpones death. Hospice exists in the hope and belief that through appropriate care, and the promotion of a caring community sensitive to their needs that individuals and their families may be free to attain a degree of satisfaction in preparation for death. Hospice recognizes that human growth and development can be a lifelong process. Hospice seeks to preserve and promote the inherent potential for growth within individuals and families during the last phase of

life. Hospice offers palliative care for all individuals and their families without regard to age, gender, nationality, race, creed, sexual orientation, disability, diagnosis, availability of a primary caregiver, or ability to pay.

Hospice programs provide state-of-the-art palliative care and supportive services to individuals at the end of their lives, their family members, and significant others, 24 hours a day, seven days a week, in both the home and facility-based care settings. Physical, social, spiritual, and emotional care are provided by a clinically directed interdisciplinary team consisting of patients and their families, professionals, and volunteers during the:

1. Last stages of an illness;
2. Dying process; and
3. Bereavement period.

The National Hospice and Palliative Care Organization (NHPCO) defines palliative care as treatment that enhances comfort and improves the quality of an individual's life during the last phase of life. No specific therapy is excluded from consideration. The test of palliative care lies in the agreement between the individual, physician(s), primary caregiver, and the hospice team that the expected outcome is relief from distressing symptoms, the easing of pain, and/or enhancing the quality of life. The decision to intervene with active palliative care is based on an ability to meet stated goals rather than affect the underlying disease. An individual's needs must continue to be assessed and all treatment options explored and evaluated in the context of the individual's values and symptoms. The individual's choices and decisions regarding care are paramount and must be followed at all times (p. *iii*).

The word *palliative* to describe care for the dying was originally used by Dr. Balfour Mount at the Royal Victoria Hospital in Montreal, Quebec. The word *hospice* in French is understood to mean "home for the destitute" and was seen as an unacceptable term in francophone Quebec. The word *palliate* originates from the Greek and translates as "to cloak," meaning that when we care for the dying, our interventions are meant to cloak or to prevent seeing or experiencing pain or other distressing symptoms.

The Hospice Movement

Why is there a hospice movement? Throughout the 20th century, modern medicine has transformed the experience of dying from a part of daily life to a highly technological event. Before the widespread use of antibiotics following the Second World War, people died at a younger age and with less forewarning. Physicians could do little but visit and attend to the dying by relieving their suffering. People were less apt to be rushed to the hospital, and they convalesced at home with the help of their families.

After the Second World War, great advances were made in the science of medicine. Many pharmaceutical agents were developed to treat illness, and techniques and equipment were invented to ward off the dying process. A seemingly unconscious goal was the elimination of death. Dying patients were not acknowledged. People died in institutions, not at home. They did not die; they "expired." They had to be kept alive at all costs; to do less was a failure. The wife of one of my patients responded to a nurse, who wanted to discuss what to do when her husband "expired," by saying, "If he is expired, can I get him renewed?"

Many health care professionals were frustrated in this climate. Many family members of the dying were angry at the way that care was depersonalized. Physicians and nurses were not trained to care for the dying. Most were uncomfortable with the notion. They tended to visit dying patients less often; unrealistic optimism led to a "conspiracy of silence," where the family and medical staff knew the truth, but withheld it from the patient (Glaser & Strauss, 1965). There was a widespread belief that to tell a patient she or he was dying would cause harm and lead to premature demise. Patients were expected to follow physicians' recommendations without question. If death occurred, it was an unintended event.

In this atmosphere of denial, many caregivers were dissatisfied. There had to be a better way to treat the dying. The United States in the 1970s was a society undergoing rapid change. Most institutions were being challenged, and people were experimenting with new ways to solve old problems. Cancer patients were demanding more participation in treatment decisions, and support groups were being formed to give information and counseling. Those involved in treating dying patients began hearing about a new approach to care being used in the United Kingdom called hospice.

Brief History

It is generally held that the first hospices were established in the 11th century by the Crusaders. Until that time, incurable patients were not admitted to places of healing. Their presence was viewed as a detriment to the healing process of others. The first hospices were places where travelers to and from the Holy Land were cared for and refreshed. Travelers as well as the sick and the dying were cared for. The Knights Hospitallers of St. John of Jerusalem founded a way station in Jerusalem for sick and weary pilgrims, but were forced by the Crusades to move on to Tyre, and then to Acre, and eventually to the island of Cyprus.

The Hospitallers were recognized by the pope as a military order in 1113 and gained support carrying pilgrims to and from the Holy Land. In 1309, they stormed Rhodes and held it for two centuries. It was here that they founded a hospice hospital that cared for the sick, for travelers, and for incurables. The knights developed a special tradition of caring for "our lords the sick and dying." They were treated royally with great dignity and the finest foods, linens, and treatments the order could offer. The knights themselves, having taken a vow of poverty, dined on plainer fare and were under strict orders forbidding any mistreatment. Their spiritual foundations were nourished by their work tending to the sick and dying.

The hospice tradition of the Middle Ages passed into history. It was reborn in the 17th century through the efforts of St. Vincent de Paul, who founded the Sisters of Charity in Paris. The sisters opened a number of houses to care for orphans, the poor, the sick, and the dying. The Irish Sisters of Charity founded Our Lady's Hospice for care of the dying in Dublin. In 1900, the Irish Sisters founded a convent in London's East End. Their ministry included visiting the sick in their homes. In 1902, they founded St. Joseph's Hospice for the dying poor in London. More than 50 years later, Cicely Saunders came to work there and developed her approaches to managing pain and the total needs of dying patients. Her philosophy of using a team to treat the whole person has become the foundation for hospice care throughout the world.

Dame Saunders, who trained first as a nurse, then as a social worker, and finally as a physician, envisioned a center for excellence in care of the dying patient. This center included teaching and research facilities. In 1967, she opened St. Christopher's Hospice outside London in Sydenham. As matriarch of the worldwide hospice movement, she inspired caregivers to carry on her mission of caring for the dying.

St. Christopher's continues today to carry out its mission of caring for the neighboring communities and as a beacon for hospice development worldwide. The research and education center has continued to promote improvement in palliative care and to share knowledge of palliative care gained from 40 years of experience. Since Cicely Saunders's death, St. Christopher's has been guided by new CEO Barbara Monroe, who as leader of psychosocial services there for many years continues the tradition of sharing the best of palliative care with pioneers worldwide.

Hospice first came to North America in 1971. Hospice Inc., in New Haven, Connecticut, was founded by Florence Wald, dean of nursing at Yale, and a few others following invited lectures given by Cicely Saunders. A home care service began there in 1973. By 1980, Hospice Inc. had opened a 44-bed inpatient facility in Branford, Connecticut, exclusively for the care of dying patients. In the mid-1970s, a small but committed hospice movement had begun to take shape throughout the United States and Canada. From Marin, Monterey, and Fresno in California to Tucson, Arizona; to

Boonton, New Jersey; to Montreal, Quebec, Canada; and to St. Luke's Hospital in New York, various models of hospice care were being tested.

The National Hospice Organization was founded in 1978 and began holding annual educational conferences. The first national directory of hospices was published in 1978, and by 1980 there were 138 provider members listed. The U.S. hospice movement had a slant distinctly toward home care. Most Americans surveyed showed a preference for dying in their homes. There was a greater emphasis on use of volunteers and more focus on psychological preparation for death than in English hospices.

In the early years of the American hospice movement, reimbursement for hospice care was limited to payment for components of care such as acute hospitalization and home health agency services. In 1982, hospice care was added as a Medicare benefit. This benefit eventually encouraged tremendous growth in the number of patients served by hospices and brought some standardization to the types of services a hospice could deliver.

The most recent in-depth census data on hospices from the NHPCO revealed that in 2008 there were about 4,700 unique locations delivering hospice care. There were about 3,700 companies or organizations providing hospice care with around 1,000 satellite locations. Satellite locations are multiple locations operated by the same company. Given that there were a total of about 3,100 hospice locations in 1998, that is over 50% growth in 10 years. Approximately 93% of hospices are Medicare certified. Hospices that are not certified for Medicare payment and primarily use volunteers continue to operate and represent about 7% of programs (NHPCO, 2008).

Medicare records indicate that in 2007, a total of 48.6% of Medicare-certified hospice organizations were nonprofit entities, and 47.1% were for-profit. The remaining 4.3% were governmentally controlled (NHPCO, 2008). This is a huge sea change in the field of hospice care, which has been historically almost all charitable organizations (see chapter 8 for a discussion of the differences between proprietary and nonproprietary organizations). The great majority of growth in hospice ownership in the last 10 years has been proprietarily owned companies. The vast majority of hospices are fairly small programs with an average daily patient census of 90 (median 51.8) and an average of 580 admissions a year (median 304). There is some skewing of the group, with some very large hospices. The more accurate number is the median size for a hospice.

The greatest source of revenue for hospices is Medicare reimbursement, which accounts for 83.6% of income based on admissions. Another 5% comes from Medicaid, and 8.5% from private insurance payments (NHPCO, 2008).

The average length of service in 2007 was 67.4 days, with 13.1% of hospice patients living more than 180 days and 30.8% of patients enrolled for

7 days or less. The median is a more accurate measure of central tendency in hospice length of stay at only 20 days.

One of the most significant trends in the hospice population is the proportion of patients served who have cancer as their primary diagnosis. In the early days of hospice in the United States, well over 90% of patients served had an oncology diagnosis. In 2007, the proportion of cancer patients had dropped to 41%. This is understandable as cancer represents only 24% of U.S. deaths. The rise in noncancer hospice patients was also driven by the NHPCO's policy recommendation to members that it was discriminatory to refuse to admit noncancer patients. In 2007, 11.8% of all admissions were patients with a primary diagnosis of heart disease, 11.2% had debility (frailty and/or old age), 10% had a dementia, 7.9% had lung disease, and only 0.6% had HIV/AIDS.

Up-to-date information on hospice usage can be found at http://www.nhpco.org by searching for the "Facts and Figures" on hospice care.

Palliative Care in the United States

All hospice care is palliative; however, not all palliative care is hospice care. In the early 1990s, as hospice began to grow, it became clear that many patients with life-threatening conditions would not qualify for hospice care, due to restrictions on curative treatment, uncertain prognosis, and a resistance to the idea of acknowledging the likelihood of death. Many of these patients were dying in hospitals and other institutions without the resources to be cared for at home by hospices.

To meet this perceived unmet need, health care professionals and some hospices began to develop care programs, usually hospital based, that provided many of the same services delivered by hospices but without any requirements for prognosis or treatment limitations. An important study documenting the need for hospital-based palliative care was funded by the Robert Wood Johnson Foundation (SUPPORT Investigators, 1995). This study documented the problems associated with dying in acute care facilities, especially teaching hospitals. Study findings included the need for better pain management and for honoring the documented treatment and resuscitation preferences of patients.

By 2008, according to a Center to Advance Palliative Care (CAPC) analysis of the latest data released from the 2008 American Hospital Association (AHA) Annual Survey of Hospitals (CAPC, 2008), U.S. hospitals continue to implement palliative care programs at a rapid pace. The CAPC analysis showed that 1,299 hospitals (31%) nationwide provide palliative care programs. This was compared to just 632 programs in 2000. Most significantly, hospitals with over 50 beds—the most likely to have a program—show a penetration of 47%. Of the 4,136 hospitals appropriate for palliative care programs (psychiatric and rehab hospitals are excluded),

- 31% have a program.
- 47% with over 50 beds have a program.
- 77% with over 250 beds (large-sized hospitals) have a program.

A national palliative care research center has been created also at Mt. Sinai in New York as a partner to CAPC and is continuing to support the development of new researchers in palliative care. CAPC has many useful resources and training materials to assist the development of palliative care generally.

Characteristics

In the United States, a set of characteristics has been developed that universally describes the essential components of a hospice program. Since the mid-1970s, these 10 characteristics have been a necessary part of every hospice, and now also palliative care programs.

1. *The patient and family are the unit of care.* Hospices do not admit a patient in isolation. They see each patient as part of a family system. Often the family's needs are equal to or greater than the dying person's. *Family* means those bonded to the patient by blood or emotional ties, that is, the patient's most immediate attachment network.
2. *Care is provided in the home and in inpatient facilities.* The philosophy of palliative care is to allow people to die where they want. Most people prefer to be cared for in their homes; others need or chose to be in a facility. Hospice and palliative care should be available to patients in all settings.
3. *Symptom management is the focus of treatment.* Hospice patients understand at some level that there is no definitive cure for their illnesses. They seek relief from pain and other symptoms of terminal illness. Palliative care is directed at treating the symptoms, not curing the disease.
4. *Palliative care treats the whole person.* People are not just physical. Palliative care is designed to address physical, social, psychological, spiritual, and practical needs of patients with life-limiting illness.
5. *Services are available 24 hours a day, 7 days a week.* People die and have problems at all hours of the day and night. Services must be available 24 hours a day, 7 days a week, including weekends and at 2:00 a.m. if needed.

6. *Palliative care is interdisciplinary.* The hospice team draws on the skills of people in a variety of disciplines who work collaboratively in meeting the patients' various needs. The hospice and palliative care team includes physicians, nurses, social workers and other mental health professionals, chaplains, therapists, pharmacists, and volunteers.

7. *Palliative care is physician directed.* The patient's attending physician must determine that the patient has an incurable condition with a limited life expectancy and must order all palliative care delivered. The hospice medical director oversees the care of all hospice patients and supplements the services of the attending physician. Palliative care specialists can provide consultative services valuable to the attending physician.

8. *Volunteers are an integral part of hospice and palliative care.* Those at the end of life respond uniquely to volunteers. Volunteers work with people facing death out of human concern. Often, they have experienced death in their lives and can appreciate how hard it is for families to handle difficult situations.

9. *Palliative care is community based care and is provided without regard to ability to pay.* Hospice and palliative care services meet the needs of people with life-limiting illness within their communities and do not deny services on the basis of inability to pay. When reimbursement is exhausted, care to the patient is not diminished.

10. *Bereavement services are provided to families on the basis of need.* Hospice provides a program of bereavement support to all families for at least a year following a patient's death. Palliative care programs also need to provide bereavement services. Grief counseling is begun before a patient's death. Bereavement support may also be extended to those grieving in the community at large, and all bereavement support should be based on need and expressed desire for help.

Palliative care programs strive to provide care to a broad population of patients with life-limiting conditions and symptom problems. Admission to a hospice program is generally limited to those diagnosed with a life-threatening illness with a limited life span. For Medicare to pay for hospice care, a prognosis of 6 months or less is required, if the disease runs its normal course. To become a hospice patient means that at some level patients acknowledge that they cannot be cured of their illnesses. This is not to say that one must accept death or abandon all hope to be served by hospice. Hospices view their role as one that accompanies another on life's last journey. No one knows how long any patient has to live; one can only help them to live until death comes.

Philosophy

Many of the underpinnings of hospice and palliative care can be found in the philosophy of humanism. Any individual has the right to determine how to be treated when facing a life-threatening illness. Those who refuse to acknowledge the possibility of their death may not want the services of a hospice. They choose to continue efforts to be cured through aggressive medical intervention. Hospice patients prefer to concentrate on living as comfortably as they can and keeping the troubling symptoms of illness at bay.

The right to determine treatment has many implications for hospice care. It means that the person may choose not to die in his or her own home, may express continued ambivalence about treatment and prolongation of life, and may change his or her mind along the way. This requires hospice workers to remain flexible with patients as they travel along this last journey. In all the public opinion polls taken on Americans' desires at the end of life, a common pattern emerges. Nine out of 10 people say they prefer to be cared for and to die in their own homes, and 3 out of 4 are very interested in hospice care when it was described to them.

A philosophy of humanism requires palliative care workers to accept patients unconditionally. As hospices grow and serves a larger segment of the population as a whole, a wider variety of lifestyles are seen, including some families whose values conflict with those of hospice workers or whose lifelong history of dysfunction is difficult to tolerate. Palliative care workers learn not only to tolerate, but also to respect individual differences in the human family. Hospices still have a long way to go to fully understand different cultures and their responses to death. They will still continue to promote a reverence for the universal human experience of preparation for death.

This respectful reverence began with the Knights Hospitallers' admonitions about how to care for "our lords the sick and dying." It is a core part of hospice philosophy that to approach the human encounter with death is to face what is noblest in humanity. Even the poorest in spirit can be transformed by the experience.

One of the critical advantages to the hospice approach is that it allows an opportunity to prepare for death. If one only seeks a cure for the disease against all odds, the reality of impending death is never faced. Facing the imminent possibility of the end of life creates important opportunities. It allows people to say goodbye to the ones they love, it allows them to resolve any interpersonal conflicts that have been left incomplete, it allows a time for review of their lives to perhaps find meaning, and it allows practical preparations for death, including all the paperwork and bureaucracy of death that are so hard on survivors afterward.

Unlike those who would pit theology against humanism, hospice philosophy embraces the spiritual life. Hospices were founded by religious orders, and many who work in hospices see their work as an expression of their spiritual values; seeking to relieve suffering, to help others come closer to God while preparing for death, and to put service above self are hallmarks of the religious life.

Another philosophical underpinning of the hospice movement comes from the writings of Victor Frankl, described in *Man's Search for Meaning* (1963). As many existential philosophers have done, Frankl emphasized the essential human need to find meaning in terrible circumstances. Patients at the end of life often strive to find meaning when faced with the knowledge of impending death. Frankl's work has inspired others to further develop ways of helping patients and grieving families to cope with the need for value and meaning, including dignity therapy, developed by Harvey Chochinov (Chochinov et al., 2005); William Breitbart's meaning-centered psychotherapy (Brietbart & Heller, 2002); and the contributions to constructivist psychotherapy of Robert Neimeyer (Neimeyer & Mahoney, 1999).

Some have criticized palliative care programs for avoiding the issue of impending death, and thus opportunities for life completion because no acknowledgment of limited life expectancy is generally required to receive palliative care services. This is a false criticism in that good palliative care most certainly helps people at their own pace to come to terms with dying. The most important philosophical issue here is the critical understanding that each person's death is his or her own and that our insistence on coming to terms with death may be more about our own needs than the dying person's.

Personal Spheres

Human beings are complex organisms who operate simultaneously on a number of levels. Maslow's (1967) conceptualization of the hierarchy of needs helps one to understand the dilemma of the dying patient. One's physical needs must be tended to before one can focus on emotional needs. Spiritual needs are difficult to attend to if emotional needs are unmet.

The hospice palliative approach recognizes this paradigm of wholeness. It first focuses on the physical comfort of its patients. Control of their symptoms is paramount. A patient must have pain controlled, nausea and vomiting relieved, bowels functioning, mind alert, skin intact, and breathlessness relieved before anything else. Once there is a physical sense of well-being and the environment is safe, emotional reactions can emerge.

People have many and varied reactions to dying. Every human emotion can be evoked. The ability to express thoughts and feelings is central to recovery from trauma. Most people also need a great deal of information about their illnesses. Those who are cognitively oriented best handle difficulty with facts and forewarnings. Thoughts and feelings need expression before questions of deeper meaning can be considered.

If comfort is achieved and thoughts and feelings are worked through, some have an opportunity to find meaning before death. Some find it in their religious beliefs, and others in their philosophy of life. Life is examined and reviewed, and a sense of perspective is gained. Each person seeks to understand his or her personal reason for being. Those patients who have this awareness can use this time between living and dying to shed the distractions of daily life and find their unique meaning.

Palliative care means recognizing a person as a whole being, not just a body part. In medicine, it is not uncommon to hear patients referred to as "the lung patient" or "the liver patient." In hospice and palliative care, each person is recognized as a unique being with a life history and perspective. It is recognized that illness affects not only the body but the soul and psyche as well.

Psychosocial Aspects of Hospice and Palliative Care

One way of understanding how people react to the knowledge of impending death is to look at loss theory and how people grieve. A dying person must face many losses in the time leading up to physical death. These small deaths include the loss of being a healthy person, of being able to work, of friends, of being able to care for oneself, of a future self, and so forth. These losses vary depending on age, perspective, and which losses have already occurred during the life span.

How the dying person reacts to these losses will vary widely depending on many factors. There is no predictable road map to the grieving process. Each human being faces death in his or her own way, some with complete avoidance, others with terror, and some with anticipation. All the reactions, stages, and tasks that have been proposed in the literature are ways in which people react or cope, but these reactions and stages do not tell how one individual will respond. There is no such thing as a typical death.

When someone loses a loved one, they must react to a disequilibrium that occurs. One of the general schemas from loss theory (Bowlby, 1980) that helps us understand this is the progression from protest, to despair, to detachment, to resolution or integration. It is common for people to protest the reality of the loss in a variety of ways. When none of this protest changes anything, they may begin to despair; as they tire of despairing, they sometimes begin to detach themselves from the relationship. Gradually, people integrate the relationship into who they are and go on with life.

A different view of the grieving process discards the notion that all people must grieve or feel the pain of loss (Wortman & Silver, 1989), and a new paradigm proposes that we do not have to detach ourselves from those we've loved and lost (Klass, Silverman, & Nickman, 1996). Our relationships with those who've died continue throughout our lives in new ways.

The difficult issue for the dying person is that there is little time to go through this progression. With malignancy, there is usually a short period from the point at which there is no more treatment available to death. This is certainly less than 6 months, and it is more often weeks to a few months, sometimes only days. In some cases, attempts at curative treatment continue until the moment of death. For noncancer patients, there may be even more uncertainty and ambivalence.

There are a number of important issues that need to be kept in mind by those who work with people facing death. The first is to always remember that the person dying has to set the agenda. Hospice and palliative care workers cannot impose their ideas of how one should react or respond. They may have the idea that dying people should always say goodbye to their families. This is laudable, but in each life there are many different relationships, and not all of them can be resolved. All people die with some unfinished business.

Second, hospice workers should direct their efforts at tying up loose ends, not uncovering issues. If they are fortunate enough to be invited by the patient into a therapeutic relationship, they must realize that it is never therapeutic to open up issues that they will not be able to work through with the patient prior to death. Relationships with the dying have a unique quality. Because they know their time is limited, patients can more quickly develop a close working relationship. Transference can occur earlier and more intensely. Another way of seeing this is that people who are dying cut through superficiality and want to deal with important issues in their lives. It is tempting to go with them and to want to do in-depth psychotherapy. It is critical to be careful to work only toward resolution.

Third, it is helpful to understand that people who are dying are a reflection of society as a whole: Some are insightful, others are not; some are intelligent, others are not; some are caring, others may be insensitive or just plain mean. Hospice and palliative care programs care not just for normal folks, but also for people who have a long history of mental illness or disability. It is helpful to bring clinical knowledge of how to respond to and treat emotional problems.

It is also very important not to pathologize the dying process. Dying is not a mental illness. People facing terminal illness are under one of life's greatest stresses. They may use their less adaptive ways of coping under this stress. They may act out and be very difficult to be around. It is best to understand this and to not take it personally; working with the dying demands great tolerance and patience.

Standards

Hospices, in their early development, resisted the idea of standardization. The creation of the modern hospice has required as much creativity as it has scientific knowledge. To attempt to codify the operations of a hospice could have the unintended effect of preventing the hospice from responding to the most significant needs of dying patients and their families in a particular locale. The founders of the hospice movement tended to be leaders with tremendous personal integrity and moral character. Unselfish devotion to the needs of the dying was their primary motivation. There was not too much concern with needing to protect a vulnerable public.

As the hospice and palliative care movement has grown, there are some who view hospice's reputation for excellent care and good works with envy. The word *hospice* conjures up the best qualities of the helping profession. Just using the word helps to raise funds. The proliferation of hospices and palliative care programs in the United States and other countries has caused concerns about how to maintain some measure of quality. New programs are formed with the idea that any service to dying patients means hospice care. Older hospice programs sometimes cling to outmoded palliative care concepts and practices that deprive their patients of services and more effective symptom management.

It was inevitable that the practice of hospice care and now palliative care would need to be specified in operating standards that would help to say what hospice is and thus what it is not. A standard of practice is developed from scientific evidence demonstrating best outcomes and where such evidence is lacking, a consensus among experts about how services need to be delivered for good outcomes to occur. There are principally four types of standards in health care.

Licensing standards generally specify the minimum requirements needed to deliver services to the public. They are concerned with safety and protection of the consumer. Certification requirements are standards that must be met to receive payment for services delivered. Professional association standards are developed to further raise the level of quality of services provided and are those deemed necessary to belong to a recognized national or regional organization that represents providers. Finally, accreditation standards are developed to reflect the state of the art in services provided and are voluntarily sought by organizations wishing to hold themselves out to the public as providers who meet the highest quality of care.

The characteristics of hospice and palliative care previously mentioned were the first standards in that they all needed to be present for an organization to be considered a hospice. One of the first groups to develop guidelines for care of dying patients was the International Work Group on Death, Dying, and Bereavement. A set of *Assumptions and Principles Underlying Standards of Care for the Terminally III* was developed and finalized by this group in 1978.

This document and others were used by the NHPCO to develop the first *Standards for a Hospice Program of Care*. These standards were first developed in 1979, were revised and disseminated a number of times in the early 1980s, and were published in 1987.

In 1984, the Joint Commission on Accreditation of Hospitals (JCAHO, 1984) initiated an accreditation program for hospices. The standards for this program were developed with the hospice community under a grant from the Kellogg Foundation. For 6 years, the program accredited mostly hospital-based hospice programs. It was discontinued in 1990 by JCAHO because of cost and lack of participation by the larger hospice community.

In response to the discontinuation of JCAHO's program, NHPCO saw the need to develop more extensive standards for its members. The NHPCO's (then the National Hospice Organization, or NHO) Standards and Accreditation Committee was charged with rewriting the *Standards of a Hospice Program of Care*. These standards were published in 1993 and have continued to be revised since then. They currently represent the best in U.S. hospice care (see, e.g., NHPCO, 2006b).

Beginning in 1995, JCAHO decided to offer accreditation again to hospice programs. The hospice accreditation program is now part of Joint Commission's Home Care Accreditation Program. Joint Commission is now the new name for JCAHO. Some hospices are concerned that Joint Commission's new program attempts make them look like home health agencies and do not include adequate detail in areas central to good hospice practice. Two other organizations accredit hospices. They are the Community Health Accreditation Program (CHAP) and the Accreditation Commission on Health Care (ACHC).

Case Illustration

Mary

The following case history illustrates a hospice scenario with a well-functioning family that was able to fully benefit from hospice intervention.

Mary was a 68-year-old patient with metastatic breast cancer who was referred to hospice by her physician while in the hospital for disease recurrence. She had failed chemotherapy and was having pain problems as a result of bone metastases. She lived with her spouse of 45 years, John, who was very supportive, but had recently had a minor heart attack. They had two grown children who had families of their own, but were in the area and were very supportive. The referring physician had given them the facts of her condition, but sensed that they were having difficulty accepting her condition and prognosis.

During hospice intake, their hopes and fears about her condition were explored. Mary was very fearful about her spouse. She was afraid her condition might aggravate his heart condition. In their families of origin, each of their fathers had died before their mothers. They believed that it was abnormal for her to die before him. While exploring these issues, they were able to understand why they were having difficulty facing the reality of her condition. As we talked, it became more apparent that each knew the seriousness of her condition, but each was afraid to level with the other for fear that it would be harmful.

As this conspiracy of silence was dropped, their communication improved and they were able to make plans. Her pain was controlled by means of oral morphine and nonsteroidal anti-inflammatory medication. The relief of improved communication with her family also seemed to help lessen her pain. She came to understand that her husband was devoted to her and that his participation in caregiving would not worsen his health.

She remained stable for a few months and gradually began to weaken. During this time, the nurse visited regularly and taught her and the family what to expect as her condition worsened. The chaplain visited and helped her to explore a relationship with God that had grown distant in her later years. A home health aide was assigned to begin providing personal care. A volunteer visited weekly to become acquainted and to help with errands.

One evening 9 weeks after her admission, our on-call nurse received a call from Mary's husband that she was having pain. The nurse went to the house to assess and after talking with the physician on call increased her morphine; the next day, her regular nurse visited and found Mary to be comfortable but weaker. She was spending more time in bed now. The social worker asked for a family meeting with her children to talk about how to help care for Mary as she got sicker. A schedule was made out so John would have help in caring for her. A hospital bed was set up at home in the living room so she could be cared for in the common living area. Once a week, the volunteer agreed to be available to stay with Mary for 4 hours so John could go out during the day to shop.

As the next few weeks progressed, Mary gradually became weaker. Her children and grandchildren spent time with her, and she reminisced about their lives. Her discomfort increased but was controlled with adjustments in her medications. She began to sleep more and to talk less with her family. Her hospice nurse held a family meeting to describe again how the dying process normally progressed. She was starting to show symptoms of decreased urine output and irregular breathing. Instructions were given about how to position Mary and to relieve symptoms. John was tired, but holding up. He slept on a cot next to Mary so he could tend to her and be with her to the end.

As death approached, both children came over, and a family vigil began. On Friday night, Mary stopped eating and swallowing. Following instructions from hospice, Mary was given her morphine in concentrated form (sublingually) under her tongue. She continued to sleep most of the time. Her head up in the hospital bed, she began having periods of apnea on Sunday. At 6:00 p.m., she took her last breath with her children at the bedside. John had just left the room for a few minutes.

The hospice on-call nurse came to the house about 7:00 p.m. to help with the death. The family was sad, but feeling good about having kept her at home to the end, as she had wished. John was feeling sad that he had not been with Mary at the moment she died after having cared for her so long. The nurse told him that it was very common for people to die when their spouse was not there. It was almost as if they could not leave while in the presence of the one they were most close to. This was a relief for John.

The on-call nurse arranged for the funeral home to pick up the body and helped everyone to talk about what had happened. The funeral had been planned and was arranged for the following Wednesday. The hospice chaplain had been asked to officiate. The hospice nurse and social worker came to pay respects. Mary had helped plan the event, including picking one of her favorite readings.

A few weeks passed. Family and friends began to call less often. John began to feel lonely. He did not want to burden others with the many conflicting feelings he had. About a month after Mary's death, a hospice bereavement volunteer called to introduce himself. He had a long talk with John about the events surrounding Mary's death. They agreed to get together in a few weeks. Over the next 15 months, they talked and met 8 times to revisit the events surrounding Mary's life and death. John received information about grief every other month from the hospice. He came to the hospice's grief support group and met another widower about his age. They became friends and reminisced about their wives. He knew the anniversary of Mary's death would be hard. He planned a family gathering with the children and grandchildren. They all talked about Mary and how much they missed her. They had dinner and enjoyed each other's company. Mary lived on in their lives.

This chapter gave a general overview of hospice and palliative care. In the next chapter, the interdisciplinary team, the foundation of hospice practice, is described in detail.

Recommended Reading

Beresford, L. (1993). *The hospice handbook: A complete guide.* Boston: Little, Brown.

Byock, I. (1997). *Dying well.* New York: Putnam.

Clark, D. (2002). *Cicely Saunders: Selected writings 1959–1999.* Oxford: Oxford University Press.

Corr, C., Nabe, C., & Corr, D. (2008). *Death and dying: Life and living* (6th ed.). New York: Springer.

DeSpelder, L., & Strickland, A. (2004). *The last dance: Encountering death and dying* (7th ed.). New York: McGraw-Hill.

Jaffe, C., & Ehrlich, C. (1997). *All kinds of love: Experiencing hospice.* Amityville, NY: Baywood.

Lattanzi-Licht, M., Mahoney, J. J., & Miller, G. W. (1998). *The hospice choice: In pursuit of a peaceful death.* New York: Firestone, Simon & Schuster.

National Hospice and Palliative Care Organization. (2006). *Standards of practice for a hospice program.* Alexandria, VA: Author.

Saunders, C., & Kastenbaum, R. (1997). *Hospice care on the international scene.* New York: Springer.

Stoddard, S. (1992). *The hospice movement: A better way of caring for the dying* (Rev. ed.). New York: Vintage.

Web Resources

Caring Connections: http://www.caringinfo.org

Center to Advance Palliative Care: http://www.capc.org

Growth House: http://www.growthhouse.org

National Hospice and Palliative Care Organization: http://www.nhpco.org

National Palliative Care Research Center: http://www.npcrc.org

CHAPTER **2**

The Interdisciplinary Team

If they don't have scars, they haven't worked on a team.

—**Balfour Mount**

The Team Concept

Hospice care and palliative care are delivered by interdisciplinary teams. For this chapter, we will usually use the term *palliative care* to mean both hospice and palliative care. Unlike most health care settings where there is a hierarchical structure, palliative care considers all team members' input to have equal value. For a given patient and family, one team member may develop the closest relationship; it may be the home health aide, the chaplain, the physician, the social worker, the psychologist, the nurse, or the volunteer in whom the patient confides the most. Each patient and family served is a unique collection of life histories that combine to face death in different ways; to understand how best to treat each patient–family unit requires many different perspectives.

Unidisciplinary to Transdisciplinary Teams

To understand teams, let us explore the evolution of team dynamics as originally described by Larson (1993). First, there is the unidisciplinary team. This is a team made up of individuals who are all of the same discipline (imagine a setting where there are all social workers or engineers). In this instance, there is a collection of individuals, and everyone performs the same function. There is little team dynamic in that each is responsible for the same activity. There may be advice and consultation, but not much team interaction.

The second team concept is the multidisciplinary team. In this instance, there are people of different disciplines who work together toward a common purpose, but each has a distinct area of responsibility and works independently. Most health care settings function in this way. The interaction is usually hierarchical in that the most important discipline takes the lead. In health care, physicians take the top rung and are usually in charge and determine how care is to be delivered.

In home health care, it is the physician who orders all care and technically directs the care, even though it is usually the nurses who set everything up for the physician to approve. There is little interaction among the disciplines, and the job of each is clearly defined. Many palliative care programs operate on a de facto multidisciplinary model.

The preferred model for palliative care is the interdisciplinary model. In this approach, hierarchy is less important. There is interaction among the disciplines. Each adds to the picture of the whole patient. An interdisciplinary team values the input of all members. There are boundaries as to what each member is expected to do and focus on, but there is some blurring of boundaries. The nurse pays attention to psychosocial concerns, and the social worker attends to how symptoms may be affecting the person's ability to meet emotional needs. The home health aide may be the one the patient wants to pray with, and the chaplain may hear about the family's financial concerns (Connor, Egan, Kwilosz, Larson, & Reese, 2002).

All of this is part of the flux of how families face death. Palliative care may do its best work when it avoids being rigid and attends to the needs of the moment. This is not to say that it is OK to violate law or regulation or to go outside one's area of expertise. It would not work for the social worker to try to change a patient's medication dosage or for the nurse to try to do in-depth psychotherapy. Some boundaries are necessary for the safety of the patient and family.

We then move toward the area of the transdisciplinary team, in which there is no hierarchical structure, each team member acts for the patient by accessing whatever the patient and family need at the time, and each member is part of a whole, be they volunteer, physician, or housekeeper. The following essay from the Hospice of the Western Reserve shows how this model can work at its best.

Case Example: Transdisciplinary Team Philosophy—a Conscious Evolving Culture

Hospice of the Western Reserve (HWR) is an independent not-for-profit community-based organization that serves five counties in

Northeast Ohio. It operates out of eight satellite facilities in addition to its headquarters campus in Cleveland, which includes Hospice House, an inpatient-residential 42-bed facility that overlooks Lake Erie. HWR's service area has a population of 2.2 million and 21,000 deaths per year. The organization's 2003 budget was $56 million, its daily census is 1,000, and it has 575 paid staff and 800 volunteer staff.

HWR's team and organizational philosophy are rooted in and informed by a profound foundational insight proffered by Dame Cicely Saunders. That is the concept of "total pain" (Clark, 1999). This definition incorporates physical, psychological, social, emotional, and spiritual elements of pain. From that perspective, it is clear that no one discipline or professional domain is adequate on its own to assure comfort from pain, freedom from distressing symptoms, and relief of suffering. The understanding of total pain leads directly to the appreciation of the team. Only a comprehensive team approach can effectively address the array of pain issues that patients experience.

In addition, at HWR there is a dynamic and robust "transdisciplinary" team culture. This approach to team deemphasizes lines that tend to separate various disciplines and instead affirms the common ground that various team members share. Moreover, it recognizes that like a hologram, each part or team member carries the entire team. Every team member may at some time need to be attuned to spiritual and existential aspects of suffering, to the impact that family dynamics may have on a patient's capacity to achieve comfort, or to a cultural belief about sickness and of course physical pain. No team member may ignore the expectation to be an active listener and observer. No team member may use the specialization of a particular profession or discipline by responding to a presented problem with "It's not my job."

It is not surprising that we associate the idea of the transdisciplinary team with the person who gave us the paradigm of total pain, herself a nurse, social worker, and physician.

In addition to the team being the optimal approach to total pain, this philosophy also serves the organization well by reducing or eliminating two unhealthy dynamics that sometimes emerge in "nonteam," department-based organizations. These are *territorialism* and *blame*. Territorialism supports separateness by demanding that people stay out of a particular area. Such intrusion may even be interpreted as a threat. Blame arises when something goes wrong and each department strives to document how it did the right thing by following procedures and protocols. The transdisciplinary team culture diminishes these dynamics. In the transdisciplinary team model, the totality is the responsibility of all. When something goes wrong, there is an emphasis on finding a solution rather than assigning blame and finding a culprit.

There are several concrete ways in which the transdisciplinary team philosophy manifests itself at HWR. These have evolved over nearly 20 years. Here are some examples:

- All clinical team members (nursing assistants, physicians, nurses, social workers, etc.) are encouraged and expected to expand their particular area of expertise in order to more holistically serve patients and families.
- Staff members are not organized and the program is not managed through a discipline-based structure, nor do we have a "matrix" organization. Instead, team leaders are empowered to hire, manage, evaluate, direct, and if necessary terminate team members. Although most clinical team leaders have been nurses, this is not a requirement. In this model, the team leader's hiring responsibility includes selecting staff from disciplines other than their own. Thus, there is no director of nursing, director of social services, and so on.
- Support staff, financial services staff, community outreach, marketing, housekeeping, maintenance, development, public relations, and other components of the organization are also designated as teams. There is a conscious cultural avoidance of the word *department*. There is a development team, a human resources team, a financial services team, and so on.
- Management is also imbued with a transdisciplinary culture. The management team is composed of all directors and team leaders in addition to the eight staff who report directly to the CEO. All management decisions are made through this group (now more than 30 people). All policies are vetted through this group. The role of each management team member extends to the entire organization. Management meetings are not comparable to what some organizations call department head meetings, which tend to be primarily information-sharing sessions. Each participant is expected to think globally and not parochially about his or her team or area of expertise. Each member is expected to understand the relationship of mission and resources. Resources are defined to include people, equipment, supplies, funds, information, space, time, and talent. It is as appropriate, expected, and matter of course for a clinical team member to inquire about, offer opinions on, and make recommendations concerning financial services, development, or other areas as it is for a facility services or development team member to participate in the creation of clinical policies and programs. This attitude supports the probability that the best ideas emerge, and ultimately it fosters broader ownership

of all decisions. This approach to management also tends to flatten organizational hierarchy.

- Office space configuration also embodies the transdisciplinary concept. Where possible, team leaders are not separated from their team members. Modular units in open space are utilized wherever possible. There is no segregation of disciplines in team rooms. The staff area at Hospice House, our inpatient-residential facility, is not referred to as a nurse's station. It is a team station since it is a place used by many disciplines in addition to nursing.
- The notion is also extended to volunteers. We speak of staff as either compensated or uncompensated. They are all equally employed and equally team members. We consciously avoid the reference "staff and volunteers," since they are indeed all staff.

Several years ago, all occurrences of the terms *interdisciplinary* or *multidisciplinary* in policy and procedure manuals were replaced with *transdisciplinary*.

The COO, CFO, director of planning and evaluation, and CEO share a common office space. This models team and fosters rich informal communication and conversation. This was implemented in April 2001 on a trial basis when individual office space was abandoned in favor of this arrangement. It has been adopted as an effective approach in a transdisciplinary team culture.

Developing an organizational culture requires thoughtful adherence to core beliefs and values as well as the creation of structures and practices that reflect them and are harmonious with them. We believe that we have been achieving such harmony. We have also learned that such an endeavor is progressive and evolutionary. What we now know and have achieved during the past two decades will be the foundation for the next phases of our organization. We look ahead with open minds.

Note: The transdisciplinary concept was introduced to us at the first Management and Leadership Conference hosted by NHPCO (then the National Hospice Organization, or NHO) in 1985 in St. Paul, Minnesota. It was articulated by Dr. Dale Larson, to whom we are indebted for his insight and grateful for his sharing.

Nurses

Nurses could be thought of as the backbone of palliative care. This is meant in the true anatomical sense: They keep all parts of palliative care moving. Nurses often function as case managers in palliative care. In this, they are responsible for making sure all disciplines and activities are moving in the right direction. Without nurses, there would be no effective symptom management, there would be no coordination of care, there would be little education and preparation for patients and families—there really would be no patient care!

Nursing is the principal means of delivering patient care in palliative care. Without nurses, there would be no palliative care. So what is it that palliative care nurses do? The principal activities of palliative care nursing can be described as educating, treating, and managing.

The largest single activity that palliative care nurses perform is education. In palliative care, caregivers are encouraged and empowered to do as much as possible for the patient and often more than they thought possible. Palliative care nurses show families and caregivers how to provide hands-on patient care. They provide a road map for them on what to expect as the disease progresses and what to do. This removes fear and uncertainty and allows those caring to stay involved up until death. After death, those who were able to provide care have a lower mortality rate and lower health care utilization post death (Christakis & Iwashyna, 2003; Connor, 1996a). Hands-on contact with the dying person alleviates feelings of guilt and makes the experience of the patient's death more visceral and real.

Examples of educational interventions include teaching about:

- Administration of medications orally, rectally, or parenterally
- Management of the following:
  - Bleeding
  - Catheter care
  - Colostomy irrigation
  - Management of constipation
  - Management of dehydration
  - Diarrhea
  - Elevated temperature
  - Enteral feedings
  - Infection control
  - Mouth care
  - Pain management
  - Nausea
  - Oral and nasopharyngeal suction
  - Oxygen therapy and safety
  - Relaxation
  - Respiratory care
  - Seizure precautions
  - Safety
  - Signs and symptoms of approaching death
  - Skin care
  - Tracheostomy care

Palliative care nurses treat patients. Treatments for patients with life-limiting conditions vary widely but are generally focused on relieving distressing symptoms. All treatments are based on accurate assessment. Good hospice care nurses have learned to do in-depth assessments of patients' needs. Examples of palliative care nursing procedures, in addition to the above, include changing dressings, administering medication, collecting specimens, and performing enemas, colostomy irrigation, tube insertions, impaction removal, equipment management, and postmortem care.

Hospice nurses are case managers. They are responsible for making sure that all disciplines are involved in and meeting the patient's needs. They are responsible for developing the largest part of the care plan. They are the link to the patient's primary care physician, seeing that all orders for care are obtained. The palliative care nurse works with the social worker to make sure all psychological and social concerns are addressed. She or he works with the chaplain to see that all spiritual concerns are being responded to. The nurse supervises the home health aide providing personal care and hears from the volunteer about support needs.

Hospice nurses see that the durable medical equipment the patient needs is ordered and delivered. They bring out or order all medical supplies needed, including eggcrate mattresses, adult diapers, dressings, catheters, and so forth. When medications are needed, they arrange for them to be provided. If the patient needs hospitalization for respite or symptom management, the nurses arrange for transportation and admission, prepare a transfer summary, and give a report to the facility. They visit the patient when he or she is hospitalized and continue the palliative plan of care during the inpatient stay.

Each weekday evening and all weekends and holidays, a nurse is on call to give after-hour medical advice and to make home visits as necessary. Any palliative care patient and family that have a question or problem can reach a hospice nurse to discuss it 24 hours a day. Most problems can be resolved over the phone, but a substantial number require a nurse to visit. These visits can be for a leaky catheter, a patient near death or who has just died, a suddenly agitated patient, or a patient who is having a seizure or pain that is out of control. It does not matter that it may be 2:00 a.m.; palliative care nurses know that when the need arises, they must respond.

Social Workers

Facing death has a profound psychological impact on the family. The person dying gradually confronts the loss of everything. Good palliative care is distinguished by recognition of the psychological and social needs of patients and their families. Hospice and palliative care workers in the United States have responded to these needs mainly through provision of social work services. The social worker is the primary provider of emotional support for the patient and family. He or she functions as both counselor and practical guide to the dying process.

On the practical side, social workers help arrange for community resources that may help everyone cope better. For example, if Meals on Wheels or help from a food bank is needed, they arrange for it. If insurance coverage is confusing, they straighten it out. If the phone is disconnected, they are the patient's advocate to see that it gets turned back on. If respite is needed, a volunteer or short inpatient stay is arranged. When it's time to leave the hospital, the social worker helps to do the discharge planning. Social workers help patients and families to face the difficult decisions about discontinuation of treatment and life support, funeral planning, and estate planning.

On the counseling side, the social worker can go as far as the patient and family wish. Some families are severely disrupted and require in-the-home family therapy. Most everyone needs to ventilate feelings that often are unacceptable to express. The social worker is an outsider who can share the burden. A nonthreatening way for the patient to help begin to deal with his or her impending loss is to do life review. The social worker can help the patient to do an oral history of his or her life, which includes important milestones in the family, values or beliefs to impart, instructions for survivors, and genealogical information. The process of doing this often helps the patient to gain perspective on life and to find meaning. It also helps identify any unfinished business the patient may want to attend to before death—such as things that need to be said to others, like "Thank you," "I'm sorry," or "I love you."

Providing counseling or emotional support can be done by any of the palliative care disciplines, and in some programs counselors, psychologists, marriage and family counselors, psychiatric nurses, or others may provide these services. The advantage of using social workers is that they can provide the needed case and resource management services along with psychological services. In effect, you get two services for the price of one. Social work has become a vital and core part of the palliative care team.

Physicians

The physician member of the palliative care team is most often the patient's attending physician. As a team member, he or she helps formulate and approve the patient's plan of care. The physician approves all orders and helps to achieve symptom management. Along with the palliative care medical director, the physician is responsible for determining the patient's prognosis.

The relationship of the patient's physician to the palliative care team varies greatly. Some physicians work in a very collaborative fashion, and others resist input and insist on controlling all aspects of care. The degree of cooperation depends on the physician's practice patterns and on his or her experience using palliative care services. If the doctor adopts a unidisciplinary approach to practice, there is little room for collaboration. Most physicians being trained today have learned to appreciate the multidisciplinary approach, and some even understand interdisciplinary care; few understand transdiscipliary care.

If the physician's experience with palliative care has been positive, he or she is more likely to refer and to trust palliative care staff input. If palliative care workers demonstrate professionalism and their recommendations result in better patient care, most physicians can be won over. Because physicans are responsible for any order they approve, they must have a high level of trust to sign off. As this trust level builds, they appreciate that palliative care can shoulder much of the burdens of caring for a dying patient.

After approving a patient's entry into hospice or palliative care, the attending physician may not see the patient as often. The palliative care staff becomes the physician's eyes and ears. They report any change in condition and give periodic updates. The palliative care plan of care is reviewed and approved periodically. If there is an unresolved problem or symptom, the patient is sent in for an office appointment or sometimes directly admitted to the hospital for more extensive assessment and treatment. All efforts and diagnostics are aimed at symptom relief.

The medical director works in concert with the attending physician. In most cases, the medical director does not take over the patient's care. Exceptions to this are when the attending physician asks for palliative care to provide all physician services, when there is no other physician to direct the patient's care, or when the patient requests the palliative care program to provide attending physician services.

Hospice and palliative care programs prefer to work with other community physicians in caring for their patients. If the program took over all the physician care, this could threaten the medical community, and there would be little opportunity to educate community physicians about palliative care.

The medical director usually serves as a consultant to the medical community. If there is a problem with the way care is being managed, the medical director can intercede for the palliative care staff to help correct the situation. Most attending physicians will not make home visits, and palliative care patients often cannot travel comfortably. The medical director can see the patient at home and give treatment recommendations to the attending physician.

The primary role of the medical director is to oversee the medical care of all palliative care patients and the palliative care staff's provision of clinical care. This includes providing education for palliative care staff and being a resource at all interdisciplinary team meetings. The medical director's role extends into review of all clinical policies, procedures, and protocols. There is even a role as part of the marketing efforts. Community physicians should know that the medical director is involved in the supervision of palliative care staff and will ensure that the highest quality of care is delivered. If the specialist hospice and palliative medicine physician is respected by the local medical community, they will encourage physicians to use palliative care to care for their dying patients.

Hospice and palliative medicine has now been accepted as a recognized subspecialization by the American Board of Medical Specialties. Many specialties including internal medicine and family medicine have included hospice and palliative care as a subspecialization. Having the training required to qualify as a hospice and palliative medicine subspecialist is a good indication to both the medical community and the public that the physician is competent to provide quality palliative care.

Home Health Aides

Home health aides play a critical role in palliative care. The aide is especially valued by the patient's family. Of all the disciplines in palliative care, aides provide probably the most tangible assistance. It is the aide's job to provide personal care to the patient. This includes bathing, feeding, and grooming patients who are too weak or ill to care for themselves.

The family also does personal care, but the aide helps lift some of this burden from them. Often, it is uncomfortable for grown children to provide care that is personal and intimate to a parent. Elderly spouses also are often debilitated and stressed and appreciate the aide's assistance.

In addition to personal care, the aide can assist with some nursing functions under the nurse's supervision. Aides give enemas to constipated patients, replace simple dressings, do range-of-motion exercises, assist with transferring the patient, give suppositories, give massage, provide skin care, and provide reassurance and emotional support. They report changes in condition to the nurse and reinforce education.

In hospice care, the aide can also assist with some homemaker chore services. If needed, the aide can help with laundry, light housekeeping, cooking, and errands. Aides become almost a part of the family if they are able to be involved very long. For some patients, the personal and physical nature of the aide's work allows them to share some of their most intimate thoughts and feelings. The best palliative care aides are those who are able to share more of themselves than their labor.

Chaplains

Providing for the spiritual needs of dying patients has long been one of the facets of palliative care that has set it apart from other health care providers. Facing death inherently means facing issues of meaning and transcendence. People strive to understand what their lives have meant and what comes next after life. They agonize over past transgressions and seek forgiveness. They may seek to solidify their faith and to be more acceptable to God. They may hope to find a faith that has eluded them throughout life or to embrace a philosophical or existential position that is an expression of their being.

Whatever the struggle, spiritual support staff is there to help walk with the patient or family. Palliative care has always framed this as more than a question of religion. Certainly palliative care is available to help with religious services. If the patient wants to pray or get in contact with a priest, minister, imam, or rabbi for religious services, it is taken care of. What distinguishes palliative care is its willingness to broaden this opportunity to include any spiritual concern. Palliative care, then, is nondenominational in its approach to questions of meaning and the transcendent. Palliative or hospice care programs may use a Baptist minister or a Catholic sister to respond to spiritual needs, but they all respond to the person and set aside their denominational role.

Chaplain services vary considerably among different palliative care programs. Some programs have no one on staff but assign someone, often a social worker, to coordinate with community clergy. Others have a cadre of staff chaplains of a variety of faiths. Each palliative care patient and family must have their need for spiritual support assessed by someone who is competent to evaluate. This assessment needs to address not only history of religious affiliations but also the presence of common spiritual concerns such as guilt, fear of death, anger at God, estrangement, and fundamentally how they see themselves in relation to a higher power (if at all). The palliative care program must be capable of responding to any spiritual need identified in the assessment.

One of the difficult issues faced by chaplains is providing service without being intrusive. Many times, patients are unaware that they are dealing with a spiritual problem or that there is potential for spiritual growth as death nears. If the chaplain is too aggressive in presenting this to the patient, it is easy to turn the patient off. Certainly, one does not want to force any religious discussion on a patient when not wanted. The worst outcome would be if the patient were made to feel bad as a result of the intervention. Proselytizing is not condoned in palliative care. The chaplain meets the patient where he or she is and tries to offer the patient support and opportunities. If the patient chooses to take advantage of what the chaplain has to offer and invites the chaplain into his or her spiritual life, then the care provided is richer.

Families also struggle with spiritual concerns. Many are angry at God for taking their loved one. Others are faced for the first time with their own mortality and need to sort out their spiritual beliefs. Facing death offers the patient and family an opportunity to bring their spiritual or philosophical issues into focus.

Counselors

The role of counseling in palliative care needs to be highlighted even though it is not the exclusive responsibility of any one discipline. In fact, all disciplines have a role in counseling the patient and family. By *counseling*, I mean the provision of education and emotional support. It is the giving of guidance or advice through an exchange of opinions and ideas. There are many misconceptions about terminal illness and death. Facing death is a frightening prospect for most patients and families. Usually, the more information they have, the better they are able to cope. Palliative care workers accept as a major charge the provision of education. Families who are prepared for the symptoms surrounding death feel more in control and confident in their caregiving.

Often, however, more is needed than education and support. Palliative care workers may need to plan interventions that help patients and families to overcome problems or maladaptive coping. These interventions can be as simple as a relaxation exercise or as complex as having the whole team apply different psychological support strategies for each individual family member. Current mental health treatment offers many different tools that can help palliative care workers in doing short-term counseling and intervention. For example, solutions therapy can help families focus on how they have overcome other obstacles and draw on their adaptive resources.

Psychologists and psychiatrists have usually played an ancillary role in hospice care and are more often utilized in palliative care programs. Since the social worker can meet most counseling needs and because hospice is obligated to pay for all counseling services related to the terminal condition, not many psychologists are part of core hospice teams. However, they can be most useful in case consultations, especially for families with complex dynamics or preexisting mental health conditions. Psychiatrists can bill for care as consulting physicians under hospice, and psychologists can sometimes bill separately from hospice for preexisting or unrelated mental health treatment (Connor, Lycan, & Schumacher, 2006).

Various forms of family therapy are often used in palliative care programs to help families cope. Palliative care psychosocial assessments often include a genogram, which usually shows a three-generational description of a family including births, deaths, divorces, or other family allegiances and rivalries. How people handle death in a family is often colored by multigenerational factors. For an in-depth account of family therapy for families facing terminal illness, see *Families Facing Death* (Rosen, 1990).

Discussion of patient care, symptom management, and the dying process is likely to arouse strong feelings that also need expression. Palliative care workers provide emotional support during the process of preparing the patient and family for death. They have to be sensitive to how much the family can absorb without becoming overwhelmed. The last thing anyone wants is for the patient or family to be forced to deal with painful facts they are unprepared for and then to receive no help with their emotional responses.

Lack of preparation and follow-up is not an uncommon scenario in the health care system. What distinguishes palliative care is sensitivity to these issues. Good palliative care practice always involves meeting the patient and family where they are in their readiness to hear information. Palliative care workers never want to beat people over the head with information. They would not want to be accused of being full of doom and gloom. Rather, palliative care workers want families to eagerly anticipate their visits. Some families make it clear that they never want to discuss dying. Others are eager for any and all information about the process.

The ability to understand where the patient and family are in their desire for education and support is crucial to good palliative care. Palliative care workers must be very adept at this assessment and empathetic to the emotional state of the patient and family.

The role of counseling is most often associated with the team's social worker. Social workers are responsible for assessing the family system, including levels of emotional distress and coping styles. They have much information to impart and are often the ones to address painful issues such as treatment wishes, advance directives, and funeral planning. Nurses also play a prominent role in counseling. It is the nurse who does the teaching of physical care and signs and symptoms of approaching death. Nurses view counseling as a major intervention, and many nursing diagnoses include correcting knowledge deficits. As an extension of the nurse, the home health aide is often called on to provide emotional support as the patient or family processes the information and emotions surrounding death.

Palliative care chaplains, of course, mainly provide counseling around the spiritual aspects of facing death. Sometimes other team members are also called on to provide spiritual support. The aide or nurse may be asked to pray with the patient, or the volunteer may discuss spiritual pain. Bereavement follow-up is provided for at least a year after the death of the patient. A bereavement counselor is available to coordinate all bereavement efforts. Some of this counseling may be provided by volunteers. The staff usually do initial bereavement visits right after the patient's death, including attendance at funerals, wakes, and so forth. This allows them to say goodbye to the family. For difficult bereavement reactions, the bereavement counselor is available, and the program must have access to mental health professionals who can respond in situations where complicated or prolonged grief is present. Whatever the need, palliative care workers must be prepared to face many of life's most difficult questions.

Volunteers

In the United States, hospice and palliative care were founded by volunteers. All those who labored to create the first hospice and palliative care programs did so on a voluntary basis. Initially there were no reimbursements or funding sources. All who labored to start palliative care did so because they believed that care of the dying had to be improved and that palliative care was the way to do it.

Many social movements started by volunteers changed when funding became available. Services were provided by professionals, and the volunteers were brushed aside. This has happened to some degree in hospice care in that volunteers have stopped functioning in most professional roles. However, the role of the volunteer in U.S. hospice care remains an essential one. The use of volunteers in palliative care adds a major dimension to the way care is perceived by patients and families.

Paid caregivers are greatly valued, but they are in the role of employees. Volunteers are there to help because they choose to give service selflessly. Patients and families who accept the help of volunteers experience this as a higher level of human activity. Volunteers are often people who have learned from their loss experiences and choose to give back something to others. Volunteers help transform palliative care into a community service rather than just a health care provider.

Volunteers are used in many roles in hospice care. The primary role is in serving patients and families. Patient care volunteers usually provide support in the form of practical assistance. They help by sitting with the patient while the family goes out and being a substitute primary caregiver. They can do just about anything to help, including errands, homemaker assistance, babysitting, massage, transport, and so forth. They always are a source of emotional support to all. Some hospice care programs use volunteers in professional roles, and some are still run entirely by volunteers.

Volunteers usually spend a block of time at least once a week at the patient's home. They can spend a great deal of time helping and often have the time to really get to know the family. Some programs use volunteers to sit with the patient in the hospital or home as death approaches if the family is not available. Inpatient volunteers assist the staff with many patient care tasks and may provide hands-on care or emotional support. Many times people will share things with their volunteer that they might not share with others because the volunteer is seen as nonthreatening.

Lay volunteers are usually taught how to handle basic patient care needs such as how to safely transfer or toilet the patient, how to give assistance when other staff are rendering care, and how to identify problems that need to be reported to the medical staff. They receive training in communication and principles of palliative care. A volunteer coordinator is usually on the staff to coordinate the efforts of volunteers. The coordinator attends team meetings, receives volunteer requests, makes assignments, and supervises and trains the volunteers.

Volunteers are used in many other ways in hospice care. Ongoing bereavement support for most families can be provided by volunteers who call, visit with, and send written materials to bereaved families during the year after the death. They also help provide office assistance in hospice care and help with fundraising and other community projects. Volunteers continue to be an essential part of the palliative care team and are one of the components of care that distinguishes palliative care from other forms of care.

Therapists

Although not usually part of the palliative care core team, there are a number of other disciplines that round out the group. The most prominent of the therapies are those provided by physical, occupational, speech, respiratory, music, art (expressive), and massage therapists. The first four specialists are usually available on contract to the hospice program, and in hospital-based palliative care they are usually available as part of the inpatient team. Because these services are often focused on rehabilitation and because palliative care patients are declining, they may not be used frequently. However, the role of rehabilitation in palliative care can be important and can help with restoration or maintenance of important abilities to function even as the end of life approaches.

Physical Therapist

The physical therapist is the most commonly used therapist in palliative care. Physical therapists help patients who have difficulty ambulating or transferring. They help teach patients and families how best to move the patient and try to help maintain muscle strength through range-of-motion exercises. Patients with basic needs can be taught by the nurse. Patients with complex problems or fractures can benefit from physical therapist help in using special equipment if they are likely to live for some time.

Occupational, Speech, Respiratory, and Enterostomal Therapists

Occupational therapy can help debilitated patients continue to function longer. When used in palliative care, occupational therapists teach the patient and family to use special devices so the patient can continue to eat and provide personal care longer. The speech therapist is used in palliative care to assist patients who have trouble communicating. A patient who has a brain tumor or lesion and who has lost speech or has other aphasic symptoms can use a speech therapist to regain some ability to communicate with family. The respiratory therapist administers breathing treatments to patients who have difficulty breathing. In addition, an enterostomal therapist can be very helpful in solving problems with stomas and is an expert in skin care management.

Expressive Therapists

The art, music, play, movement, and/or expressive therapists most often work with children. They help them to express feelings that they may be unable to verbalize. This may also help create an environment for the dying person that is conducive to growth.

Massage Therapists, Pet Therapists, and Aromatherapists

Massage therapy services have grown popular in many palliative care programs. In some programs, there is a group of massage therapy volunteers who are available to work on the patient's or family members' aches and pains. Massage therapy has been shown to reduce pain in hospice patient populations (Wilke et al., 2000). It offers an adjunct that many patients enjoy and that adds to their quality of life. In some programs, there are volunteers who use pets for therapy. Animals are brought around to visit the patients, as they can have a beneficial effect. Aromatherapy is more common in the United Kingdom. The use of herbs and the use of smell can have a very beneficial effect on quality of life.

The Patient and Family

The patient and family are a critical part of the palliative care team. Patients can play a significant role in their own care if they are taught how at an early enough point in their illness. The patient is also the only one who can really establish the goals of care. Palliative care workers can empower the patient to guide them in all they do.

In most cases, family members actually deliver most of the care given to a dying patient. They are the ones who are there with the patient day and night while hospice workers come and go. They are usually eager to learn all they can about how to deliver care. They may need care as much as or more than the patient in order to give care. They benefit in many ways by being involved in care delivery and are really the ones who deserve the credit when things go well.

One of the really unique things about palliative care is the extent to which families are allowed to be involved in the caregiving process. Nearly anything the patient needs, the family can be taught to do. With palliative care, families are able to do more than they thought possible in caring for their loved one, and involvement in hands-on provision of care can help the family cope better during bereavement.

The Administrative Team

The administrative team is often overlooked as a critical part of palliative care delivery. The office team supports the clinical staff in the areas of medical records maintenance, supply ordering and stocking, billing services, accounts receivable and payable, marketing, physician relations, public relations, secretarial services, computer operations and training, and sometimes scheduling and intake. Without the administrative team, palliative care could not be delivered. Someone has to be there to answer the phone, to page the nurse when a crisis occurs, to keep the records straight, to bill for services so everyone gets their paychecks, to prepare the paychecks, to make sure supplies are there when needed, to help order the equipment, and so on. Care works best if the office staff members are seen as part of the palliative care team.

Some programs use functional unit management processes or self-directed work processes in which operations staff are assigned to a team or service and are accountable to that group rather than to an office supervisor. However the program is organized, it is important for office staff to realize that the clinical staff is their customer and to strive to improve their services. Clinical staff who see the office support staff as part of the palliative care delivery process and who value the services provided find that everything runs more smoothly.

Teamwork

Now that the individual disciplines in palliative care have been described, it is helpful to explore how they work together to provide interdisciplinary or transdisciplinary care. After a patient has been screened for palliative care eligibility, an admission–assessment visit is usually done. Some programs have a nurse and/or social worker do the admission assessments. Assessments are done after explaining all services and obtaining informed consent.

The nurse does a complete physical assessment, including all bodily systems, activities of daily living, and a thorough pain assessment. The social worker usually does the psychosocial and sometimes spiritual assessments. These assessments lead to the creation of an interdisciplinary team care plan that guides the activities of all team members.

The interdisciplinary team plan could, for example, include goals for controlling pain, educating family, meeting the patient's personal care needs, addressing family anxiety and patient depression, and helping resolve the patient's alienation from his or her faith community. The palliative care nurse might visit daily until pain control is achieved. The nurse could assign a home health aide to bathe the patient at home a number of times per week and also help do the laundry.

Simultaneously, the social worker could call a family meeting to help arrange a schedule for staying with the patient. The nurse would come to the meeting to help answer questions about care and disease progression and to lessen family anxiety. The social worker would also visit privately with the patient to learn more about emotional symptoms. With the patient's permission, the palliative care chaplain contacts the patient's minister to arrange home visits.

Team collaboration often occurs in office hallways or in weekly team meetings where everyone shares their perceptions of the patient. If the patient seems most concerned with getting symptoms controlled, the nurse takes the lead. If fear of dying is causing the most distress, the chaplain may take the lead. All team members focus on the areas of greatest concern.

These, then, are the components of the palliative care caregiving team. The next chapter reviews how the palliative care team successfully manages the distressing physical symptoms of terminal illness.

Recommended Reading

Chang, R. Y. (1994). *Success through teamwork: A practical guide to international team dynamics*. Irvine, CA: Chang Associates.

Drinka, T., & Clark, P. (2000). *Health care teamwork: Interdisciplinary practice and teaching*. Westport, Conn: Greenwood.

Katzenbaum, J. R., & Smith, D. K. (1993). *The wisdom of teams: Creating the high performance organization*. Boston: Harvard Business School Press.

Larson, D. (1993). *The helper's journey: Working with people facing grief, loss, and life threatening illness*. Champaign, IL: Research Press.

Parker, G. M. (1996). *Team players and teamwork: The new competitive business strategy*. San Francisco: Jossey-Bass.

Robbins, H., & Finley, M. (1995). *Why teams don't work: What went wrong and how to make it right*. Princeton, NJ: Peterson's Guides.

Sanborn, M. (1995). *Teambuilt: Making teamwork work*. New York: Mastermedia.

Sayer, C., & Connolly C. (1996). *How teamwork works: The dynamics of effective team development.* New York: McGraw-Hill.

Towery, T. L. (1995). *The wisdom of wolves: Nature's way to organizational success.* Valparaison, Indiana: Wessex House.

Wellins, R. S., Byham, W. C., & Wilson, J. M. (1991). *Empowered teams: Creating self directed work groups that improve quality, productivity and participation.* San Francisco: Jossey-Bass.

West, M. (2004). *Effective teamwork: Lessons from organizational research.* Malden, MA: Blackwell.

Whyte, D. (1996). *The heart aroused: Poetry and preservation of the soul.* New York: Bantam Doubleday Dell.

CHAPTER 3

Symptom Management and Physical Care

Total pain is suffering that encompasses all of a person's physical, psychological, spiritual and practical struggles.

—Dame Cicely Saunders

If you ask people who are terminally ill what they fear most, it usually is dying, not death itself. In our culture, terminal illness is equated with suffering. To face death is to confront the knowledge that one may have to endure unimaginable distress. Perhaps this is why in some cultures, it is thought preferable to withhold the truth from those found to be incurably ill.

Unfortunately, in the United States and most of the rest of the world, dying can still be an agonizing process. Either there is no knowledge of palliative medicine or there are too few resources to provide adequate care— or both. Ours is a world where to face death usually means to experience unrelieved symptoms, indignity, and the loss of all that is meaningful. It is not so surprising that some people seek out assisted suicide.

A seminal report (SUPPORT Investigators, 1995) on efforts to improve care for seriously ill hospitalized patients reveals some troubling findings. One half of the patients who died had moderate or severe pain during their final 3 days of life. Only 41% of patients reported talking to their physicians about prognosis or cardiopulmonary resuscitation (CPR). Physicians misunderstood patient preferences regarding CPR in 80% of cases. When patients wanted CPR withheld, a do-not-resuscitate order was never written in 50% of cases.

If the hospice and palliative care movement has taught us anything, it is that dying does not have to be this way. The great majority of hospice patients are free of physical pain in the time leading up to their deaths. A study by the National Hospice and Palliative Care Organization (NHPCO) looked at how well pain was controlled in the last 30 days of life for hospice patients. Readings were taken from patients' reports at each nursing visit by means of a scale ranging from 0 to 10, with 0 equaling *no pain* and 10 equaling *the worst imaginable pain*. Mean scores were summed for each patient, and those means were then averaged to derive a global mean pain level for each hospice. The overall mean for the 11 hospices participating was 1.67. This meant that, overall, these hospices kept their patients' pain well controlled up to the time of death (NHPCO, 1995).

In a more sophisticated analysis of pain among hospice patients the National Hospice Outcomes Study, funded by the Robert Wood Johnson Foundation, pain outcomes were analyzed at the episode level (NHPCO, manuscript in preparation). Pain assessment data for 835 patients where at least two pain assessments were available were analyzed to determine how often pain control was achieved. For patients with pain, 82% of the pain episodes resulted in control, and in 18% of the episodes, pain was not controlled. Increased length of service was correlated with improved pain control.

Hospices also understand that suffering encompasses a broader sphere than pain alone. Eric Cassell (1982), in his classic article "The Nature of Suffering and the Goals of Medicine," showed that suffering can occur in different dimensions of the person. Physical distress may cause suffering or may be viewed as redemptive or as leading to a goal, as in childbirth. Cassell argued that "suffering occurs when an impending destruction of the person is perceived; it continues until the threat of disintegration has passed or until the integrity of the person can be restored in some other manner" (p. 640).

Hospices attempt to help patients deal with as many of the different dimensions of suffering as possible. If the patient is experiencing spiritual pain, increasing the morphine dose will not solve the problem; intervention by the chaplain may be necessary. If the patient develops neuropathic pain, supportive counseling will be less effective than adding a coanalgesic. Care of dying patients requires very careful assessment.

Trajectories of Dying

Most cancer patients follow a fairly predictable downhill course as the disease progresses. There are increasing symptoms, and functional ability decreases. The enormous expansion of hospice care to people with different disease categories has taught hospice and palliative care workers that there are very different pathways of illness progression and decline depending on diagnosis. Lunney, Lynn, Foley, Lipson, and Guralnik (2003) proposed that there are four major disease trajectories leading to death: the sudden death (nonpalliative care) scenario, the cancer trajectory, the solid organ failure trajectory, and finally the dementia and frailty trajectory. While the cancer trajectory is more predictable, the solid organ failure trajectory (e.g., chronic obstructive pulmonary disease [COPD], congestive heart failure [CHF], or liver or kidney failure) is much more unpredictable with periods of relative stability punctuated by exacerbations of severe illness. The dementia and frailty trajectory is noted for low levels of functional ability with a slow but steady decline.

Hospice and palliative care may modify some of these trajectories, particularly the solid organ failure and dementia and frailty ones, by reducing the severity of some of the exacerbations of illness (Figure 3.1) and improving the performance status of some patients.

While the cancer trajectory has been seen as relatively predictable, medical oncology is undergoing significant changes. Though the absolute number of cancer deaths continues to increase, the overall cancer death rate has recently declined and there are now many new treatments available. There have been significant improvements in the prognoses for people with Hodgkin's disease, testicular and breast cancer, and some leukemias.

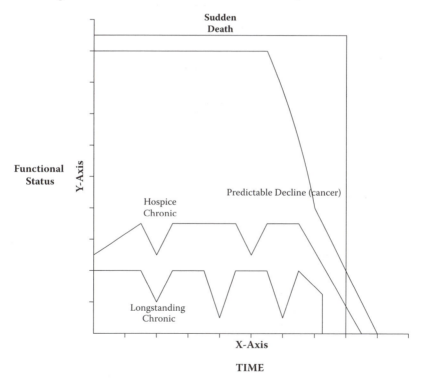

Figure 3.1 Trajectories of Death and Decline

Some patients with prostate cancer can look forward to such slow disease progression that they will likely die of conditions other than their cancer.

With many chronic, life-threatening illnesses such as COPD and CHF, there are often periods of exacerbation followed by periods of stability. A patient with congestive heart failure may have many life-threatening episodes requiring hospitalization. While the person is an inpatient, medical intervention can stabilize symptoms to the point where the patient returns home. This cycle can repeat for years until the patient's body simply gives out or until the patient decides to let the disease run its natural course without aggressive intervention.

It is often the decision about how to treat the patient that determines if the patient is at a "terminal" stage. For many people with these chronic conditions, how exacerbations are treated determines when they are terminal. For the patient with chronic obstructive pulmonary disease, it may be the decision to forgo ventilator treatment; for the Alzheimer's patient, it may be the point when a decision is reached to not treat generalized infection. For the cancer patient, it may be when the burden of experiencing aggressive chemotherapeutic side effects outweighs the possible benefit of prolonging life.

In palliative care, there is more attention to the prevention of these exacerbations of illness through close monitoring. For hospice patients, we may see fewer of these exacerbations and they may be less severe (Figure 3.1).

The provision of palliative care itself may alter the patient's prognosis. In a study of patients matched based on disease severity prior to death, hospice patients were found to have an average of 29 days of increased survival compared to nonhospice patients (Connor, Pyenson, Fitch, & Spence, 2007). While palliative care may not be proven to improve survival, the notion that patients die earlier because they utilize hospice or palliative care seems unfounded. It may be that some palliative care patients simply avoid many of the hazards of overexposure to the health care system and excessive treatment.

For hospice care, the issue of being terminally ill is relevant; however, for palliative care generally, the decision to forgo treatment is not necessary. Palliative care is provided for anyone with a life-threatening illness without regard to treatment choices. Ideally, patients will get appropriate palliative care from diagnosis to death, and referral to hospice should be made at the appropriate point. In addition, attention to good management of pain and other symptoms should be a routine part of health care in general. It's just good health care.

However, once this turning point is reached, the focus of care can shift to the goal of comfort. The aim is not to fight for cure of the disease but to simply live as fully as possible for as long as possible. To reach this goal, the patient must be relieved of distress. In the Maslovian (Maslow, 1967) view, the patient must first be free from physical pain and other symptoms such as nausea, constipation, confusion, and shortness of breath. This has to be accomplished before any psychological, emotional, social, or transcendent issues can be attended to and resolved. In this hierarchy, pain is usually attended to first.

Pain Management

It is not within the scope of this work to undertake a thorough explanation of pain management. There are several excellent references and resources for the reader who wishes to delve more deeply into the subject (see the list of recommended readings at the end of the chapter). Some of the key distinguishing factors that make the hospice approach more effective are reviewed here. Treatment of pain requires a well-developed knowledge of assessment.

The International Association for the Study of Pain defined pain as "an unpleasant sensory and emotional experience associated with actual or potential tissue damage" (Foley, 1985, p. 25). Pain is always subjective; there is no way to distinguish pain occurring in the absence of tissue damage from pain resulting from tissue damage. Pain is what the patient says is pain. Caregivers must always be alert to the reality that pain is multidimensional. In addition to physical pain, there is the potential for enormous psychological, social, and spiritual pain.

The first distinction in assessment of physical pain is between chronic and acute pain. Acute pain is associated with a well-defined onset due to an external insult or internal event, and results in hyperactivity of the autonomic nervous system. Chronic pain has a less well-defined temporal onset and persists for longer than 6 months. The autonomic nervous system adapts, and there are fewer objective signs. Rather, there are significant changes in personality, functional ability, and lifestyle that require treating not only the pain but also its complications.

Hospice and palliative care patients are generally faced with chronic pain from their illnesses. There are periods when hospice patients are faced with acute pain episodes related to their primary diagnosis or its treatment, but the vast majority of pain problems are chronic in nature. Many patients with noncancer life-limiting illnesses do experience pain, and it is critical to good palliative care for all patients to be assessed and treated for pain. The incidence of pain in HIV/AIDS increases as the disease progresses. We most often associate malignant disease with pain syndromes. Pain associated with cancer is primarily one of two types: nociceptive or neuropathic.

Two common forms of nociceptive pain are somatic or visceral pain and occur as a result of activation of nociceptors in cutaneous and deep tissues. This pain is usually well localized and constant, and is often described as aching or gnawing. Painful bone metastasis is an example of somatic pain.

Visceral pain results from stretching or distending the viscera, usually as a result of metastatic tumor. This is also a common cancer pain, is not well localized, and is often described as squeezing or pressure pain. Metastatic infiltration of the liver is an example of visceral pain.

The other major type of cancer pain is neuropathic pain, which is the result of injury to the peripheral or central nervous systems, or to both. This is due to tumor compression or infiltration of the nerves. It can also occur as a result of surgery, chemotherapy, or radiation (Foley, 1985). Neuropathic pain can be quite severe and is often described as a constant dull ache punctuated with episodes of burning or electrical shock-like sensations. Examples of neuropathic pain include metastatic or treatment-induced lumbosacral or brachial plexopathies.

In addition to physical pain, clinicians should be alert to the possibility that experienced pain can be of psychogenic orgin.

Proper control of pain requires an accurate assessment of the type of pain the patient experiences. Most somatic and visceral pain responds to narcotic and nonnarcotic agents. Neuropathic pain is often poorly tolerated and difficult to control. Many patients have more than one type of pain. It is critical for staff to assess each pain source carefully. Palliative care uses a variety of pharmacologic and psychological approaches to the management of pain.

There are several important palliative care principles that hospices apply in the treatment of chronic pain. First, for constant pain, medication must be given around the clock. If the drug is immediate-release morphine, it must be given about every 4 hours. It is more common today to use long-acting narcotics whose duration of action is 8–24 hours. This allows for less frequent dosing and avoidance of sleep interruption. Regular around-the-clock dosing is critical to controlling pain. Many patients are still put on an as-needed (*pro re nata*, or PRN) dosing of medication. This creates a vicious cycle of yo-yoing back and forth between pain relief and the return of pain. Regular use of pain medication stops this cycle and eliminates the patient's memory and fear of pain.

A second principle is to give or titrate the proper amount of medication. Some clinicians fear giving large doses of narcotics. They are usually afraid of overdosing the patient. Palliative care has yet to find a ceiling to how much opioid medication can be safely given. The art is to give enough to control the pain without causing sedation or unwanted side effects. When starting out, it is best to give enough to make sure the pain is controlled. Good pain control is not achieved by sneaking up on the pain. It is often necessary to give a significant dose increase to get on top of the pain. Once this is accomplished, the dose can be adjusted on the basis of feedback from the patient.

Another cardinal rule in controlling pain is that, as mentioned above, pain is what the patient says is pain. The only one who can accurately measure pain and pain relief is the patient. Studies of surrogate measurement of pain find that medical staff and family do not give accurate ratings of pain when compared with the patient's own ratings (Grossman, Sheidler, Swedeen, Mucenski, & Piantadosi, 1991; Teske, Dant, & Cleeland, 1983). Continuous titration of the patient's medication dosage is critical to the control of pain. Hospice and palliative care nurses often use a pain measurement scale, such as a simple 0–10 scale, with 0 being *pain free* and 10 being *the worst imaginable pain*. Most patients want to be pain free, but some are quite content with keeping the pain at 3 or below on this scale. It is best to establish the patient's goals for pain relief.

When titrating pain medication, the focus is usually on breakthrough pain. This is the pain experienced before the next dose of medication is due. When using a long-acting opioid, there is usually a short-acting agent available as a supplement. When the use of the short-acting analgesic reaches a large enough dose, the dose of the long-acting drug is increased.

Pharmacologic treatment is often divided, using the World Health Organization (1990) three-step analgesic ladder, into mild, moderate, and severe pain. Newer research (Maltoni et al., 2005) is suggesting that a two-step approach may be better passing directly from step one to step three. Mild pain is treated with nonopioids with or without an adjuvant. Moderate pain is treated with an opioid for mild to moderate pain, and with a nonopioid analgesic with or without an adjuvant. Severe pain is treated with an opioid for moderate to severe pain, with or without nonopioid and adjuvant treatment.

Other Symptoms

Other symptoms that can often accompany terminal illness include nausea and vomiting, dyspnea, diarrhea and constipation, anorexia, and confusion. (For a more thorough discussion of symptom management in terminally ill persons, refer to the list of recommended readings at the end of the chapter.)

Nausea and Vomiting

Nausea and vomiting occur in 60% of terminal cancer patients at some stage but tend to be intermittent (Kaye, 1993). Nausea can have numerous causes, and careful assessment is imperative. According to Kaye, the most common causes are as follows:

- Drug side effects
- Oral thrush
- Brain metastases
- Anxiety

- Gastric irritation
- Intestinal obstruction
- Constipation
- Small stomach syndrome
- Hypercalcemia
- Uremia
- Low grade urinary tract or pulmonary infection

Nausea usually has more than one cause and can become a conditioned response. Many different drugs can cause nausea, and it is a good idea to avoid polypharmacy. Using the right antiemetic by the appropriate route is critical. The oral route is best for prophylaxis, whereas suppositories or injections are usually needed during the first 24 hours. A continuous subcutaneous infusion may be useful for severe nausea and vomiting.

Other recommendations include the use of more than one antiemetic, the use of steroids or an H_2 receptor antagonist, a change of opioid drug, behavioral treatment, and, in rare instances, a celiac plexus block. Vomiting with little or no nausea can occur with high intestinal obstruction, regurgitation, or raised intracranial pressure. Some patients can tolerate occasional vomiting if nausea is controlled.

Dyspnea

Pang (1994) found that the incidence of dyspnea in advanced malignancies varied from 48% to 78.6% of patients. Breathlessness is a frequent part of the dying process and can usually be managed with palliative measures. Shortness of breath during the course of illness can be due to multiple causes, including:

- Anemia
- Ascites
- Bronchiospasm
- Cardiac failure
- Lung collapse
- Lung infection
- Pericardial effusion
- Pleural effusion
- Pneumothorax
- Pulmonary emboli
- Superior vena cava obstruction

Treatment varies, depending on the etiology of the dyspnea and condition of the patient. If the patient is far from the end stage, it may make sense to treat anemia with transfusion or a lung infection with an antibiotic, whereas in end-stage or chronic breathlessness, the more conservative palliative measures would include the use of morphine and ativan with relaxation therapy, reassurance, and oxygen or possibly an electric fan.

There is disagreement over the effectiveness of oxygen in terminal dyspnea. A review of the best research for the Cochrane Collaborative found a failure to demonstrate beneficial effects for oxygen breathing over air breathing in cancer or cardiac failure (Cranston, Crockett, & Currow, 2008). Oxygen use in COPD has shown short-term benefits, but studies on this question are limited.

Diarrhea and Constipation

Although these are thought of as opposites, they are often connected and are part of a continuum of gastrointestinal disturbances. Constipation is a very frequent complaint of terminally ill persons, often as a side effect of narcotic use. Kaye (1993) reported that in a study of 200 hospice patients, 75% needed rectal measures (enema or bowel protocol) within a week of admission. Other frequent causes of constipation are as follows:

- Low-fiber diet
- Failure to heed the urge or reduced defecation
- Dehydration
- Depression
- Hypercalcemia

In addition to opioids, diuretics and anticholinergics can cause constipation.

The most frequent cause of constipation in terminal patients is the regular use of opioids without the concurrent use of adequate doses of laxatives and stool softeners. Even patients with little intake should not go more than 3 days without a bowel movement. Laxative treatment should include both a fecal softener and a mild stimulant laxative. Bulk-forming laxatives can be contraindicated as they may lead to impaction. Patients with impaction will need an enema or manual disimpaction.

Diarrhea is found in patients with impaction as small amounts of liquid feces leak past the fecal mass. Other causes of diarrhea include the following:

- Steatorrhea (due to malabsorption of fat)
- Malignant intestinal obstruction
- Laxative imbalance
- Rectal tumor
- Fecal incontinence due to loss of sphincter control or a rectovaginal fistula
- Carcinoid tumor

Anorexia

Loss of appetite occurs in the majority of palliative patients as illness progresses. It is a normal consequence of disease progression and not due to poor eating habits on the patient's part, as many families seem to think. Factors contributing to anorexia include the following:

- Oral thrush
- Constipation
- Nausea
- Hypercalcemia
- Chemotherapy
- Depression

Treatment of anorexia includes administration of steroids to increase appetite, attention to attractive meal preparation, and patient–family education. Generally, patients are more likely to eat if they are presented with small, more frequent meals or snacks. Attention to presentation can include the use of garnish, care to avoid strong odors, concentration on bland foods, and a bit of detective work in an effort to serve meals that the patient prefers.

Education of the family is very important. They can feel rejection as the patient refuses to eat. They need to understand that taste abnormalities are common in seriously ill people, that the body needs less intake when inactive, and that they can continue to give the patient whatever he or she wants, especially fluids, up until the end.

Confusion

Various changes in mental status are common in terminally ill persons. Confusion is found in about 30% of cancer patients at some point in their illness. The causes of confusion include the following:

- Drugs
- Full bladder
- Pain
- Impaction
- Brain metastases
- Infection
- Metabolic imbalance
- Anxiety
- Withdrawal from alcohol or benzodiazepines
- Delirium

Most psychoactive medication can cause confusion, usually because of deterioration in liver or kidney functioning. Many other medications can cause confusion, including diuretics, beta blockers, anti-Parkinsonian drugs, and sulfonamides. As death approaches, it is not uncommon for patients to experience delirium as part of the end-stage process.

One of the most difficult symptoms to manage is severe agitated confusion. In this state, the patient may become aggressive, paranoid, terrified, or greatly distressed. Immediate sedation may be needed. Families have a very hard time managing patients who are up all night trying to get out of bed without pharmaceutical intervention.

Symptom management is important to the patient's quality of life. Without good symptom management, it is difficult to have quality of life. However, having good symptom management does not ensure quality of life.

Management of Impending Death

Effective management of the symptoms found at the end stage of the illness is critical to achieving a good death. For cancer and most other chronic diseases, there is a symptom complex as death nears that has a number of distinguishing characteristics.

This cluster of symptoms usually includes lowered body temperature, increased somnolence, confusion, incontinence, congestion in the lungs or throat, restlessness, withdrawal or detachment from others, visionlike experiences, decreased intake of fluid and foods, decreased urine output, and changes in breathing.

Common interventions that help manage the symptoms of impending death are shown in Table 3.1.

Education and Caregiving

Good physical care for a dying patient is very important to comfort. Having the right medication and psychosocial support is not enough if one is lying all day in wet sheets because there is no one there to change the bed. Hospices do not usually provide around-the-clock caregivers. Family, friends, or paid caregivers must be identified to deliver this basic care to the patient under the hospice's supervision.

Some hospices offer private-duty caregivers that the patient must pay for to provide care around the clock. There are many private duty services available in most communities. Under the Hospice Medicare Benefit, there is also provision for continuous care during periods of crisis where hospice can send in a combination of nurses and nurse aides for 8–24 hours in a day. Still, the bulk of care must be provided by non-hospice caregivers.

Table 3.1 Signs and Symptoms of Approaching Death

Symptom	Intervention
Coolness	Warm the patient, but not with an electric blanket.
Somnolence	A normal reaction; sit with the patient.
Confusion	Speak softly, clearly, and truthfully.
Incontinence	Catheter, chucks, or adult diapers.
Congestion in lungs or throat	Position head to the side; clear mouth or airway. Medication or suction may be used if necessary.
Restlessness	Light massage, quiet voice, and/or soothing music.
Withdrawal or detachment from others	Give space; encourage interpersonal communication to the extent comfortable to the person; assess for depression.
Visionlike experiences	Do not discount; ask for details. Try to understand symbolic meanings. Offer reassurance if troubled.
Decreased intake of fluid and foods	Give supplements as tolerated. Pay attention to presentation of food and fluids. Maintain good mouth care. Use ice chips.
Decreased urine output	Monitor intake and output. Consider a Foley catheter. Usually a sign that death is nearing.
Changes in breathing	Irregular breathing, periods of apnea, Cheyne-Stokes respiration, and wet respirations. Elevate the head; turn patient on side. Hold hand. Speak gently.

The primary caregiver is often a spouse or other family member. This person usually has little experience in caring for a seriously ill person. Home hospices have developed training materials to familiarize people with how to provide basic safe care. The hospice nurse or aide always demonstrates how to perform a procedure and usually gives written instruction for reference.

The kinds of procedures typically taught to hospice families include the following:

- Medication administration
- Catheter care

- How to handle bleeding
- Dressing changes
- Colostomy care
- Constipation
- Signs and symptoms of approaching death
- Dehydration
- Diarrhea
- Elevated temperature
- Infection control
- Durable medical equipment operation
- Hospital bed change
- Body mechanics to avoid injury
- IV therapy
- Mouth care
- Nausea
- Oral and nasopharyngeal suction
- Oxygen safety
- Relaxation
- Seizure precautions
- Skin care
- Pericare
- Tracheostomy care
- Pain control

The type of teaching needed will depend on the needs of the patient. The more that caregivers know about the needs of the patient, the better they are able to cope. Hospice staff has to be able to assess how much a caregiver can be expected to do. Some are able to learn right away, whereas others are too emotionally upset to learn. Sometimes, the relationship precludes doing care. Many children have a difficult time with the thought of doing personal care for a parent.

Empowering caregivers to do more than they thought they could in caring for the patient is healthy. Spousal involvement in caregiving may powerfully mediate the somatic effects of grief (Christakis & Iwashyna, 2003; Connor, 1996a). There is much anecdotal experience in hospice that suggests that patients live longer if they receive competent and consistent care from a primary caregiver.

Case Illustration

John

John was a 56-year-old non-small cell lung cancer patient with metastatic disease to the bone who was admitted to hospice while in the hospital. He had been treated unsuccessfully with chemotherapy and wanted to return home. On admission, he was still nauseated from chemotherapy and was too weak to get out of bed without assistance. He had residual movement pain from bone metastases.

He had difficulty breathing and was on oxygen in the hospital. At hospice admission, his medications included Percocet (10 mg as needed), Tigan (250 mg 3 times a day), and IV fluids. He had not had a bowel movement in 3 days, and he rated his pain as 5 on the 0–10 scale.

He lived with his wife and two teenage sons; an older daughter lived nearby. His wife worked as a sales clerk, and up until his diagnosis 5 months earlier he had worked as a car mechanic. He was generally angry and impatient with the indignities of being in the health care system.

He was transferred to the hospice unit to prepare for discharge home. On transfer, his medications were changed to MS-Contin (30 mg twice daily), Naprosyn (500 mg twice daily), Compazine (5 mg three times daily), and Senekot-S. He was given an enema and disempacted. Hospice nurses began teaching him and his family about care in the home and what to expect.

After 24 hours, he reported that his pain was at 1 on the 0–10 scale and that his nausea was controlled. He was able to get up out of bed and had less shortness of breath. He had resisted getting up due to movement pain, and he now reported only very mild pain when ambulating. His IV was removed, and he was able to eat a diet as tolerated.

Plans for his discharge were made, and he went home with his family. Before discharge, a hospital bed and an oxygen tank were delivered. He no longer needed continuous oxygen as the morphine relieved his respiratory distress; the tank was there for reassurance and for occasional use should he become short of breath. He was sent home with a supply of medication, and once there was visited by his hospice home care nurse. She assessed the home and made sure he and his family felt prepared to handle his care.

A home health aide was assigned to come the next day to help John with his personal care. The social worker and chaplain had visits scheduled during the week. On Thursday night, John's wife called the hospice on-call service because John was having an episode of anxiety. He was short of breath and could not get comfortable. The nurse on call got an order from the patient's physician for 2 mg of Ativan to be given twice daily. The order was called into the pharmacy and was picked up by the nurse on her way to visit the home. Within an hour of taking the Ativan, John felt more comfortable. The nurse also instructed the patient in the use of a relaxation exercise to control anxiety.

John's care went smoothly for another 3 weeks until he began to develop more pain. He was started on an oral morphine solution (5 mg per cc) for breakthrough pain. His oral morphine solution dose gradually increased until his MS-Contin dose was moved to 60 mg twice daily. At first, he needed no oral morphine solution, but gradually he began to have breakthrough pain. As his pain increased, the long-acting and immediate-release doses of morphine were adjusted to stay on top of his pain.

John gradually got weaker and was confined to bed. As death approached, he began to have trouble swallowing. His MS-Contin dose was put into small gelatin capsules, and his family was taught how to give them rectally. He was able to take liquids and ice chips. He died peacefully at home with his wife and three children at his side. The hospice nurse came to the house and called the funeral home. She complimented the family on the care they were able to give John, and they talked about how life would be without him. She reminded them of the bereavement support services available for the next year, and the funeral home arrived to take John's body.

Once the physical symptoms of terminal illness are under control, it is possible to begin to deal with psychological and spiritual concerns. In the next chapter, some of the more common psychosocial and spiritual concerns of the dying are addressed.

Recommended Reading

Ferrell, B., & Coyle, N. (Eds). (2005). *Textbook of palliative nursing*. New York: Oxford University Press.

Hanks, G., Portenoy, R., Christakis, N., Cherny, N., Kaasa, N., & Fallon, M. (Eds.). (2009). *Oxford textbook of palliative medicine* (4th ed.). New York: Oxford University Press.

Kaye, P. (1994). *A–Z pocketbook of symptom control*. Essex, CT: PCM Books.

Kinzbrunner, B. (2001). *Twenty common problems: End of life care*. New York: McGraw-Hill Professional.

Walsh, D., Caracini, A., Fainsinger, R., Foley, K., Glare, P., Goh, C., et al. (Eds). (2009). *Palliative medicine: Expert consult online and print*. Philadelphia: Mosby Elsevier.

Woodruff, R. (1996). *Palliative medicine: Symptomatic and supportive care for patients with advanced cancer and AIDS*. Melbourne: Asperula.

Web Resources

American Pain Society: http://www.ampainsoc.org

Fast Facts (end-of-life/palliative education resource center): http://www.eperc.mcw.edu

International Association for the Study of Pain: http://www.iasp.org

PC-FACS (fast article critical summaries for palliative care clinicians): http://www.aahpm.org/membership/pcfacs.html

Stop Pain (Beth Israel Medical Center): http://www.stoppain.org

CHAPTER 4

Psychosocial and Spiritual Care

The more complete one's life is, the more … one's creative capacities
are fulfilled, the less one fears death.… People are not afraid of death
per se, but of the incompleteness of their lives.

—Lisl Marburg Goodman

The knowledge of impending death has profound psychological and social
impact on human beings. Humans are believed to be the only animals who
know their own mortality. In an attempt to understand how humans cope
with this knowledge, some have attempted to develop theories that give a
road map for how to prepare for death.

The psychological and spiritual aspects of coping with impending death
are intertwined. It is an arena where psychology and religion overlap. How
people cope emotionally is affected by their spiritual belief system, and
their capacity for spiritual growth is influenced by psychological health.

Reactions to the Knowledge of Imminent Death

Death defines life. It gives people's lives meaning and context, yet nothing
is as feared or as assiduously avoided. There are probably as many reactions
to dying as there are people who die. It is intriguing how individuals faced
with comparable tragedies can respond so differently. One person may be
incapacitated with anxiety and dread; another reacts with stoic resignation. Once, a patient said he felt that "death was a big present with a bow
on it." He couldn't wait to find out what was inside.

Weisman (1972) originated the concept of "appropriate death." He
described this as a purposeful death. Appropriate death should be pain

free, with emotional and social impoverishments kept to a minimum. The person should be able to function as effectively as possible as long as possible before dying. Conflicts should be recognized and resolved, and remaining wishes should be satisfied. Control should be yielded to others in whom the dying person has confidence. However, what might be an appropriate death for one person might be unsuitable for another.

Some research has pointed to the view that in adults, age is negatively correlated with fear of death. Bengston, Ceullar, and Ragan (1977) studied three age groups: 45–55, 55–64, and 65–74 years. The youngest cohort expressed the most fear of death, whereas the oldest expressed the least. Similar results were found by Kalish and Reynolds (1977), Wass (1977), Devins (1979), Cappon (1978), and Kastenbaum and Aisenberg (1972).

A number of factors account for this tendency. Elderly people are more often confronted with death among their peers. Death is viewed culturally as the natural conclusion to the life cycle. Older persons are more likely to believe in an afterlife (Kalish & Reynolds, 1977). They may be less concerned about survivors and less concerned about having additional life experiences.

Other research has found that fear of death is moderated by a number of factors, including age, religiosity, gender, and diagnosis. Cicirelli (2006) found that fear of death increased in some who were mid-old age, as the reality of death begins to come to the foreground, but less in old-old age. It is common to want to live to about 85 years (Lang, Baltes, & Wagner, 2007), and fear of loss of independence may be greater than fear of death.

Is it true that people die as they lived? In the sense that people cope with death the way they have coped with other problems in life, perhaps yes. Yet there are times when the dying process inflicts indignities that seem so inappropriate to a loving, caring person or when death seems so easy for the hard-hearted.

People's responses to the knowledge of impending death are not linear. They are characterized by vacillations in emotional and cognitive responses. Most often, the human reaction is ambivalence—the coexistence of fearful avoidance and the desire for release.

Rather than being contradictory, ambivalence seems a natural part of the dying process. Death as the ultimate unknown is usually feared. Underneath people's managed exterior is a raw terror of annihilation. In life, people attempt to control events; at the moment of death, control is gone. In juxtaposition to fear, many grow weary of the struggle to stay alive. They may also be curious as to what lies ahead. At times, death may also be seen as a solution to life's unanswered questions.

Stage Theory

People have a great need for landmarks and labels when dealing with the mysteries of the dying process. They feel more comfortable and less helpless if there is a predictable road map to follow. This may explain why Elisabeth Kübler-Ross's (1969) 5 stages of dying (denial, anger, depression, bargaining, and acceptance) became so universally accepted as *the* explanation of the dying process.

As a metaphor for dealing with all losses, Kübler-Ross's (1969) theory seems to fit with human experience; however, it was developed to explain the dying process and should not be confused with the experience people have in bereavement. She provided a new language that can be useful if not used too concretely. Kastenbaum (1974) stated that the problems with stage theories of dying are that they reckon little with the symptoms and trajectories of a particular disease state, with the person's personality, or with the person's environment. He also criticized the lack of any scientific evidence for the 5 stages (Kastenbaum & Kastenbaum, 1989).

Recently, however, the 5 stages were studied, and some support for this theory was presented (Maciejewski, Zhang, Block, & Prigerson, 2007). This new research attempted to validate the "stage" theory of grief using 5 single-item measures of disbelief, yearning, anger, depression, and acceptance from the Inventory of Complicated Grief—Revised. The 5 indicators reached their maximum values in the predicted sequence within 6 months post loss. This study has been criticized as too simplified, relying on single-item measures and looking only at the frequency of these reactions, not their severity.

Garfield (1978) challenged the notion that all people—regardless of belief system, age, race, culture, and historical period—die in a uniform sequence. Kalish (1978) questioned whether all patients go through stages and highlighted the influence of the medical care system on the patient's reactions to illness. The goals of cure and rehabilitation can encourage reactions such as denial and anger.

Dying persons show a variety of emotions that ebb and flow throughout their lives. These emotional reactions or stages can vary from minute to minute. A wide variety of emotions are seen in dying people, with some displaying a few, and some a great many. Instead of defining a universal, sequential order of stages of dying, it may be more helpful to describe phases of dying and courses of illness that demand different coping strategies at different times.

Holland (1989) described several possible courses for the patient following a cancer diagnosis:

- Treatment leading to long survival and cure

- Treatment leading to survival with no evidence of disease, followed by recurrence
- Treatment with poor response and no disease-free interval, followed by palliative treatment and death
- No primary treatment possible, followed by palliative treatment and death

For the patient who experiences many remissions, there may be considerable uncertainty, ambiguity, and several episodes of heightened anxiety and preparation for death. There is also uncertainty as to length of remission (or "cure") and when recurrence will occur.

Another view of the phases involved in dying of a terminal illness was offered by Weisman (Pattison, 1978). These include the following:

- The acute crisis-of-knowledge phase
- The chronic, living–dying interval (middle knowledge)
- The terminal phase

Weisman added that, given the same disease, people do not follow the same sequence and do not die at the same rate, of the same causes, or in the same circumstances. There is no well-recognized succession of emotional responses that are typical of people facing death. Pattison believed that the concept of stages of dying is not only inaccurate but also misleading to both the dying person and his or her helpers. There are no typical deaths. Dying may be stageless.

Psychosocial Care of Dying Persons and Their Families

The International Work Group (IWG) on Death, Dying, and Bereavement is a voluntary nonprofit organization composed of recognized leaders in the field. The group was formed in 1974 to help promote and advance understanding of the needs of dying persons and their families. The members meet at approximately 18-month intervals to advance knowledge in the field and to develop consensus documents on important areas of concern in the care of dying patients and their families. These IWG documents are usually statements of assumptions and principles.

IWG documents have been produced on terminal care, ethics, bereavement, care of the dying and bereaved in developing countries, spiritual care, education, HIV, palliative care for children, death and the arts, research and practice, and violence.

A "Statement of Assumptions and Principles Concerning Psychosocial Care of Dying Persons and Their Families" was developed in a work group I chaired (International Work Group on Death, Dying, and Bereavement,

1993). These assumptions and principles address the important psychosocial issues facing the dying, their families, and caregivers and offer advice about handling them. They are reprinted here for the reader's reference.

Statement of Assumptions and Principles Concerning Psychosocial Care of Dying Persons and Their Families

Introduction

The dying and their families face numerous psychosocial issues as death approaches.[1] In writing the following assumptions and principles concerning these issues we hope to counteract the tendency to focus too much on physical and technical care, to stimulate readers to test the following assumptions against their own experience, and to incorporate them into their work.

By psychosocial we mean the emotional, intellectual, spiritual, interpersonal, social, cultural, and economic dimensions of the human experience. Assumptions and principles for spiritual care have been developed by other work groups of the IWG.

By family we mean those individuals who are part of the dying person's most immediate attachment network, regardless of blood or matrimonial ties. The family, which includes the dying person, is the unit of care. By caregivers we mean those professionals and volunteers who provide care to dying persons and their families. We have separated the dying person, the family, and caregivers for the purpose of discussion only. Many of these assumptions and principles apply equally to dying persons and their families. They may not apply to all cultures and belief systems.

Issues for Dying Persons

Assumptions	Principles
1. Dying persons may choose to acknowledge or not acknowledge their impending death.	1. Caregivers must recognize and respect the person's right to deny or not communicate about his or her impending death. Caregivers may be helpful to family members and others in understanding or accepting the dying person's position, which may change with time.

2. Dying persons can communicate about their impending death in different cultural ways, encompassing verbal, nonverbal, or symbolic ways of communicating.

2. Caregivers must seek understanding and knowledge of the dying person's cultural and life-style experiences. Caregivers need to be astutely sensitive to nonverbal and symbolic ways of communicating and recognize that these modalities may be more significant to the dying person than verbal expression.

3. Dying persons have the right to information on their changing physical status, and the right to choose whether or not to be told they are dying.

3. Caregivers need to be sensitive and perceptive to the different ways the person may be requesting information about his or her condition.

4. Dying persons may be preoccupied with dying, [with] death itself, or with what happens after death.

4. The caregiving team needs to be aware of the dying person's concerns and fears in order to provide care that is responsive and supportive.

5. Dying persons can have a deep-seated fear of abandonment. They may therefore continue treatment for the sake of the family or physician rather than in the belief that it will be of personal benefit.

5. Caregivers can be helpful to the dying person in identifying feelings that may affect treatment decisions.
Caregivers may also be helpful in opening communication between the dying patient and family or physician that may clearly reflect the patient's goal for treatment.

6. Many dying persons experience multiple physical and psychological losses before their death.

6. Caregivers may be helpful in facilitating the expression of grief related to the multiple losses of terminal illness. Caregivers may also be helpful in supporting the dying person's need for continued autonomy, satisfying roles and activities, and meaning despite these losses.

7. Dying persons exhibit a variety of coping strategies in facing death.

7. Caregivers need to be able to recognize the utility of adaptive coping mechanisms and be tolerant of the patient's or families' need to use or abandon such mechanisms. Caregivers can help to foster an environment that encourages the use of effective ways of coping by accurately addressing the dying person's concern.

8. Dying persons generally need to express feelings.

8. Dying persons should not be isolated but given the opportunity to communicate.

9. Dying persons communicate when they feel safe and secure.

9. Caregivers should strive to create an environment in which communication can be facilitated, paying special attention to physical comfort, symptom management, physical surroundings, privacy, confidentiality, adequate time, acceptance of feelings, and shared expectations.

10. Dying persons may find it helpful to communicate with others who are terminally ill.

10. Opportunities should be encouraged for patient interaction such as peer or professionally facilitated support groups, social functions, or designated areas within treatment settings where patients may informally gather.

11. A dying person's communication of concern about death may be inhibited by a number of psychosocial and culturally determined expectations.

11. Caregivers can be helpful in breaking through the barriers that inhibit the dying person's true expression of feelings.

12. Dying persons have a right to be acknowledged as living human beings until their death.

12. Even when they seem severely impaired, dying persons are still able to sense their own surroundings. Caregivers need to facilitate this awareness. Caregivers should encourage behavior, touch, and communication, which continue to demonstrate respect for the dying person.

13. Dying persons' psychological suffering may be greater than their physical pain or discomfort.

13. Caregivers should recognize, and attend to, the psychological component of suffering.

14. Dying persons may have difficulty in dealing with the different or conflicting needs of family members.

14. Caregivers need to be aware of the dynamics within each family and recognize the importance of dealing with individual members as well as the family unit. Caregivers should be sensitive to the presence of conflicts between family members, and may need to maintain a position of neutrality in order to be effective.

Issues for Families

Assumptions	Principles
1. Families have fundamental needs to care and be cared for.	1. Families should be encouraged to provide whatever care they can. Caregivers should not supplant the family in the caregiver role except where the family lacks physical or emotional resources, knowledge, or desire to provide care. By providing care to family members, caregivers may be better able to care for the dying person.
2. The need to care and the need to be cared for sometimes conflict.	2. Those who sacrifice their own needs for care in order to care for others need to be encouraged to accept help for themselves. Some need to receive care before they can give care.
3. People vary in their coping abilities and personal resources. Moreover, competing priorities may hamper the amount and quality of care people are able to give.	3. Caregivers should not impose their own expectations on a family's ability to care. Caregivers may need to explore with the family what is reasonable for each person to provide.
4. The approach of death may disrupt the structure and functioning of the family.	4. Many families need counseling and support to prepare for the dying person's death and its consequences.
5. Families need to have information about a dying person's condition, although in cases of conflict his or her desire for confidentiality must be respected.	5. The dying person and caregiving team share the responsibility for informing the family about the person's condition, depending on his or her ability to participate. Whenever possible, the dying person and appropriate caregivers need to agree on the source and extent of information to be given to the family.
6. Families often need to be involved with the dying person in decision making.	6. Guided by the dying person's wishes, caregivers can be helpful in facilitating joint decision making.
7. Families have a right to know that their affairs will be shared only with those that have a need to know.	7. Confidentiality must be maintained at all times and its meaning taught to all caregivers.

8. Family members need to maintain self-esteem and self-respect.

8. Caregivers should show respect at all times. Caregivers do this by paying attention to family wishes, feelings, and concerns.

9. Sexual needs may continue up to the point of death.

9. Caregivers should acknowledge dying persons' and their partners' need to express their sexuality both verbally and physically, with easy access to privacy without embarrassment.

10. Families coping with terminal illness frequently have financial concerns.

10. Caregivers need to assure that families have access to informed advice and assistance on financial issues. These issues represent present or anticipated problems that may or may not be realistic.

11. Faced with death the family may imagine that changes will be greater than they are.

11. Caregivers can often allay fears with information and support.

12. Families have a need and a right to express grief for the multiple losses associated with illness, and for impending death.

12. Caregivers can help families by encouraging communication between families and the dying person about their shared losses, and encouraging the expression of grief.

Issues for Caregivers

Assumptions	Principles
1. Caregivers need education and experience in addressing the psychosocial needs of dying persons and their families.	1. A combination of specialized courses in death and dying, and clinical practicums in care of the terminally ill and their families, may help us to prepare caregivers to deal with the physical and psychosocial needs of dying persons.
2. Caregivers need to be aware of the dying person's and family's psychosocial frame of reference in acknowledging and coping with impending death.	2. Caregivers need to be sensitive to the dying person's and family's current willingness to acknowledge the reality of their situation. Caregivers must not impose their own expectation of how dying persons face death.

3. Caregivers bring their own values, attitudes, feelings, and fears into the dying person's setting.	3. Caregivers must recognize that they cannot take away all the pain experienced in the dying process. Caregivers need to be reassured that it is not a lack of professionalism to display and share emotions. Caregivers need to be aware of the way in which their coping strategies affect their communication of emotional involvement with the dying person and family.
4. Caregivers are exposed to repeated intense emotional experiences, loss, and confrontation with their own death in their work with dying persons.	4. Caregivers need to receive adequate support and opportunity to work through their own accumulated emotions. Caregivers working with dying persons need sound motivation, emotional maturity, versatility, tolerance, and a special ability to deal with loss.
5. Caregivers dealing with family groups sometimes experience conflicting needs and requests for information and confidentiality.	5. Caregivers need to be prepared to deal with complex family dynamics and to assist the family in resolving their own conflicts.
6. Caregivers may sometimes not communicate with each other about their own needs and feelings.	6. Caregivers need to be tolerant, caring, and nonjudgemental with each other in order to promote cooperation that will benefit the dying person's care.

Note: Developed by the Psychosocial Work Group of the IWG: Dr. Thelma Bates (United Kingdom), Rev. David Head (United Kingdom), Ms. Constance Connor (United States), Ms. Shirley Henen (South Africa), Dr. Stephen Connor (United States), Dr. Isa Jaramillo (Colombia), Ms. Donna Corr (United States), Dr. Scott Long (United States), Ms. Esther Gjertsen (Norway), and Dr. Colin M. Parkes (United Kingdom).

To be effective, those who provide psychosocial services to those with life-limiting illness and their families must develop a considerable sensitivity to the above issues. They must also learn to meet each dying patient as a unique individual with his or her own way of dying. Hospice can help patients grow emotionally and spiritually, but only if they wish to do so.

Some believe that dying patients should be offered an opportunity for growth by suggesting ways that they can develop themselves at the end of life. Others feel that the dying patient should determine the agenda and that encouraging the patient to deal with death and dying issues is intrusive.

There is some truth to both positions. It would be a mistake to be intrusive to patients and to expect them to be able to deal with their grief and unfinished interpersonal business before death. It would also be a mistake to passively avoid suggesting to them the same possibilities. Those facing death do not have prior experience on how best to die. The best one can do is offer them the possibility that there are opportunities to explore. If they show interest in dealing with feelings and relationships, hospice and palliative care workers have permission to move forward. If they express discomfort, workers know to back off.

Case Illustration

Howard

Howard was the patriarch of a large family. At 78 years old, he had five children, 14 grandchildren, and 8 great-grandchildren. His wife had died of a stroke 4 years earlier, and he was still feeling sad at her loss when he was diagnosed with stage 4 colon cancer. He opted for no oncology treatment and was admitted to hospice service.

As hospice staff got to know Howard, they began to learn more about his extraordinary life. He had traveled all over the world as a merchant seaman. He had become an engineer and had three patents registered. During World War II, he was parachuted behind enemy lines to sabotage enemy installations. He had been wealthy and had lost all his money on bad investments.

His family knew little of his exploits. One of his grandchildren was particularly interested in family history. The hospice social worker helped Howard to understand the importance of sharing his oral history with his family. Not only would their lives be enriched but his would be as well. Howard agreed to talk on videotape, beginning with what he could remember of his ancestors. He recounted the important details of his life. Finally, he shared his personal philosophy of life and thoughts on death and afterlife.

In the course of summarizing his life, he remembered some who had been major influences on him. He decided to write to two who were still living to thank them for their support and guidance. He also wrote a former business colleague who had been responsible for an important business failure. He forgave this old friend. As Howard's death approached, he thanked the hospice workers for helping him to reach closure on some important parts of his life.

Truth Telling

Elisabeth Kübler-Ross has said that she used a rule of thumb about truth telling. She told her patients the truth three times, and if after that they refused it she did not bring it up again (Connor, personal communication, May 5, 1979). Clinical instincts can be helpful here. Timing is very important in any relationship. The first time you tell someone bad news, they often refuse to believe it. After they have had enough time to muster their more adaptive coping resources, they usually are able to hear it.

Robert Buckman (1992) gives some helpful guidance in *How to Break Bad News: A Guide for Health Care Professionals*. Buckman suggested a six-step protocol for breaking bad news. Step 1 is getting started by attending to the environment in which the bad news is given. Make sure there is enough privacy, be sure you are both sitting down, and try to relax. Step 2 is to find out how much the patient knows. Ask open questions and look for factual knowledge as well as emotional content. Step 3 is to find out how much the patient wants to know. Again, it is best to ask open questions and try to discover at what level the patient wants to be informed. Questions like "Would you like to know the full details of what's wrong or just hear about the treatment plan?" are helpful. The fourth step is to share the information. Use of good communication skills is essential. Other suggestions include using plain English rather than "med-speak," giving information in small chunks, using visual or written cues, and encouraging questions. Step 5 is responding to the patient's feelings. A large number of responses are possible, including shock, denial, disbelief, fear, anxiety, anger, blame, guilt, hope, despair, depression, dependency, sadness, relief, joy, humor, bargaining, and a search for meaning. Finally, Step 6 includes planning and follow-through. It is advisable to summarize what was said, to be sure all the options are explained, and to agree on the next steps. If there are no options, it is important to identify sources of support. Rather than being contradictory, it is possible to plan for the worst while hoping for the best.

Hospice and palliative care programs are often in the difficult position of having to help people deal with the worst news they have ever received. Although patients are usually informed of their prognosis by a physician, it is often the hospice worker who must help the patient and family to process this information. Once their shock wears off, there are numerous reactions. The significance of the patient's situation often has to be worked through over and over again.

In some respects, much of palliative care is helping people to face the truth. Patients and families have to be continuously reassessed to discern their readiness to digest more information. This becomes a delicate balancing act as the patients' conditions are continually changing.

When John (who we met in chapter 3) was referred to hospice, he said he knew he was not supposed to recover but he preferred not to discuss it or think about it. The hospice team supported his request until one day a month later, when he had an episode of incontinence. He laughed at himself as the home health aide changed his clothes and bathed him. He told his nurse that if he was going to keep from soiling himself, he had better know more about his condition. This opened the door to talking about why he was losing bladder control, what other things might happen, and how he could prepare. John discovered that he could cope better if he knew what to expect. His outlook changed, and he was less fearful and depressed.

Psychopathology

While most palliative patients' reactions are relatively normal, there is a subset of patients who have a history of mental illness or whose reactions are severe enough to rise to the level of a mental disorder. In one of the few studies of the incidence of mental disorders in the cancer population, Derogatis et al. (1983) reported that overall in 47% of 215 randomly assigned new inpatient cancer admissions, some disorder was diagnosed. Of the 47%, the most common disorder was adjustment disorder, which occurred in 68% of cases. Also, 13% of patients were diagnosed with a major affective disorder (depression), 8% had an organic mental disorder, 7% had a personality disorder, and 4% had an anxiety disorder. Overall, 85% had features of anxiety or depression, and a large majority had treatable conditions.

Similarly, Minagawa, Uchitomi, Yamawaki, and Ishitani (1996) studied 97 cancer patients admitted within one week of inpatient admission and found that 53.7% met the DSM-III-R criteria for a psychiatric disorder; including 28% for delirium, 10.7% for dementia, 7.5% for adjustment disorder; 3.2% for amnestic disorder and major depression, and 1.1% for general anxiety disorder. Their findings differed from those of Derogatis et al. (1983), probably due to the fact that the unit used specialized in neurological treatment.

Jacobsen et al. (2005) have suggested a simple single-item screening tool for psychological distress called the Distress Thermometer. Patients are asked to circle a number from 0 to 10 on a visual thermometer that best describes how much distress they have been experiencing in the past week, including today. Those indicating 5 or above should be considered for referral to a psychosocial professional.

General Guidelines and Use of Mental Health Professionals

As described in chapter 2, psychosocial professionals are a very important component of the hospice team. Social workers can do most of the delivery of counseling services along with other team members, but there are many patients with either preexisting mental health conditions or diagnoses that may be exacerbated by the illness, including severe anxiety, clinical depression, obsessive–compulsive disorders, personality disorders, bipolar disorder, and organic mental disorders, to name a few, that need more advanced diagnosis and treatment. Well-trained and experienced clinical social workers, psychologists, and psychiatrists are essential consultants to the team.

For those whose mental health or response to life-limiting illness does not rise to the level of a mental disorder, there are still many who may experience some significant psychological distress and need competent mental health treatment.

The need to make meaning is very common among patients at the end of life. Helping patients to discover a coherent narrative for their life and to be able to put their illness and impending death in a context that fits that narrative can be a powerful psychological and spiritual intervention.

For many patients, assistance may be needed to help them shift from the idea that they are seeking cure to the concept of healing. Healing can occur on many levels, not just the physical. If the disease is the enemy, then how do I separate myself from my body? If I am fighting the disease, am I fighting myself? If I have some power to cure myself, did I somehow participate in causing my disease in the first place?

For many patients, there may be a pursuit of wellness to achieve cure that requires an attitude of continual positive thinking. There is a fear that negative thoughts may cause the illness to advance. Those around the patient, not wanting to deal with the reality of the patient's impending demise, may criticize the patient if fears are expressed and say, "Just think positively." Lazarus (1985) has referred to this as the trivialization of distress. There is no evidence whatsoever that expressing fears and concerns leads to an early demise.

Weil (2005) describes healing as something that comes from within. Treatments come from outside, and at best treatments only facilitate healing. Healing is about wholeness, whether or not you are cured of the disease.

Spirituality and Acceptance of Death

Are religious and spiritual needs synonymous? Hospice clinicians prefer to focus on patients' spiritual needs rather than limiting themselves to the religious. It is seen as a broader frame that encompasses both concerns with the rites, rituals, and rules of conventional religion and concerns with the individual's desire to develop spiritually.

Zerwekh (1993) described spirituality as the essence of personhood, the longing for meaning in existence, experience of God, experience of ultimate values, and trust in the transcendent. This is a broader frame that suits the situation of all dying patients whether they are religious, spiritual, or neither. If one tries to understand patients' transcendent needs, one captures their religious, spiritual, philosophical, and existential concerns. By definition, any concern with why one is here or what happens after death concerns transcendence. People transcend their individual existences and are concerned with more than themselves.

Hospice chaplains and all providers of palliative care strive to help the patients get their transcendent issues in focus and to come to some resolution. The resolution can range from returning to good standing in their church, mosque, or synagogue, to resolving their guilt over past transgressions, to feeling at peace with themselves and their notion of a universal power, to understanding what it is they needed to learn from their life, and to acceptance or a sense that their life is complete and that they are ready to die.

Standards for Provision of Spiritual Care

The NHPCO Standards (2006b) address spiritual care in a variety of areas that call for thorough assessment of spiritual history and needs and inclusion in the interdisciplinary team's plan of care. The section on the interdisciplinary team under workforce excellence gives the following guidance for the provision of spiritual care in hospice.

Interdisciplinary Team: Spiritual Care

Standard

WE 17 Hospice spiritual care and services are based on an initial and ongoing documented assessment of the patient's and family's spiritual needs by qualified members of the interdisciplinary team (clergy person or someone with equivalent education, training and experience) and provided according to the interdisciplinary team's plan of care.
WE 17.1 Spiritual care and services include:

1. Assessing the spiritual status of the patient, family and caregiver;
2. Documenting the spiritual assessment, goals for spiritual care, services provided and the patient's and family's response to spiritual care;
3. Acknowledging and respecting the patient's and family's beliefs, culture and values related to life's meaning including suffering and loss and desire for services/support;
4. Meditation, counseling, prayer, sacred rituals or practices, active listening and supportive presence;
5. Assisting with funerals and memorial services;
6. Communicating with and supporting the involvement of local clergy and/or spiritual counselors as possible and as desired by the patient, family and caregiver; and
7. Consulting and providing education to the interdisciplinary team members and patients and families about spirituality and related care and services.

Practice Examples

- The hospice chaplain coordinates spiritual services thereby assuring that the patient's and family's needs are met by their own clergy or the hospice chaplain.
- The hospice chaplain prays with the patient who requests prayer.
- The hospice chaplain explains to the team the specific beliefs of a patient and the team discusses the effect of such beliefs on that patient's care.
- Other members of the interdisciplinary team identifying spiritual needs of the patient/family consult with the hospice chaplain about how to best address such needs.

Many patients and families are concerned about their religious beliefs as well as their spiritual lives. They may only know how to demonstrate their spirituality through religious expression. Hospice and palliative care providers should always support the patient and family in the expression of their specific religious beliefs and practices and strive to learn those they are unfamiliar with.

Often, religious expression is influenced by cultural background. Each culture adapts religious expression to more comfortably fit cultural norms. Palliative care providers are more effective when they understand these norms. Cultural beliefs and practices around death and dying are especially important for hospices to understand and support. For instance, hospice may help make it possible for an Islamic family to be able to wash and wrap the patient's body following death according to cultural and religious practice. The ability to carry out such perideath rituals can have a very positive impact on the bereavement process (see Irish, 1993, for more details on such practices).

Acceptance is more than just resignation toward death. Resignation is like learned helplessness. No matter what a person does, the illness progresses and one has to give in. There is no more point in fighting. Accepting death is an embracing of what comes next. It is a feeling of completeness with one's life without bitterness or regret. Patients may describe a sense of wonder about what lies ahead.

A number of useful writings on spiritual growth at the end of life have been contributed by insightful authors including Stephen Levine, Rachael Naomi Remen, Ram Dass, Joan Halifax, and others (see the recommended readings at the end of this chapter).

The following case illustrates some of the difficult emotional challenges that face hospice providers and the potential to change a tragic situation into one in which there is some resolution.

Case Illustration

Janine

Janine was too young to die—only 37 years old with two small children, Josh (9) and Jackie (11). She had been fighting metastatic breast cancer for 4 years. Besides the tragedy of knowing she would not live to see her children grow up, there was a conflicted relationship with her ex-husband and a distant relationship with her parents. She had many friends and what she viewed as a good support system of other women.

Janine came to hospice after failing a round of chemotherapy. She was in need of help emotionally and physically, but she was not so sure about throwing in the towel. She could not say goodbye to her kids, and she felt very conflicted about her life. She was gradually getting weaker and spent most of her time in bed. Janine came into the hospice unit for pain control shortly after becoming a hospice patient. She could not get comfortable with increases in her morphine and was eventually put on a continuous subcutaneous infusion.

It became clear that increased doses of morphine were not affecting her pain. As we came to know Janine more, it became clear that she was agitated about who would care for her children when she was gone. She felt little trust for her ex-husband, who had cheated on her, and she felt distant from her parents.

We explored with Janine what she could do to become more resolved about her children. We arranged for her parents to come and visit. They had not known how serious her illness had become. She invited her ex-husband to visit, but he would not show up when he said he would. Janine agreed that she would start a videotape of her life to leave for the children.

As her parents visited in the hospice unit, it became clear that the estrangement with her parents came from rebellion against them as a young adult. They had rejected her lifestyle, and each had not forgiven the other for the angry things said. The conflict seemed almost trivial now that her life was near an end. They began to explore her life growing up to help with the video and to help her to put together a photo album. There was much sadness as they forgave each other and regret over the time they had lost.

Janine's pain was finally controlled, and she worked hard on the videotape project. She included special messages for her children. She left an oral history of her life, her philosophy, and her wishes. She went home to the care of her parents and friends. Arrangements were made for custody of the children to be given to her parents. Her ex-husband finally visited and asked for forgiveness for his behavior. He agreed to the custody arrangements and visited a few times, although he was unable to stay long or to help with her care.

A week before she died, Janine finished her tape and family album. She spent as much time with Josh and Jackie as she could, and they helped with her care. She died peacefully in her bed with her parents, children, and friends around her. Two days later, they held a service that she had helped plan. Her children read some of her favorite poetry, and everyone celebrated her short but full life.

The dying face many intense emotional and spiritual concerns as death approaches. Grief is a central dynamic to the dying and especially to their families. In the next chapter, grief and bereavement are given more detailed attention.

Recommended Reading

Buckman, R. (1992). *How to break bad news: A guide for health care professionals.* Toronto: University of Toronto Press.

Callanan, M., & Kelly, P. (1992). *Final gifts.* New York: Bantam.

Corless, I., Germino, B., & Pittman, M. (2006). *Death, dying, and bereavement: A challenge for living* (2nd ed.). New York: Springer.

Corless, I., Germino, B., & Pittman, M. (Eds.). (1994). *Dying, death and bereavement: Theoretical perspectives and other ways of knowing.* Boston: Jones & Bartlett.

Dass, R. (1971). *Remember, be here now.* San Cristobal, NM: Lama Foundation.

Dass, R. (2001). *Still here: Embracing aging, changing, and dying.* New York: Riverhead.

Doka, K. (2008). *Counseling individuals with life-threatening illness.* New York: Springer.

Garfield, C. (Ed.). (1978). *Psychosocial care of the dying patient.* New York: McGraw-Hill.

Halifax, J. (N.d.). [Articles]. Retrieved October 24, 2008, from http://www.upaya.org

Kastenbaum, R. (2000). *The psychology of death* (3rd ed.). New York: Springer.

Kübler-Ross, E. (1969). *On death and dying*. New York: Macmillan.

Levine, S. (1989a). *A gradual awakening*. New York: Anchor.

Levine, S. (1989b). *Meetings at the edge*. New York: Doubleday.

Levine, S. (1989c). *Who dies? An investigation of conscious living and conscious dying*. New York: Anchor.

Remen, R. (1997). *Kitchen table wisdom: Stories that heal*. New York: Riverhead.

Rosen, E. (1990). *Families facing death: Family dynamics of terminal illness*. Lexington, MA: Lexington Books.

Wass, H., & Neimeyer, R. (Eds.). (1995). *Dying: Facing the facts* (3rd ed.). Washington, DC: Taylor & Francis.

Weenelson, P. (1996). *The art of dying: How to leave this world with dignity and grace, at peace with yourself and loved ones*. New York: St. Martin's.

Werth, J., & Blevins, D. (2006). *Psychosocial issues near the end of life: A resource for professional care providers*. Washington, DC: American Psychological Association.

Web Resources

Association for Death Education and Counseling: http://www.adec.org

Growth House, Inc.: http://www.growthhouse.org

International Work Group on Death, Dying, and Bereavement: http://www.iwgddb.org

CHAPTER 5

Grief and Bereavement

A man's dying is more the survivor's affair than his own.

—Thomas Mann

The central psychological concern of patients and families facing death is reaction to loss. The patient faces the loss of everything, including health, occupation, body image, pleasures, significant relationships, and future. The family who will be left behind faces the loss of a loved one who is an integral part of a family system.

Hospices recognize that helping people deal with loss and grief is essential to providing good care. People do not begin to mourn a loss after the death; they begin as soon as the impending loss is acknowledged (Rando, 2000). This predeath reaction is known as anticipatory mourning. It is generally accepted that some grieving is done before the loss; however, it is also held that the tasks of grieving cannot be completed before the actual loss.

There are a number of excellent texts on grief that the reader may wish to consult for a more in-depth exploration of the field (see the recommended readings at the end of the chapter). This chapter focuses on how hospices and palliative care programs provide bereavement services to families as well as to the community at large. Special considerations for grieving children, prediction of bereavement risk, pathological grief identification, the impact of bereavement intervention, and the cost-effectiveness of bereavement support are also covered.

Need for Bereavement Support

It would be fair to ask why hospices provide bereavement support in the first place. Isn't it the job of mental health agencies and churches to provide this service? To understand why hospices have emphasized a specialized bereavement support service, one needs to look at how society views the needs of the bereaved.

There is a tendency to minimize the impact of death on functioning. People are expected to be back to work or school and ready to function within a few days of the death. The average person thinks it should only take days or weeks to get over a death. The reality is that the first days or weeks are a period of shock. It is only after this time passes that a person is able to begin to deal with the loss.

There has been a breakdown in our sense of community. People have less time for friendship and often do not even know their neighbors. There is less social support available, and that support is critical to getting through a major loss. There are few cultural rituals to help people express grief in Western culture. There is no commonly agreed-on etiquette for the public display of grief. People have fewer ties to organized religion and have reduced access to rituals and support from communities of faith. For those with such strong faith that they believed God would heal them, there may be a sense of failure or disappointment with God.

There is an assumption that clergy and mental health professionals are well trained in handling grief counseling. Few of these professionals receive any training in grief counseling or grief therapy. A few specialize in helping the bereaved, but the great majority have little knowledge or training in this area.

Bereavement Follow-Up Services

Hospices provide follow-up counseling, education, and support to families for a minimum of 1 year following the death. Hospice bereavement follow-up usually includes the following components:

1. Hospice clinical staff assigned to the case visits the family to say goodbye and to attend the funeral or visitation.
2. A staff member or specially trained volunteer is assigned to contact the family at regular intervals in the year after the death.
3. Educational mailings are sent to families at regular intervals on aspects of grieving. Topics may include common reactions and feelings, journaling, poetry, self-esteem, next steps, and coping with holidays.

4. Hospice staff or volunteers are assigned to visit or call families at intervals determined by need. For those families without special needs, contact is often after 1, 3, 6, 9, and 12 months. For families having trouble coping with grief, contact is more frequent or may require referral to a competent mental health professional with expertise in grief and loss.
5. Regular grief support groups are held, and all families are invited. These groups may include emotional support, educational components, or both. Some programs also include a social component.

The bereavement follow-up to a hospice family should be based on the needs identified. It may be helpful to see families as falling into one of four categories: those who refuse follow-up, those who need routine follow-up, those who need enhanced follow-up, and those whose mourning is complicated and who need professional intervention.

There are commonly a small number of families who ask for no further contact from hospice after the death. Usually, it is because they are having some difficulty with their grief and prefer to use avoidance as a coping style. It may also be due to low self-esteem or tied to cultural expectations. Hospices respect this request and discontinue contact. However, it is recommended that at least one follow-up attempt be made after about 6 months to make sure that there has not been a change of heart. A significant number of these reluctant people find that their avoidance is ineffective and respond positively to follow-up. A hospice worker may hear, "I'm really glad you called; we're having more trouble dealing with this than I thought, and it would be good to talk about it."

The second group includes those who welcome the contact from hospice and are coping well. These are the large majority of hospice families who have good support and coping resources. They do fine with a modest amount of follow-up. About 75% of families fall into this category.

The third group includes those who need enhanced follow-up. These are the people who are having some difficulty with their grief and are having trouble coping. They may need or request more frequent contact from hospice. They are encouraged to come to the support groups and may require as much as weekly contact with hospice staff or volunteers.

The fourth group consists of those who have complicated or prolonged grief. This may be manifested by severe depression, suicidal ideation, extreme difficulty in functioning, or unremitting distress. These family members are not responding to supportive intervention. They may need to be helped to accept a referral for professional intervention. Hospice will have available or will have a referral relationship with mental health professionals in the community who are knowledgeable about treatment of grieving people. Not uncommonly in this group, there is an underlying mental health problem that preceded the loss.

Palliative care programs provide a variety of bereavement services to families depending on need and available resources. Standards for bereavement services for palliative care programs are offered in the *Clinical Practice Guidelines for Quality Palliative Care* (National Consensus Project, 2008).

Community Bereavement Support

In a survey of U.S. hospices (Connor & Lattanzi-Licht, 1995), 88% reported that they provide bereavement services to the community at large, not just to families served by hospice. The most common community service was group counseling (94%), followed by phone support (82%), short-term counseling (72%), and educational mailings (72%). Other, less frequent types of support included an assigned volunteer (52%), long-term counseling (25%), expressive therapies (25%), and camp experiences (25%). Some hospices have even begun providing education and support through computer services and the Internet.

Often, it is the families who were not served by hospice who use its bereavement services. Those served by hospice are usually more prepared for the death and may have fewer emotional complications afterward. Many communities view hospice as having expertise in handling grief and are turning to hospice programs for help in times of crisis.

Bereavement services for children tend to be more easily accepted and valued by the community. Many hospices have developed special programs for schools and families with children. In the school system, hospices have led grief education programs, conducted group sessions after the deaths of students, and taught educators about grief and mourning. Some hospices use expressive therapists to work with children. These therapists use art, play, movement, storytelling, and other modalities to help children to express their grief.

Providing bereavement services for children and teens is especially important as a preventive measure. Children sometimes blame themselves for the death of a family member. They may feel that they either caused the death or should have prevented it. A 5-year-old who had seen the movie *Twister* thought he caused a tornado because he had yelled out, "Twister, twister," a while before a tornado destroyed the homes of most of his neighbors.

Teens have considerable fear of the public expression of grief for fear that it will alienate them from other, nongrieving peers. Both children and teens may be hesitant to bring up the subject of a loved one's death for fear that it might upset other family members. In some ways, providing services to children and teens is a way of reaching adults. It may be more acceptable for parents to seek help for their child than for themselves. In the process, they can receive help and education about their own grief.

The Center for Prevention Research at Arizona State University has conducted longitudinal research on the needs of bereaved children and has found that certain interventions are most correlated with better outcomes at 6 years post loss (Haine, Ayers, Wolchik, & Sandler, 2008). They include the following: teaching positive parenting, defined as increased warmth and appropriate discipline; more positive parental affect; fewer negative life stressors; fewer caregiver mental health problems; increased child adaptive control beliefs and feeling understood; lower inhibition of emotional expression; increased coping efficacy; and lower threat appraisal for stressful events. A 12-session psychoeducational program has been developed from this research that includes both surviving parents and their children.

Camps

Another popular community bereavement service is grief camps. This is a program where children go to a camp for a weekend or a number of days with hospice grief counselors and volunteers. There are entertaining and therapeutic activities planned. These might include craft programs designed to address grief such as making dream catchers to eliminate nightmares, worry dolls, and ornament decoration with objects from the deceased.

Activity programs at these camps might include physically challenging experiences, such as ropes courses where group effort is necessary for success or mock survival situations. Art activity can help children express feelings and unresolved conflicts. Art or expressive therapists can help children understand the images or just reinforce the enjoyment of artistic creation.

Group rituals, where, for instance, participants may be asked to write down burdens that are then thrown into a fire, are common. Candles may be lit or other items may be sent floating down a river to symbolize loss. Trees may be decorated and then planted. Other group activities might include a memorial service, nondenominational religious observance, or family activity. The emphasis is on reducing the child's sense of isolation and feeling that he or she is the only one experiencing feelings of loss. It is also helpful for the child to deal with fears of losing other important people and guilt over perceived responsibility for the loss.

In most camps, the children come by themselves. There are some that both young and older children attend, and others that are designed for teens or preteens only; some are designed for the whole family to attend. There is usually some type of follow-up activity after the camp through either support groups or reunions. Participants describe the experience as a turning point where the loss finally was acknowledged or when the bad dreams finally went away.

Groups

Hospice grief support groups are usually open to the community at large. They are professionally facilitated self-help groups that are part of the common concern group movement that has flourished in the United States since the early 1970s. The structure and content of grief support groups vary. Some are open; others are closed. Open groups allow participants to come and go as they please. Closed groups usually require a commitment and are for a preset number of sessions. There are structured and unstructured group formats. Structured groups may offer a preset educational program with different topics for each session. Unstructured groups tend to follow the needs of the individuals who attend a particular session. Some offer a combination of topic for the session followed by an open support component.

Some hospices provide social occasions for the bereaved to attend. These are often potluck meals where widows and widowers come for good food, conversation, and sharing. As social support is an important factor in grief recovery, these occasions serve a therapeutic function. They have also been a springboard for other social contact and relationship building. Successful hospice socials have led to travel groups, bridge clubs, and sometimes new marriages.

Counseling

Hospices and palliative care programs vary in the amount of bereavement counseling offered. Most provide at least short-term counseling for anyone experiencing problems with grief. Some offer longer term counseling either using hospice staff or through arrangements with community therapists. This is often on a sliding-scale fee basis. The objective of short-term counseling is to express grief and to help the person to progress through the normal tasks of mourning.

Worden (2009) has distinguished this from grief therapy, which aims to help someone whose grief is not progressing normally. Complicated or prolonged grief may be due to preexisting psychological problems and may require a longer term therapy. Worden's conceptualization of grief work involves successfully completing four tasks. The first is accepting the reality of the loss. The second is to process the pain of grief. The third is to adjust to a world without the deceased person, and the fourth is to find an enduring connection with the deceased in the midst of embarking on a new life (Worden, 2009, Chapter 2).

There has been discussion of the qualifications necessary to do grief counseling or therapy. The only recognized certification available is certification in thanatology, through the Association for Death Education and Counseling. Hospice staff who do grief counseling usually have a background in social work or pastoral care and receive on-the-job train-ing. The majority of family members' grief support needs can be met by using volunteers. Most hospices train volunteers to assist in providing support to the bereaved. In the United States, regular trained hospice vol-unteers will sometimes specialize in bereavement follow-up and be given some additional training.

In the United Kingdom, the Cruse Bereavement Care program was developed to provide a nationwide network of trained volunteers for the bereaved. This program makes available free bereavement care for every grieving citizen in the country. Training for Cruse volunteers involves an initial 10-evening introduction followed by basic counseling training and a 2-year supervised probation. The Cruse volunteer counselors continue to be supervised as long as they stay in the program. There are Cruse branches throughout the United Kingdom.

Also in the United Kingdom, specially trained individuals who receive more than 300 hours of training can be designated as grief counselors. These individuals handle all the needs of the bereaved. In the United States, grief therapy is usually reserved for licensed mental health profes-sionals with special expertise in grief work.

This dichotomy raises an interesting question about whether grief should be considered an abnormality. Most who work in hospice view grief as a fundamentally inherent part of the human experience. It is both a powerful human emotion and something that helps define who one is. The experience of loss can devastate but can also promote resiliency and strengthen the ties that bind people to others. Grief counseling may have emerged as a new social ritual to compensate for the loss of other forms of grief expression.

Normal versus Pathological Grief

Past thinking in the mental health community was that bereavement can be a legitimate focus of treatment, but it does not constitute a mental dis-order. Yet there are some whose reactions to loss are so overwhelming that they become unable to function.

Examples of complicated mourning include the following: unresolved grief, complicated grief, chronic grief, delayed grief, and exaggerated grief (Worden, 2009). It is important to note that the range for what is normal grief is quite wide. Many times, people seek counseling because they do not seem to be living up to society's unrealistic expectations that people simply pull up their bootstraps and get on with their life after a significant death. It is people's discomfort in having to acknowledge the griever's feel-ings that seems to push them to cut off the person's expression of grief.

A person with chronic grief experiences grief that is excessive in dura-tion, though that will vary considerably depending on many factors,

including who the person was, the nature of the attachment in the relationship, how the person died, previous experiences with loss, personality
characteristics, the grieving person's social context, and the level of current stressors. Chronic grief never comes to a successful conclusion. Grief
in this situation can be very prolonged and can continue in some cases for
10, 15, 20, or more years.

In exaggerated grief, the person is flooded with grief and intense emotions and is unable to stop grieving. Day and night, they feel pain and
express painful emotion. Although it is helpful to express the pain of loss
(Elisabeth Kübler-Ross, 1969, called this emptying one's pool of pain), if it
becomes a bottomless pit, help is needed. Sometimes this pain is not simply a result of the death but is related to other losses or traumas that have
been unexpressed.

Delayed grief is found in those who after many months are unable to
grieve and are distressed that they are unable to move on. The flip side of
this is prolonged grief, where a person continues to grieve for years and
cannot seem to stop.

In some cases, there is an obvious problem with a preexisting emotional
problem that complicates grief. In other cases, though, there is no evidence
of a mental disorder such as clinical depression or character disorder. Yet
the person's ability to function is greatly impaired for a significant period.

Recent research (Lichtenthal, Cruess, & Prigerson, 2004) has suggested
that there may be a unique disorder related to reaction to loss (traumatic,
complicated, or prolonged grief disorder) that could affect 5–15% of the
bereaved. A set of criteria has been proposed that distinguishes this proposed disorder from other diagnoses such as major depressive disorder.
These criteria include those given in Table 5.1.

The Grief Work Hypothesis

Most theorists believe that major emotional expression is needed for grief to
be resolved. Wortman and Silver (1989) questioned this need and claimed
that some can resolve their grief without "feeling the pain." The expression
of grief can take many forms and is as varied as human nature. Certainly
the nature of the relationship and one's cultural background have an enormous influence on the expression of mourning.

Can grief ever be resolved? Phyllis Silverman (2004) is a proponent of
the life cycle model for understanding grief. This view is that grief is simply part of the normal life cycle. People grieve all their lives in one way
or another. Grief helps to define who they are. Silverman objected to the
medical model of grief as a wound that needs to be healed. One never fin-
ishes grieving, and to expect people to do so may set them up for failure.
This view is consistent with the report of many who say they will never
completely get over their loss. If getting over the loss means the lack of any

Table 5.1 Proposed Diagnostic Criteria for Complicated Grief

Criterion A	Criterion B
• Person has experienced the death of a significant other, and response involves 3 of the 4 following symptoms experienced at least daily or to a marked degree:	• In response to the death, 4 of the following 8 symptoms experienced at least daily or to a marked degree:
1. Intrusive thoughts about deceased 2. Yearning for deceased 3. Searching for deceased 4. Excessive loneliness since the death	1. Purposelessness, feelings of futility about future 2. Subjective sense of numbness, detachment, or absence of emotional responsiveness 3. Difficulty acknowledging the death (disbelief) 4. Feeling life is empty or meaningless 5. Feeling that part of oneself has died 6. Shattered worldview (lost sense of security, trust, and control) 7. Assumes symptoms or harmful behaviors of, or related to, the deceased 8. Excessive irritability, bitterness, or anger related to the death
Criterion C	**Criterion D**
• Duration of disturbance (symptoms listed) is at least 6 months.	• The disturbance causes clinically significant impairment in social, occupational, or other important areas of functioning.

Source: Lichtenthal, Cruess, & Prigerson (2004).

emotional connection to the deceased person, then most would prefer not to fully recover. This is not to say that it is not desirable to reach a place where grief does not preoccupy life.

Klass, Silverman, and Nickman (1996), in their book *Continuing Bonds*, explored the need for expanding the understanding of the grief process. Most theorists have explained grief and mourning as a process aimed at cutting bonds with the deceased. Unhealthy grief is defined by how much the mourner continues to hold on to the dead person.

Yet experience with the bereaved helps one to understand that a continuing inner relationship with the deceased may not be unhealthy at all. Healthy resolution of grief enables people to maintain a continuing bond with the deceased that does not have to interfere with new relationships.

Bill Worden (2009) said that the most significant symptom that someone is having complicated grief is when the person is unable to be without an object of the deceased. He referred to this as a linking object. This object is usually a personal item that the bereaved has to have with him or her or know the location of at all times. The linking object signifies that the deceased remains the central emotional object in the life of the mourner. The grief of Queen Victoria is an example of someone whose life remained fixated on a lost relationship. She refused to stop mourning after the death of Prince Albert. His clothes were laid out daily, and his place set at the table. She refused to accept the reality of his loss.

Grief and Depression

One of the most difficult clinical distinctions is between grief and depression. They have many of the same characteristics, but the most distinguishing differences are that in depression there is a pervasive disturbance of self-esteem, hopelessness, psychomotor retardation, or suicidal gestures that greatly affect social and occupational functioning (Jacobs & Leiberman, 1987). There are more vegetative signs and symptoms in depression, which are less typical of an acute stress reaction. In grief the pain of loss is recognized, whereas in depression it is unrecognized and denied. Anger is more easily expressed in grief than in depression. Grieving people are more preoccupied with the deceased, whereas depressed people are more focused on themselves. Grievers usually respond well to support, whereas depressed people do not and will tend to drive others away.

Another difficult grief reaction is feeling excessive guilt. Probably most mourners experience some guilt as they go over the events of the death, seeking reassurance that all was done that could be done. Illegitimate guilt may be a defense against helplessness. It is easier to take responsibility for the event than to accept the randomness of the world and not feel in control. Exploring the legitimacy of the guilt may help get at underlying assumptions. When guilt is legitimate, it can be channeled into constructive activity and, it is hoped, changed into forgiveness and feelings of regret.

One way to understand and work with grief is to focus on the stories of the bereaved. The stories of the events leading up to, during, and right after the death are of major significance to the bereaved. How the narrative evolves and is interpreted has a significant impact on the course of bereavement. Hospice families are often told that it is most helpful to tell their story, and they do it over and over again.

Robert Neimeyer (2001) has stressed the importance of meaning making through narratives.

Stroebe and Schut (1999) have proposed a cognitive stress model for understanding grief in adult life. They proposed a dual-process model for grief that accounts for the vacillation in the emotional responses seen in the bereaved. Most people have periods after a major loss where they avoid the emotional reactions characteristic of grief. There are many practical details that must be attended to after a death. These reality-based concerns allow a break from the more intense emotional work of grief.

Everyday life experience oscillates between loss-oriented activities such as grief work, intrusive emotional reactions, and untying bonds and restorative activities such as attending to life changes, doing new things, distraction from grief, and denial or avoidance of grief (Stroebe & Schut, 1999). In this model, there are no stages or phases of grief, just a continuing oscillation. Difficulty occurs when the person cannot move back and forth and stays stuck either in loss or in the restorative activities.

Most researchers have agreed that red flags for complicated grief include the following:

- When a person is thinking about hurting him or herself
- When a person feels constantly depressed and unable to find a glimmer of hope
- When a person refuses to seek medical help for health problems
- When a person starts drinking more or taking illegal drugs to soothe grief
- When a person feels constantly guilty over or angry at the deceased
- When a person refuses to talk about the deceased or has difficulty expressing any emotions

In spite of the many helpful theories about and models of grief, a truly integrated non-culture-bound universal theory of bereavement is still lacking. Researchers tend to define unhealthy grief as any behaviors that do not fit their simplistic models of how people ought to grieve.

Risk for Poor Outcome

Much of the bereavement literature concerns identification of those individuals who are at risk for poor outcome in their grief. Poor outcome usually means the development of emotional disorders, suicide, or health deterioration. There is disagreement in the literature as to whether grief can cause illness or death. In Osterweis, Solomon, and Green's (1984) *Bereavement: Reactions, Consequences, and Care*, the risk literature is reviewed and found to lack sufficient proof for grief having a causal relationship with morbidity and mortality. The cause is often attributed to grief after the fact owing to proximity.

Stroebe and Stroebe (1987) later reviewed the field in *Bereavement and Health* and came to a different view. They found evidence to support a strong relationship between widowhood and poor health outcomes. In their review of the risk literature, they showed that the only well-established risk factors were male gender, young age, and lack of forewarning. There is also quite a bit of evidence for perceived lack of social support.

There is a multiplicity of approaches to bereavement theory coming from our understandings of social constructionism, attachment theory, cognitive stress, and trauma theory, but still no comprehensive evidence-based theory for the experience of bereavement. Bereavement is now understood to have much more diverse individual trajectories with little evidence for stage theories.

Much more research is needed on risk for poor outcome and understanding the multiple interacting factors that influence the physical and emotional consequences of bereavement. Many bereaved people exhibit resilience in the face of loss, and this observation needs more understanding (Bonanno, Boerner, & Wortman, 2008). While it may not be necessary to relinquish continuing bonds with the deceased, it is not certain that maintaining such bonds is necessarily adaptive. However, achieving a sense of meaning, especially in the context of a family system, may be a principal task of coping with loss (Neimeyer, 2001).

Catherine Sanders (1993) summarized findings on risk factors in bereavement outcome and concluded that the following factors can be seriously debilitating:

- Ambivalence and dependency
- Parental bereavement
- Health before bereavement
- Concurrent crises
- Perceived lack of social support
- Age and gender (young age, male sex)
- Reduced material resources

Additional articles (Avis, Brambilla, Vass, & McKinlay, 1991; Barry & Fleming, 1988; Wolinsky & Johnson, 1992) have continued this debate about causality. One generally accepted observation is that bereaved people tend to have greater utilization of the health care system. This may be due to increased illness or to mental health reasons. After the death of a spouse, it is natural for a widowed person to seek support through accepted venues. If one is distressed, it is acceptable to go to the doctor. It may also be that taking care of one's ailments is put on hold in the period preceding a spouse's death and that these accumulated complaints are dealt with afterward.

Cost-Effectiveness of Bereavement Follow-Up

A study by this author (1996a) found that an association existed between being a widowed person who received bereavement follow-up through hospice and a decrease in the use of health care resources in the year following the death. A total of 354 widowed persons were studied over a 2-year period. In this time-series-designed study, there were three groups. The control group of 111 bereaved spouses received no follow-up. A limited-intervention group of 128 received a minimal follow-up consisting of four components. The third, extensive-intervention group of 115 received hospice services and a more extensive follow-up consisting of seven components.

Use of inpatient and outpatient health care services in the year before and year after the spouse's death was analyzed. Data on all scheduled outpatient services, both physician and nonphysician, were compiled. Data on all inpatient days were also collected for each participant. Clinic data for each group were analyzed by using a t-test for independent means to determine if the difference scores from the year before the death to the year after the death were significant. Results indicated that there was no significant difference between the no-intervention and limited-intervention groups. There was, however, a significant difference between the extensive-intervention (hospice) group and the no-intervention group ($p < .001$). This reduction amounted to an average of two clinic visits per participant.

More notable results were found in the inpatient data. Again, the limited-intervention group had a reduction in hospital use compared with the no-intervention group (345 days versus 166 days), but the difference was not significant. For the hospice group, however, there was a significant difference between it and the no-intervention group (345 days versus 49 days; $p < .0001$). This difference amounted to an average of about 3 hospital days per participant.

Hospice bereavement counseling and follow-up may be associated with reduced use of health care services. Spouses who were involved with the care of their loved one before the death and who received support before, during, and after the death seemed to have fewer health complaints. In a related study (Christakis & Iwashyna, 2003) of the impact of health care services on the health of those cared for, hospice caregivers were found to have lower mortality rates than matched controls.

Current Issues in Bereavement

The *Handbook of Bereavement Research and Practice: Advances in Theory and Intervention* (Stroebe, Hansson, Schut, & Stroebe, 2008) offers a thorough summary of some of the emerging themes, results, and controversies in the bereavement field. Current thinking on theories of grief in contemporary society are examined, and social and practical concerns are explored, including the case for prolonged grief disorder, the patterns and consequences of grief phenomena and their relational nature, and finally the development and efficacy of interventions for grief. This book expands on their two previous volumes (*Bereavement and Health*; Stroebe & Stroebe, 1987; *Handbook of Bereavement Research: Consequences, Coping, and Caring*; Stroebe, Hansson, Stroebe, & Schut, 2001).

Grief is not a universal process with typical symptoms. There are a wide range of individual and cultural differences in the way people grieve. What is normal in one culture may be quite aberrant in another. Adjustment to bereavement is a multifactorial process involving far more than emotional responses. Research is needed to look more at the full range of behavioral and cognitive reactions as well.

Stage theories may help one understand in a general way how people form attachments (Bowlby, 1980) or respond to stress (Horowitz, 1986), but they do not help one to understand a particular individual. Bereavement may not always result in distress but can usually be expected rather than seen as inevitable. Researchers do not yet understand the universality of grief, though grieflike responses have been found in very diverse societies and across species. More in-depth research is needed on the differing patterns of loss found in different cultures.

The duration of grief and recovery continues to be a controversial topic. Most agree that the majority of bereaved persons cease to grieve intensely after 6 months to 2 years. However, a return to baseline does not equal recovery. Some forms of grieving never end, and when there has been a strong attachment, emotional involvement with the deceased is likely to continue throughout life.

Are there differences in grief reactions following different types of loss? Is the loss of a limb or a farm as bad as the loss of a life partner? These questions remain hard to reconcile. Different types of loss may require that special needs are attended to for maximum benefit. Different forms of attachment may have a significant influence on grief, where those with overly strong attachments may be more vulnerable to chronic or exaggerated grief, whereas with overly weak attachment, grief may be characterized by delayed or masked grief.

Although there is evidence for an excess mortality rate among bereaved persons, there is still a great deal that researchers need to know about the impact of bereavement on health. Also, although some factors may pre-dispose someone to be more vulnerable to poor outcome in bereavement, there continues to be controversy over which factors they are and whether they are unique to bereavement or are associated with poor health in the population at large.

Progress has been made in the development of quantitative scales for measuring grief (Neimeyer, Hogan, & Laurie, 2008) from an attachment theory perspective (Bowlby, 1980), including general-purpose grief scales and specialized grief scales that look at different types of loss, and for grief in different cultures.

An examination of effective versus ineffective coping is a central research concern. Is suppression of memories an effective coping strategy, or is it essential to develop a tolerance for memories of the deceased?

Efficacy of Grief Counseling

A controversy developed in the period of 2000–2008 over an initial find-ing that those who underwent grief counseling were worse off after treat-ment than they would have been if they had been assigned to the control group. This "deterioration effect" proposed in dissertation research done by Fortner (1999) claimed that grief counseling could possibly be harm-ful. According to the dissertation research, nearly 38% of recipients of grief counseling theoretically would have fared better if assigned to the no-treatment condition. This finding was included initially in an article by Neimeyer (2000), though the results of the meta-analysis done by Fortner had not been peer reviewed or published. Subsequently a number of other authors cited Neimeyer, including Lilienfeld (2007), who listed grief coun-seling as a potential psychological treatment that can cause harm. That article was used as the basis for a segment of the ABC television show *Boston Legal*, which showed a psychologist being sued for malpractice for not informing a patient, who subsequently committed suicide, that grief counseling could be harmful. Clearly, the idea of grief counseling as inef-fective or harmful had begun to enter the realm of urban legend.

In response to this belief, two other authors (Larson & Hoyt, 2007) examined the finding of a deterioration effect and in their analysis raised serious questions about the original dissertation work. As part of an effort to unravel the source of the finding for harm, the original dissertation underwent blind post hoc peer review by two experts in meta-analysis from the American Psychological Association. They found that the statistic used to estimate the treatment-induced deterioration effect was "seriously flawed and that there was no valid basis for the claim that 38% of grief counseling clients suffered deterioration" (p. 349).

The controversy over the effectiveness of bereavement counseling continues as studies of treatment effect in grief counseling show widely varying results and are often less than for other forms of psychotherapy. Currier, Neimeyer, and Berman (2008) published a meta-analysis looking at the effectiveness of psychotherapeutic interventions for the bereaved that revealed low treatment effects. However, when looking at studies of bereavement intervention, there are many with methodological flaws, and most evaluate group interventions with people at varying periods following the death. Generally, ecologically valid studies of family members who sought out individual counseling achieved positive results from grief counseling, a closer parallel to general psychotherapy results. Grief counseling is not a standardized therapy like cognitive-behavioral therapy, so not surprisingly results will vary and those who seek treatment are likely to realize the most benefit.

Much more work is needed to identify who benefits most from which interventions at which points in the grief process. With the breakdown in social support networks, more formal support services are needed to compensate. As can be seen from the above, the bereavement field is still in need of a great deal of study.

Most would agree that how people grieve is affected a great deal by their life experiences with loss. These experiences can set a pattern for how people deal with loss throughout the life span. The following two cases are examples of how complicated grief can emerge and be dealt with.

Case Illustrations

Trudy

Trudy was a 63-year-old widow whose husband, Fred, had died of pancreatic cancer as a hospice patient. She was a social worker who was still working. She was an excellent caregiver who seemed to be coping well with her grief. After Fred's death in the hospice unit, she seemed numb for a month or so. The hospice volunteer who stayed in contact with her said she was not expressing any emotion and seemed to be stuck in her grief after several months.

Trudy came for individual counseling to assist her in moving through the grief process. She knew that Fred was dead, but she did not feel particularly sad and this bothered her. She felt mostly alone and a little overwhelmed. She missed Fred and at times had the feeling that he was still there. She thought she heard or saw him in brief glimpses.

In the course of therapy, Trudy showed a tendency to become dependent on me as her therapist and to be needy. She would become anxious if unable to make her appointment. As she recounted her life history, she focused a lot on her father. He was larger than life, and his death 20 years ago had been a great blow to her. As with Fred, she had been unable to grieve for him after he died.

As we explored the relationship with her father for clues to her current limitation, troubling memories began to come to light. She remembered that some 50 years ago, her father had molested her as a teenager. The experience had devastated her. She felt like an object rather than a person. She relived the experience as if it was yesterday.

Fred had been the savior who had taken her away, and now that he was gone she felt too vulnerable. She felt both anger and sadness about her relationship with her father. Many thoughts and feelings had to be expressed about this basic violation of trust before she could begin to express long-lost feelings of grief for her father and for the father he would never be.

Finally, she was able to express her pain at the loss of her husband. He had been a good husband and father, but she had always kept a part of herself away from him for fear that he would break her trust, too. Now that he was gone, she also grieved for the loss of the relationship she could not have with him because of her long-buried secret.

As these issues and feelings came to light, her ability to function as an independent person improved. She learned to take care of all the things Fred had done and to keep herself focused at work. As she terminated therapy, she was getting involved in many new outside activities that she had not had the courage to do before.

Margaret

Margaret was a 60-year-old widow whose husband had died 18 months earlier. She was referred by the mental health department of our medical center due to unremitting grief. Her husband had died suddenly of a heart attack. In our first session, she was convinced that nothing would help. She knew he was dead, and she was caught up in the intense pain of her grief.

Margaret had been very dependent on her husband for everything. He had made all decisions for her, and she had relied on him in a childlike manner. Her own father had died in an accident when she was 14. She felt completely alone and bereft in the world. She wanted someone to tell her that she would recover and it would be all right. In spite of this wish, she was easily angered and rejected all attempts at reassurance from friends, whom she had driven away through her continuous expression of painful grief.

She was isolated and complained of depressive symptoms. Her sleep was poor, along with her appetite. She enjoyed nothing and had difficulty thinking clearly. She had been taking an antidepressant but with little improvement.

Margaret had a long-standing history of emotional problems that preceded her bereavement. Before much progress could be made, a stable therapeutic relationship was needed. She had not developed emotionally, and it seemed like she was behaving much like a 14 year-old whose emotional outbursts could not be controlled.

After some trust was developed, we explored what had happened following the accidental death of her father. There had been a period of intense emotional reaction followed by a complete absence of grief. During her remaining teen years, she became withdrawn and could not express emotion except for occasional angry outbursts. She became very dependent on her mother. She married after high school and went from her mother's home to her husband's without ever having lived on her own.

Margaret came to see that her father's death had taken away what sense of basic trust she had had. Her response was to contain her emotions (particularly her anger at her father for leaving her) as best she could and to be dependent on others. When her husband died, it reactivated the conflicts she had never resolved as an adolescent. Over a course of therapy, she had to learn how to gain a sense of safety, control, connection, and identity, the building blocks of personhood that had not been gained following the death of her father.

I now turn from the more clinical aspects of hospice care to the larger issues of hospice's role within a community. The next chapter looks at how hospices have come to be the focal point in many communities for helping society to move toward a healthier understanding of death, dying, and bereavement.

Recommended Reading

Bowlby, J. (1980a). *Attachment and loss: Attachment.* New York: Basic Books.
Bowlby, J. (1980b). *Attachment and loss: Separation—anxiety and anger.* New York: Basic Books.
Cook, A., & Dworkin, D. S. (1992). *Helping the bereaved: Therapeutic interventions for children, adolescents and adults.* New York: Basic Books.
Dershimer, R. (1990). *Counseling the bereaved.* New York: Pergamon.
Klass, D., Silverman, P., & Nickman, S. (Eds.). (1996). *Continuing bonds: New understandings of grief.* Washington, DC: Taylor & Francis.
Lattanzi-Licht, M., Kirschling, J. M., & Fleming, S. (Eds.). (1989). *Bereavement care: A new look at hospice and community based services.* New York: Haworth.
Osterweis, M., Solomon, F., & Green, M. (Eds.). (1984). *Bereavement: Reactions, consequences, and care.* Washington, DC: National Academy Press.
Parkes, C. M. (1987). *Bereavement: Studies of grief in adult life* (2nd ed.). New York: International Universities Press.
Parkes, C. M., & Weiss, R. (1983). *Recovery from bereavement.* New York: Basic Books.
Rando, T. (2000). *Clinical dimensions of anticipatory mourning.* Champaign, IL: Research Press.
Raphael, B. (1983). *The anatomy of bereavement.* New York: Basic Books.
Silverman, P. (2004). *Widow to widow.* New York: Routledge.
Stroebe, M., Hansson, R. O., Schut, H., & Stroebe, W. (Eds.). (2008). *Handbook of bereavement research, and practice: Advances in theory and intervention.* Washington, DC: American Psychological Association.
Worden, W. J. (2008). *Grief counseling and grief therapy: A handbook for the mental health practitioner* (4th ed.). New York: Springer.

CHAPTER 6

Community and Public Engagement

Death is the only inescapable, unavoidable, sure thing. We are sentenced to die the day we're born.

—Gary Mark Gilmore

Educating the Community

Most hospices have made it a part of their mission to educate their communities about hospice and palliative care and issues around death and dying. Hospice has always been in part a consumer movement. As consumers of health care, many of the public have learned to become wary of the promises of modern medicine. Palliative care expands this movement directly into the acute care setting, where patients are at their most vulnerable.

Medicine attempts to remedy all ills and views death as an enemy to be defeated. People want to believe physicians when they say there is much that can be done to cure the disease. They want to believe surgeons when they say they got all the cancer. They want to believe that they will be one of the 5% who will respond to the new treatment. Elderly people tend to be more careful when facing medical decisions. They have seen friends and family who died alone and in pain in the hospital. They know of the disappointment after false hope has been dashed.

The SUPPORT Investigators (1995) study demonstrated that death in the U.S. health care system is still characterized by ignorance of patients' treatment wishes. As previously mentioned, this 2-year prospective observational study was an attempt to improve end-of-life decision making and to reduce the frequency of mechanically supported, painful, and prolonged dying.

A total of 4,301 patients participated in this two-phase study at five teaching hospitals in the United States. The first phase involved studying how patients died in the hospital and documented shortcomings in communication and the frequency of aggressive treatment administered. Findings from Phase 1 included that only 47% of physicians knew when their patients preferred to avoid cardiopulmonary resuscitation (CPR), 46% of physicians knew of do-not-resuscitate (DNR) orders that were written within 2 days of death, 38% of patients who died spent at least 10 days in an intensive care unit, and for 50% of conscious patients who died in the hospital, family members reported moderate to severe unrelieved pain at least half the time.

Even more troubling were findings from Phase 2 of the study. In an effort to improve the care of hospitalized dying patients, SUPPORT Investigators (1995) assigned specially trained nurse advocates to help make patients' treatment wishes known. They also developed a sophisticated algorithm that helped predict the probability of a patient's death within a time span (Lynn, Tino, & Harrell, 1995). Results of these prognostic reports were provided to physicians to help them more accurately determine which patients were nearing death.

During Phase 2 of the SUPPORT Investigators (1995) study, intervention patients experienced no improvement in patient–physician communication. Five areas were targeted to show positive outcomes: discussion of CPR preferences, timing of DNR orders, physician knowledge of CPR preferences, number of days spent in the intensive care unit, and level of reported pain. The intervention also did not reduce use of hospital resources.

These findings demonstrate what many in the hospice field already knew: that there is a great deal of room for improvement in the care of dying patients in the health care system. They also show that a concerted, well-orchestrated interdisciplinary effort is needed to deal with the complex and highly emotional issues surrounding dying.

The SUPPORT Investigators (1995) underestimated the difficulty of appropriately caring for the dying when they designed the study. They thought that all that would be needed was a little education for the patients, families, and physicians, and a major change would occur. They underestimated the tenacity of physicians in continuing to care for patients the way they always have. They did not see that for a major change to occur in the way patients were cared for, a multidisciplinary educational effort was needed.

Hospices and palliative care services know that they have a message that everyone needs to hear but that few wish to hear. In spite of 20 years of grassroots activity and concerted efforts at educating the public, most people still do not seem to have a clue as to what hospice does. There is usually a vague idea that it has to do with care of the dying, but few facts are known. A common misconception in the United States is that hospice is a place where people go to die. In the United Kingdom, this is closer to the truth.

Unless someone in your family or a close friend has used the services of hospice, it's unlikely that you will know much about it. When someone needs the services of a hospice or palliative care program, he or she is usually amazed at the services available. Yet even those who have direct experience receiving hospice or palliative care tend not to discuss it too often and relegate it along with the painful memories of the death.

In essence, the hospice and palliative care movement reminds people that death is a natural part of life and that they must take that knowledge into account whenever they make a treatment decision. How one dies is just as important as how long one lives, and dying is a human experience more than a medical event.

Avoidance

So why, after three decades of care for a large segment of the population, are hospice and palliative care still so little known? In spite of the culture's and media's fascination with unnatural or violent death, people avoid anything having to do with natural death. They prefer to ignore anything that reminds them that they will have to face their own deaths someday.

The denial that is pervasive in our society inhibits people from choosing to face the facts surrounding death and dying. Few people seek out an opportunity to become educated about death, grief, and loss. When they are exposed to the reality of death, they usually tend to put it out of mind as quickly as possible. Death happens, of course, but to other people, not ourselves; we maintain our unconscious belief in immortality. Perhaps it is like staring at the sun: a person cannot do so for long.

In annual in-services on hospice care given to hospital staff, the people attending seem to retain little from one year to the next. They ask what exactly it is that hospice does. Newsletters are sent out, educational mailings are done, articles in the newspapers are printed, and talks are given to all sorts of community groups—all to little avail. If one asked the average person what hospice is, he or she would be apt to say, "I'm not sure; I think it's a place you go when you are dying."

In the late 1990s, an organization was formed under the leadership of Dr. Joanne Lynn to help create a consumer voice for improved end-of-life care. Called Americans for Better Care of the Dying (ABCD), this organization attempted to grow a consumer membership of individuals who supported change in our health care system to demand improved care, not only from hospitals and nursing facilities but also from hospices. In spite of Dr. Lynn's personal determination and energy, the organization never grew enough to achieve its purpose. It would be very helpful if we could see a mass march, of patients and their families, on Washington to demand better care; but for the seriously and chronically ill and their tired families, however, this is not likely to ever happen. By 2007, ABCD decided to close.

Hospices have tried various strategies to make their message less difficult to hear. They have come up with various euphemisms for death. Instead of describing clients as *terminally ill*, they are now described as having a life-threatening illness or a life-limiting illness. Even the word *hospice* is a word with little prior connection to death. However, any word chosen will eventually become tainted by association with the reality of the work that is done. There has been discussion in the field about dropping the word *hospice* in favor of *palliative care*. This may reflect that hospice has become too identified with a narrowly defined set of services and structures. Whatever name is used to describe an effort to care for the dying will be difficult for people to embrace.

What is needed is a continuing effort to find the right language to speak to the public and engage them in positive ways. The National Hospice and Palliative Care Organization (NHPCO) and some of its members have made several attempts at public engagement campaigns around end-of-life care. Gallup polls have been conducted asking the public what they know about hospice and what kind of care they would want at the end of life (NHPCO, 1996c; NHF, 1999). In all these polls, it is clear that the public wants the kind of care provided by hospice and palliative care programs. However, the majority of the public still knows little about palliative and hospice care.

Based on focus groups and opinion polls, some attempts have been made to reframe or communicate positive messages about hospice and palliative care. In one campaign, the phrase used was "Comfort and compassion when it's needed most," and in another, "We come into the world with love, compassion and care: Don't we deserve the same when we leave?" In another poll of baby boom generation adults caring for aging parents, it was discovered that respondents found it easier to talk with their children about sex and drugs than their parents about death and dying. Such is the sensitivity of the subject.

Much more in-depth research is needed to develop the underlying messages that express the value of hospice and palliative care in ways that the public can hear and understand. There is not one message that will resonate with all. Different messages for the young and the old, and for different cultures and lifestyles, are needed.

Trauma Response

Some hospice programs have begun to expand their bereavement outreach programs to include services for victims of traumatic death. The whole field of trauma research and response has mushroomed in recent years. Large-scale disasters such as the 9/11 Twin Towers disaster and the Oklahoma City bombing have propelled the needs of victims into the public's eye. On the local level, there are numerous tragic events that leave victims in their wake. Hospices are a natural resource for providing ongoing support to victims.

The field of trauma response is generally divided into two major groups, the victim assistance organizations (such as the National Organization for Victim Assistance) and the emergency responder groups. Most states in the United States now have posttrauma response teams that can be readily mobilized to respond to either a major disaster or a local emergency.

These response groups are usually able to provide short-term services such as debriefing victims or emergency responders, defusing participants in an ongoing traumatic scene, or doing school intervention. Their intervention is in the period immediately after the crisis and is aimed at prevention of later posttraumatic stress responses in participants. There has been criticism of the use of critical incident stress debriefing (CISD). CISD was not developed using accepted methods and in some cases may result in retraumatizing individuals (Lilienfeld, 2007).

Except for unusual and large-scale disasters, there is little or no ongoing service to affected communities. Hospices can be part of the continuum of posttrauma response by offering a variety of services. They can assist in the longer term by providing services. Some are also working with local law enforcement to help them in responding to traumatic death by, for instance, having specially trained staff or volunteers who can accompany officers who must inform family of a traumatic death.

Hospice can add to the community response by providing ongoing services. Support groups or individual counseling can be offered to victims who continue to need to express reactions to the loss. Social support and social work assistance can be provided to the bereaved to help them adjust to life without the deceased. Chaplains can help victims cope with their anger at God. For those who are suffering more severe impairment, hospice can serve as a bridge for referral to mental health treatment.

Volunteer Training

Hospices have always relied on volunteers to help in caring for patients. All hospice volunteers must go through an extensive training program before assisting in care. They receive training in basics such as psychological reactions to death and dying, grief and loss, personal death awareness, confidentiality, documentation, and the interdisciplinary team.

Hospice volunteer-training programs act as a community education service. Many of the people who attend these programs do not end up as volunteers. They come to learn about hospice or to help them deal with their own death anxiety; as many as half of those who attend self-select themselves out of hospice volunteer training. A few are eased out by the volunteer trainers if there are apparent emotional problems or agendas for volunteering that are inconsistent with hospice. If someone has had a recent bereavement, wishes to convert others to a faith before dying, or is there to meet his or her own needs more than those of the patient and family, this person is not appropriate for work in hospice. Still, it is estimated by the NHPCO (2008d) that there are over 400,000 hospice volunteers in the United States giving over 16 million hours of care annually!

Hospice in the School System

Schools have been quite receptive to education from hospice programs. Requests for presentations on subjects such as death and dying, loss and grief, trauma, and advanced directives have proven hospice's value to the educational community.

Elementary and secondary educators are aware that there is very little opportunity to teach children about death in the current school curriculum. Children are very inquisitive about end-of-life issues, and teachers have very little experience in how to discuss the topic. Schools reflect society, which still has difficulty acknowledging that death is a part of life. Bringing in outside experts on the topic helps children learn to respond to death in healthier ways and relieves teachers who are sometimes fearful of mishandling the topic.

Where hospices have shown their expertise and given help to schools, schools have responded by giving hospices increased access and in some cases funding for their outreach activity. A typical scenario might include coming as a guest speaker for students, followed by doing training for school personnel, followed by being asked to respond to help groups of students following the death of a student, giving memorial services, and doing ongoing groups and classes for students or teachers.

As schools learn that hospices can be trusted to work within the education system, there are sometimes funds available to support outside consultation and education. These funds can be requested by hospice for services performed. Schools can also be prime referral sources for other support services for students such as grief camps, groups, or other activities put on by hospices.

Community colleges can also be forums for community education on hospice topics. Some hospices have banded together to conduct a course on hospice for the community.

There is also a growing interest in offering courses on death and dying as part of graduate and undergraduate curricula. Most psychology programs have an elective course on death and dying. Several universities also offer a degree program in thanatology, the study of death and dying.

Educational Organizations

The Association for Death Education and Counseling is a national organization that provides certification programs for death educators and counselors who specialize in working with the dying and bereaved. The association holds annual conferences and ongoing training programs for members to distinguish them as qualified to teach and counsel.

The NHPCO is the largest organization representing the interests of hospice and palliative care providers in the United States. Rather than being a trade organization, it is a nonprofit corporation that seeks to further care for the dying in the United States. The NHPCO provides education to hospices and related organizations and individuals. It conducts an annual clinical conference, an annual management conference, and several specialty conferences throughout the United States. The NHPCO provides technical assistance to hospice members throughout the United States, works closely with the Centers for Medicaid and Medicare on regulatory issues, educates members of U.S. Congress and presidential administrations, promotes quality palliative care through its quality initiatives, conducts research, and promotes the development of palliative care internationally.

The NHPCO coordinates a council of hospice and palliative professionals made up of 14 sections representing different disciplines and activities within palliative care. There are sections for CEOs and executive directors, administrators, nurses, social workers, spiritual caregivers, bereavement professionals, allied therapists, nursing assistants, public relations and development specialists, physicians, pharmacists, volunteers, and researchers, academics, and educators. Each section has regular meetings and a newsletter to share activities and to promote networking within respective hospice disciplines.

Each state has a hospice association that promotes hospice care at the state level. The NHPCO has a Council of States that is made up of the leadership of the state associations. The council attempts to coordinate education on a regional level for hospice programs. Education for hospice professionals is primarily done at the state and regional levels.

The National Hospice Foundation is affiliated with the NHPCO. It is a foundation whose purpose is to promote education and research in hospice care. The foundation has sponsored a number of important activities, including physician education teleconferences and a touring photographic exhibit on hospice care.

The Hospice Association of America is the second national organization focused on promotion of hospice care. The Hospice Association of

America is a part of the National Association for Home Care (NAHC). This association is the national trade organization that represents the home health industry in the United States. The NAHC has been trying to broaden its scope to include all health care activities that occur in the home. It is reaching out to the providers of paraprofessional services in the home, durable medical equipment providers, and home infusion and mobile health service providers. Many home health agencies that are members of the NAHC also provide hospice services. Hospice educational programs are conducted as part of the NAHC's national and regional educational programs.

The National Prison Hospice Association promotes hospice care for terminally ill inmates and those facing the prospect of dying in prison in the United States. The goal of this association is to support and assist corrections professionals and outside groups in their continuing efforts to develop patient care procedures and management programs in the prison systems. The NHPCO through its access program also promotes palliative care for prisoners.

The Canadian organization that represents the interests of palliative and hospice care providers north of the U.S. border is the Canadian Hospice Palliative Care Association. Every 2 years, an international conference on palliative care has been held in Montreal, Quebec, Canada. Dr. Balfour Mount (a pioneer palliative care physician) founded the conference, which is focused on expanding clinical knowledge of palliative care.

The European Association for Palliative Care has been formed to assist in the development of palliative care services throughout Europe. Conferences are organized, technical assistance is given, and the *European Journal of Palliative Care* is published for members and others.

Other regional palliative care organizations include the Asia Pacific Hospice and Palliative Care Network, the Latin American Association for Palliative Care, and the African Palliative Care Association. The International Association for Hospice and Palliative Care, based in Texas, has been providing support for the development of palliative care specialists throughout the world since its founding in 1980. A Worldwide Palliative Care Alliance has also formed as an alliance of all the national and regional associations (see chapter 13).

Caring Connections and the Schiavo Case

The NHPCO Caring Connections program was developed following the closure of the Robert Wood Johnson Foundation-funded Last Acts Partnership. The purpose of Caring Connections (n.d.) is to continue the effort to engage the public around the important issues surrounding end-of-life care (see http://www.caringinfo.org). Caring Connections provides free resources and information to help people make decisions about end-of-life care and services before a crisis. The program brings together community, state, and national partners working to improve end-of-life care through a national campaign called It's About How You LIVE.

Caring Connections has provided a number of consumer services including a state-specific advance directive library. Any consumer can go to the library and download an advance directive form approved for use in his or her state for free. One need only then follow the printed instructions for completion, and a legal advance directive is complete.

The importance of completion of an advance directive was highlighted by the case of Terri Schiavo. Ms. Schiavo was a woman who was in a persistent vegetative state after an apparent heart attack. Ms. Schiavo had not completed an advance directive and was kept alive on a feeding tube with around-the-clock personal care. An unfortunate and irremediable conflict arose between her husband and Ms. Schiavo's parents over whether to remove her feeding tube, as reported in the popular press. All of this conflict could have been avoided if Ms. Schiavo had completed an advance directive. Her husband, after assisting in her care for years in the hope that she might recover, contended that he had conversations with her wherein she stated that she would not want to be kept alive on tubes.

The Schiavo case involved hospice care in that when her husband first received court permission to remove her feeding tube, she was transferred to a Florida hospice inpatient facility for end-stage care. Subsequently, there were years of court battles ending finally in her tube removal and death. Throughout this ordeal, the hospice caring for Ms. Schiavo refused to abandon her and her husband and ensured that she was kept comfortable and well cared for. In spite of criticism that the hospice was complicit in her death, it was the position of the hospice program that decisions about whether to continue or discontinue medical treatments are the responsibility of the patient and his or her legally empowered surrogates, and that hospice's role was only to ensure that patients receive the best care possible at the end of life.

Educating the Medical Community

One of the hospice movement's original goals was to improve care of the dying in the health care system to such an extent that hospices would not need to exist. After more than 30 years, it appears that hospice is a long way from achieving that goal. As shown in the SUPPORT Investigators (1995) study, those dying in the health care system are still too often alone, in pain, and overtreated.

In some ways, the palliative care movement in the United States has been an effort to realize the goal of incorporating palliative care into the mainstream health care system. In 2007, the American Board of Medical

Specialties approved hospice and palliative medicine as a recognized subspecialty. This was a long-sought-after goal necessary for the acceptance of hospice and palliative care as a part of mainstream health care in the United States. Ten medical specialties have indicated a desire to add hospice and palliative care as a subspecialization, including internal medicine, family medicine, anesthesiology, physical medicine and rehabilitation, psychiatry and neurology, surgery, pediatrics, emergency medicine, radiology, and obstetrics and gynecology.

So how are health care professionals to be taught not only the skills of palliative care but also the judgment and values that are necessary when caring for those who are incurably ill? Medicine and nursing teach that the preservation of life is paramount. The pursuit of this ideal is well intentioned but can become perverted when it seeks to prolong life at any cost to the person.

Changing physician attitudes must be done as early as possible. According to information on medical school curricula, all U.S. medical schools offer some educational content on death and dying and palliative care. The average number of hours offered in these areas is less than 15 (Dickenson, 2007). Some medical schools and residency programs are starting to include opportunities to learn about palliative care, but these are not the norm. Approximately one-fourth of the schools offer students an opportunity to have a continuing relationship for several weeks with a terminally ill patient (Dickenson, 2006).

The Agency for Health Care Policy and Research (1994; now the Agency for Healthcare Research and Quality) has published guidelines for treating pain. One of its findings was that physicians received little training in pain management. In an effort to redress this lack, the National Institutes of Health recommended that funds be allocated to develop model training programs in hospice and palliative care for physicians. Proposals were received from hospices, medical schools, and residency training programs. A number of programs were funded in 1995 to develop curricula and physician–resident training models; these programs have been created by the American Academy of Hospice and Palliative Medicine; Hospice of the Florida Suncoast; the West Coast Palliative Care Center at the University of California, Davis; and Dartmouth University.

This effort was a small step in the right direction. It is only a small first attempt. What is needed is support from those who control decisions about medical school curricula. Medicine has grown so complex that there is hardly any room available in the 4-year curriculum for new content. Yet controlling pain and caring for people who are incurably ill are significant parts of a physician's duties in practice.

The American Academy of Hospice and Palliative Medicine is an association of physicians working in hospice and palliative care. The academy holds a high-level annual clinical conference and has established training programs for hospice medical directors.

In nursing, there are some efforts to provide specialized training in hospice and palliative care. The National Board for Certification of Hospice and Palliative Nurses now offers certification programs for hospice nurses, including RNs, LVN and LPNs, nursing assistants, and advanced practice nurses. A nurse must take and pass a national exam to become a certified hospice and palliative care nurse. Too often, nurses are hired to work in hospices and after a brief orientation are expected to be able to function as hospice nurses. Given the burgeoning literature on palliative care and the level of responsibility given to hospice nurses, it is reasonable to expect hospice nurses to receive considerable training before being asked to manage the care of a dying patient.

Social work standards were written for social workers who work in hospices (National Hospice Organization, 1994). These standards specify the training and experience needed for a hospice social worker. A certification program for social workers in end-of-life care began in 2008 as a joint effort between the National Association of Social Workers and NHPCO.

Support Groups

Many hospices formed out of support groups for cancer patients and those grieving a loss. These common concern groups emerged in the 1970s as part of the self-help movement (Alcoholics Anonymous, Parents without Partners, Widow to Widow Program, Compassionate Friends, etc.). People need to feel they have some sense of control over their problems. They need information and learn best from others who have faced the same problems that they are facing.

Today, support groups remain an important part of a hospice's scope of services. Hospices facilitate groups for a large variety of populations. In addition to cancer support, there are groups for people living with AIDS, caregiver support groups, and groups for specific disease populations such as breast cancer, laryngectomy, women's cancer issues, motor neuron disease, and so forth. In addition to general grief support groups, there are groups for survivors of suicide, murder victims, AIDS, the death of children, and so forth.

Groups range in style and content. Some are open, and others are closed after the first few sessions. Some are highly structured, and others vary depending on the needs of the participants attending a given session. Most include an education component. Some are nearly all educational, whereas others are nearly all support focused. Hospices often hold open sessions for the community to learn more about services. These are usually free sessions offering education to the public on topics such as preparing for death, making an advanced directive, and how to care for an ill relative. These sessions offer the public an opportunity to learn more about hospice services, to value what hospices have to offer, and to overcome misconceptions about hospice care.

Recommended Reading

Corless, I., Germino, B., & Pittman, M. (Eds.). (1995). *A challenge for living: Dying, death and bereavement.* Boston: Jones and Bartlett.
Corr, C., Nabe, C., & Corr, D. (2008). *Death and dying: Life and living* (6th ed.). New York: Springer.
DeSpelder, L., & Strickland, A. (2004). *The last dance: Encountering death and dying* (7th ed.). New York: McGraw-Hill.
Wass, H., & Neimeyer, R. (Eds.). (1995). *Dying: Facing the facts* (3rd ed.). Washington, DC: Taylor & Francis.

Web Resources

American Academy of Hospice and Palliative Medicine: http://www.aahpm.org
Caring Connections (a consumer education initiative of the NHPCO): http://www.caringinfo.org
Hospice and Palliative Nurses Association (HPNA): http://www.hpna.org
National Board for Certification of Hospice and Palliative Nurses: http://www.nbchpn.org

CHAPTER 7

Managing Hospice and Palliative Care

There go my people. I must find out where they are going so I can lead them.

—Alexandra Ledru-Rollin

We Don't Make Widgets

Providing leadership in a hospice program is one of the most challenging roles anywhere. A hospice must be run as a business and at the same time ought to function as a vehicle for the noble expression of humanity. This is not suggested out of misty-eyed sentimentality.

Where hospices may have lost their souls, it is because the demands of the business have overshadowed the essential vision of hospice: a community of people dedicated to the relief of suffering, who help make possible opportunities for growth at the end of life.

There is an ongoing tension between the demands of business survival and the need to preserve what is important and unique about hospice. There are also some who never understood hospice's mission in the first place and simply look on it as a product line, marketing device, or cost-effective way of caring for some of the more expensive patients in the health care system.

Hospital-based palliative care faces similar problems in having to justify expansion using primarily a cost-avoidance model with hospital chief financial officers who are more interested in fat revenue streams from new, cutting-edge procedures. Without a dedicated revenue stream, palliative care has learned how to use the existing channels of funding for consultations, procedures, and treatments. What isn't funded using this approach are the interdisciplinary team services found in hospice.

In most businesses, the essential purpose of the group's activity is simple. The corporation exists for self-preservation through the creation of profits. Profits are made if the product or service produced can be sold for more than it costs to produce; the greater the demand for the product or service, the larger the business.

Many businesses now realize that organizational self-preservation, profits, and growth can be enhanced by reframing the company as it exists for the purpose of delivering quality goods or services. The total quality management movement in manufacturing is spreading to the service industries. The more successful companies see themselves as existing for the purpose of providing a superior product or service to an increasingly global market.

In 1960, computer pioneer Dave Packard said:

> Many people assume, wrongly, that a company exists simply to make money. While this is an important result of a company's existence, we have to go deeper and find the real reasons for our being.... People get together and exist as ... a company so that they are able to accomplish something collectively that they could not accomplish separately—they make a contribution to society. (Carmichael, 2008)

Hospices began with the mission of providing a superior service for a vulnerable population. The need for financial survival and growth came later. Early hospices were only concerned with finding a way to meet the needs of dying patients in a local community. As the hospice movement has grown and matured, the need to improve access to hospice care has driven concerns with financial viability, management efficiency, and acceptance by the mainstream medical community. Although it is good for hospices to improve their funding and functioning, it should not be at the expense of their original purpose.

Some recent critics in the United Kingdom have questioned the continued relevance of the hospice movement. Colin Douglas (1992) has said, "The hospice movement is too good to be true and too small to be useful." He referred to the hospice movement as "deluxe dying for a minority" and expressed the most critical review by saying about hospice, "Well done, thanks, and good-bye" (p. 579).

The Business of Hospice

Hospice care is a managed care program. The reimbursement system for hospices in the United States at this writing is based on per diem payment. This is a set payment to the hospice for each day that a patient is enrolled in the program. Hospice is paid the set amount whether or not a direct service is provided that day. The hospice is responsible for making available a range of services and supplies for the terminally ill patient and family who enroll in the program.

These services include all necessary home care visitation services such as nursing, home health aide and homemaker care, social work, therapies, counseling, and volunteer visits. Also included in the per diem payment is provision of all the medical supplies, treatments, durable medical equipment, diagnostic tests, labs, outpatient procedures, and medications related to the terminal illness. These services need to be available or accessible to the patient and family 24 hours a day, 7 days a week, as determined by need. Consulting physician services can be billed for above the per diem. Hospice medical director services are covered under the per diem, but the attending physician of record can bill Medicare as usual.

Sometimes hospice is able to provide all these services to a patient and family for less cost than the amount of per diem received. If this happens, the hospice is able to keep the difference as a gain. For other patients and families, the cost of delivering all these goods and services is more than the amount paid. If this happens, the hospice loses money.

An analogy to this is that hospice is like an insurance company that accepts all applicants and cannot change the rate it charges. There is not a lot it can do to ensure that it is able to survive financially. Some of the decisions a hospice is forced to make to survive raise troubling questions. For instance, can a hospice decide not to admit a certain type of patient who is likely to require very expensive care? Can it limit the services provided?

Since the U.S. Hospice Medicare Benefit was established, hospices have operated in roughly the following way: The number of patients on whom hospice loses money should be less than those on whom it gains money. The belief is that if you cover the cost of treatments the patients want to continue, then physicians will refer more patients to you earlier and you will benefit overall. The patients wanting fewer invasive interventions subsidize those who are more expensive to take care of; overly restrictive policies that limit access to palliative treatments lead to shorter length of service and limited growth.

As the health care system has attempted to reduce expenses and coverage, there seem to be more patients who are looking to hospice to cover more and more treatments, medications, tests, and so forth. This has in some cases upset this delicate balance and caused hospices to become more cautious in patient admission. The point where access is difficult to determine continues to be the palliative-curative interface.

New developments in medicine and pharmacology are providing prolongative treatments to patients with fatal illnesses. These new drugs are not intended to cure the underlying illness or to relieve symptoms.

They are specifically intended to delay death, usually by only weeks or months.

Examples of these new treatments include Riluzole for Lou Gehrig's disease, protease inhibitors for AIDS patients, Inotropes for congestive heart failure, and newer oncologic treatments such as Taxol. These new drugs are very expensive and bring with them some ethical considerations. Is it life that is being prolonged, or is it dying? Is this expensive use of limited health care resources just, when others are forced to receive little or no medical care?

These decisions need to be made based on the individual patient's and family's values and goals. Too often, treatments are continued or instituted simply because they are available. The assumption is that life must be continued because there is a means to do so. Hospice and palliative care workers need to determine whether the treatment has value for the patient.

Often, it is the family who demands that treatment be continued. Too often, this is insisted on for reasons that have little to do with what the patient wants. Family members do not want to feel guilty for not giving the patient a treatment that could offer some continued life or benefit. The exclusive focus on the primacy of the patient as health care decision maker ought to be rethought. Patients do not make health care decisions in a vacuum. They often make treatment decisions based on the feelings of family members.

So how is a hospice to make the right decisions about serving the needs of as many dying patients as possible without going bankrupt? A number of solutions to this problem have been tried as the hospice movement has matured. These solutions include but are not limited to restricting access to some types of patients, serving patients under the home health agency model, increasing access to disease-modifying therapies, and increasing size to help spread risk.

Some programs have attempted to limit the populations served by hospice to contain risk. For example, there are programs that will not admit a patient who is receiving any chemotherapy or radiation, even if it is specifically for symptom relief. This is usually done by the hospice with the position that patients must not be receiving curative treatment while in hospice. The NHPCO has taken the position that no one should be denied hospice care with such blanket exclusions (*Hospice Service Guidelines and Definitions*; NHPCO, 2001). It is the job of the hospice program to distinguish those palliative treatments from curative treatments.

Another approach to the problem is to create new models of service delivery or to adapt old ones. Before the Medicare Hospice Benefit was created, some hospices used existing sources of reimbursement for elements of hospice care such as home health agency payment for skilled nursing, home health aide, therapy, and social work visits. These payments cover a portion of hospice service costs but have significant restrictions. The patient has to be homebound, only the skilled services of a nurse or other professional are covered, no medications are paid for (except under Medicare Part D), psychosocial services are very limited, and inpatient care is excluded. Under the new home health agency prospective payment system, there is an incentive to admit patients but to shorten episodes of care. Actually, under the home health reimbursement system, it may be advantageous for home health agencies to refer patients to hospice who meet hospice eligibility requirements. Some hospital-based palliative care programs have expanded to provide home-based palliative care utilizing the home health agency model for patients who do not qualify for hospice care due to continuation of potentially curative treatments.

So far, hospices have not had much success getting insurers to pay for services outside those covered under the Medicare Hospice Benefit. The future of hospice reimbursement may lie in hospice's ability to become more flexible in what it gets reimbursed for.

The majority of hospice programs in the United States serve a small number of patients each year. The median daily census was about 52 patients in 2007 (NHPCO, 2008). This is a small volume for the amount of overhead each hospice must carry. As the costs of delivering hospice care increase, programs must find ways to reduce expenses or to raise more financial support.

The trend is for programs to grow in size either through increased penetration of the population of terminally ill people or through acquisition or merger with other hospice programs. Increased size allows for better economies of scale, reduced costs through bulk purchasing, more ability to spread risks, and less overall overhead.

Along with increased size come new problems for the hospice. There may be less flexibility in meeting patient care needs, it becomes more difficult for the organization to function as a supportive community, and community support may diminish. Records and procedures become standardized, and processes become resistant to change. Employees feel they are part of a large company and do not know those with whom they do not work. The community perceives the nonprofit hospice as a large successful organization with reimbursement funding and no longer sees it as a charitable institution that needs financial support.

These challenges can be effectively dealt with if the organization empowers its employees to continually improve the organization, supports self-directed work teams, and seeks to meet the unique needs of the community it serves.

Hospice Care and the Curative Treatment Restriction

One of the primary reasons for the development of nonhospice palliative care in the United States is the Medicare Hospice Benefit (MHB) curative treatment restriction. Prior to the institution of the MHB, hospices admitted and cared for patients who continued chemotherapy, radiation therapy, and other treatments that in some circumstances could be considered efforts to cure disease. These therapies were rarely curative, and not many were available to patients with advanced life-limiting illnesses.

In fact, the original National Hospice Organization (NHO) standards in 1979 specifically defined hospice care as a combination of palliative and curative therapies:

Standard No. 1   *Appropriate therapy is the goal of hospice care*

   Principle: *Dying is a normal process*

Interpretation of Standard:

Appropriate medical care is always a blend of two complementary systems of therapy—curative and palliative. All patients receiving care in a hospice program are alive and needful of care regardless of the medical care required or of the length of time they are expected to live.

Curative therapies are treatments directed primarily toward eradicating a disease process. Even if they do not produce a cure, they may still be partially successful in establishing disease control. Such therapies are beneficial to the extent that they successfully remove or control the disease process causing distressing signs or symptoms. They usually do not directly benefit the patient and may temporarily increase the patient's distress before their antidisease effect becomes predominant.

Palliative therapies are those therapies directed primarily toward control of signs and symptoms. Their purpose is to control distress that results from a disease process that has not yet responded to curative endeavors, or for which cure is no longer possible. Palliative therapies do not directly affect the disease process itself.

Seldom does a patient receive therapy that is solely curative or palliative in nature. Rather, there is an equilibrium between these two systems of therapy from the time of diagnosis until the time of death.

Appropriate therapy is the blend of curative and palliative therapies that produces the greatest degree of relief from distress caused
by disease for the longest period of time with the least number of
distressing therapy-related side effects. (p. 10)

As seen in this elegantly written standard, the original intent of hospice was not to limit curative therapies but to use them appropriately.
However, when the MHB was being developed Mr. David Stockman, head
of the Reagan administration's Office of the Budget, insisted on including
a limitation on curative treatment, for fear that hospice would not be cost-
effective if allowed to provide both curative and palliative therapy. After
this provision was instituted, it became common practice for hospices to
disallow any therapy whose intent was to cure the illness, even though
most of these therapies we not in fact curative but were intended for symptom relief or in some cases a partial remission of disease or brief prolongation of life.

The Robert Wood Johnson Foundation (n.d.) established a research program titled *Promoting Excellence in End-of-Life Care*, whose intent was to
examine what happens when curative and palliative therapies were com-
bined. The program funded a variety of projects that examined this propo-
sition in numerous populations and found that the costs were no higher
when patients were allowed to continue their therapies. A number of positive benefits were found when this restriction was lifted, including greater
satisfaction, fewer symptoms, better treatment compliance, and reduced
hospitalization. For a complete review of the results of this research, go to
http://www.promotingexcellence.org.

What seems to happen when the curative treatment restriction is lifted
is that patients generally make better decisions about when to discontinue
curative, sometimes futile care. If patients lack access to palliative care,
they often are left with only the option of "What's the next treatment to
try?" When patients receive palliative care, they are more often presented
with various options and help in clarifying treatment goals, which leads to
more appropriate therapy.

Some hospice programs have attempted to circumvent the curative
treatment restrictions by admitting all terminally ill patients receiving disease-modifying therapies under the premise that none of these
disease-modifying therapies are actually curative. These programs can be
very successful in expanding hospice care but must be done with care so
that the program does not admit patients who are not qualified for the
MHB and so that the program does not cost more than the reimbursements it receives.

Managed Care

Because hospices under the Medicare/Medicaid benefit function as a kind of managed care provider, one would assume that hospice care would fit well into existing managed care systems. This is both true and false. It is true that hospices have learned to develop systems for managing and sharing financial risk. Insurers ought to embrace hospices that are striving to help patients make good decisions about end-of-life care. Inappropriate care at life's end is one of the major factors in escalating health care costs. Most studies have shown that hospice saves Medicare money.

So why is managed care seen as a threat to hospices? There are a number of reasons that have been put forward. First, insurers want the least expensive alternative for the patient. Many times, case managers view home health as less expensive. If they pay per visit and limit the visits, they are likely to pay out less for professional services than giving the hospice a per diem that is paid each day whether a visit is made or not. They often do not take into consideration that the package of services covered in the per diem, unbundled, may well cost the insurer more than the hospice's fee.

At around $140 a day for hospice care at home in 2008, insurers may feel that they are paying too much. Home health visits may run around the same price per visit but are not paid daily; however, they do not include costs for equipment, medical supplies, medication, counseling, volunteers, phone advice, and 24-hour-a-day availability.

The difficult fact is that many insurers do not want to pay for these costs. They are ratcheting down the payments for home health as well as hospice. They perceive that there is overuse in the field, and they do not want to pay for things that families may provide out of their pockets or with their own sweat.

This brings us to the second main issue in managed care. Managed care prefers to control all aspects of the delivery of health care. They would rather have home health and hospice as part of their integrated health systems. This integrated health system is controlled through a capitated payment methodology. In a capitated system, there are just so many dollars allocated for care in the home, including hospice. The managed care provider will keep this utilization under control by delivering the care directly or by using providers who agree to deliver the care for a discounted amount.

In capitated systems, there is a set income of money per member per month. After profits and so forth, there is only so much allocated for specific types of care. A provider is guaranteed to receive that allocation no matter how much actual service is provided. If the care costs less to deliver than the allocation, the provider gets to keep the difference. If more care is needed than funds allocated, the provider has a problem.

This type of system works reasonably well for care that is delivered in large volumes and is not greatly expensive (e.g., doctors' office visits).

People go to see their doctor fairly often, and it does not cost a lot per unit of service. There is an incentive to get the patient's problem solved without running a lot of expensive diagnostics and follow-up visits. In this arrangement, the doctor's office becomes a cost center rather than a revenue center. The more visits and services, the less money is made.

Hospice care does not do as well in this type of system. In a large population, terminal illness is a relatively infrequent event. It can also be a very expensive event. The cost risks can be quite high. Even one very expensive patient can skew the arrangement to cause financial difficulty for the provider. Infrequent services such as hospice should not be capitated. An anecdotal report out of Texas showed how capitation can have a negative impact on hospice. The capitated amount set out for hospice care resulted in the following. If the patient was under hospice care more than 12 days, the hospice program lost money. This creates an incentive that encourages last-minute referral and also creates barriers to hospice admission. Nonetheless, managed care seeks to capitate every cost in the health care system.

Large, seamlessly integrated health systems do not accommodate the local community hospice very well. There can be difficulty with the way they interact. There have been rare instances where patients who were good candidates for continued curative treatment have been referred for hospice admission. This may help the managed care provider's costs but is not in the patient's best interests; nor is referring the patient who will die within hours or days.

Many of the emerging integrated health care systems are adding hospice care to their continuum of care. This is being done either through acquisition of existing programs or through new start-up of programs in urban areas. New programs are more difficult to add owing to the time involved in establishing a referral base and in building a well-functioning interdisciplinary team. Many community- or home health agency-based programs are becoming more interested in securing their survival by becoming part of a larger entity.

The problem with integrated health care is that it is not yet really integrated. There is no sense of how each type of patient is best managed throughout a health care delivery system. What is really being managed is the cost of health care, not health care itself. What is needed is a seamless system of care that includes all providers and provides the right level of service when the patient needs it. Payment incentives will need to be aligned to this purpose to achieve this kind of continuity.

Leadership Style

Hospices tend to attract employees and volunteers who are very altruistic and demand a great deal of their leaders. The common dictatorial style of management found in the business world is not easily tolerated in a hospice program. The values of a hospice ought to be found in its leaders. If a hospice values teamwork, integrity, service, and caring, then it would be hypocritical for the leaders to act unilaterally, with self-interest and financial gain in mind.

Leadership in a hospice program calls on individuals to act with the utmost integrity. Hospice puts itself on a pedestal, per se, in that it claims implicitly to put service above self. Its leaders must do the same, or those they lead will refuse to follow.

On the continuum of leadership from laissez-faire to dictatorial, good hospice leaders tend to be toward the middle. They try to function democratically but are better off making disputed decisions decisively than being unable to act.

James Autry (1991), in his book *Love and Profit: The Art of Caring Leadership*, spoke to the type of management style that may work best in a hospice. Autry showed that the external rules and regulations of management are useless unless the leader really cares about the work and the people who do it. He pointed out that all real power is given to those who manage by those who are being managed.

The authoritarian "Wait until someone messes up and then pounce on them" style of management does nothing to further any enterprise. To improve morale, productivity, and success, you must really care about the people you work with, not manipulate them. Autry believed that the workplace can provide opportunities for spiritual and personal as well as financial growth.

Autry (1991) gave five guidelines for managers:

1. Avoid in-box management—stay in touch with employees regularly.
2. Care about yourself—you cannot motivate others unless your own battery is charged.
3. Be honest—if you care, you have to be willing to make critical appraisals as well as give compliments and set standards that are applied equitably.
4. Trust your employees—most management manages to make people feel mistrusted.
5. If you do not care about people, get out of management before it's too late; save your health and other people a lot of misery because the business of management is all about working with people. The policies and procedures are not important if you do not have your heart in it.

Max DePree carried forward a similar philosophy in his books *Leadership Is an Art* (1989) and *Leadership Jazz* (1992). He called leadership "liberating people to do what is required of them in the most effective and humane way" (p. 1). He saw the work relationship as a covenant between the organization and the people who work there. Effective leaders inspire people to see new possibilities.

Likewise, Jim Collins (2001) in his book *Good to Great* gives us valuable lessons in what make organizations great as opposed to just good. He identifies several characteristics of such organizations based on in-depth research. First, great organizations have leaders who have a paradoxical blend of personal humility and professional will. These (level 5) leaders have an ability to focus on the larger goal of building a great company rather than meeting personal ego needs.

Collins distinguishes between level 1 leaders, who are highly capable and make productive contributions through talent, skill, and good work habits; level 2 leaders, who contribute individual capabilities to the achievement of group objectives; level 3 leaders, who are competent managers that organize individuals and resources; and level 4 leaders, who catalyze commitment to a clear and compelling vision. The essential quality of level 5 leaders is a fierce commitment to the organization without regard to personal charisma or ambition. Level 5 leaders are quite ambitious, but their ambition is for the success of the organization, not themselves. They have both humility and incredibly intense will.

The other important characteristics of great organizations include the ability to ensure that the right people are on the team (first who, then what), the ability to confront the brutal facts facing an organization, the ability to develop a clear and focused purpose for the organization, the creation of a culture of discipline, and the accelerated use of technology. Essentially, this is the establishment of disciplined people, disciplined thought, and disciplined action. Readers are encouraged to read Collins's original works (e.g., Collins, 2001) and his adaptation of the Good to Great model to social service organizations.

Good leaders and managers are continually moving forward, not maintaining the status quo. If you are not continually reinventing your organization, then entropy is likely setting in. It helps to have a passion for management, to be truly excited about the possibilities of taking ideas and translating them into reality. It ought to give the same sense of satisfaction that an artist gets when creating an object of art.

It is easy to become weighted down by the uncertainties of the future, the overwhelming challenges that must be faced, and the sometimes petty concerns and conflicts of coworkers. Being effective as a hospice manager requires one to believe in the philosophy of hospice care, to believe in the people who are drawn to work in hospice, to trust people and be willing to delegate, and to maintain a sense of excitement about the possibilities that lie ahead. Leaders must always be looking ahead to provide a vision for what is possible, not bogged down in the day-to-day details.

To make change happen, the locus of responsibility for problem solving must shift to the people working there. Solutions to the challenges facing any company do not reside in the executive suite. They are in the collective intelligence of employees at all levels who must use each other as resources. Rather than relying on a hierarchical organizational structure in hospice, it is more effective to use a client-centered approach. Figure 7.1 diagrams the circular structure of a client-centered approach. In this structure, the patient and family are the primary focus of everyone's efforts. The clinical staff has primary responsibility to care for them. In the next circle, the administrative and operations staff focus on making sure the clinical staff have the resources and support to meet the needs of the patient and family.

Hospice as Community

Organizations use many metaphors to describe their functioning. The most popular seem to be based on sports. The team metaphor is most common

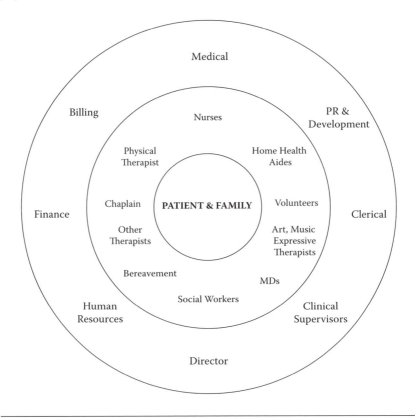

Figure 7.1 Client-Centered Organizational Chart

and denotes a closely functioning unit under tight direction by a leader, the coach. It is competitive, is always opposed to other teams, and strives to be victorious. Hospice workers describe themselves as team members, although the analogy is a poor one. Hospice team members have no one to compete with. Their success does depend a great deal on cooperation and striving toward a common goal, but the goal is not to defeat anyone except, say, the effects of a terminal illness.

Another metaphor used is that hospice people are like family. They are close to each other and support each other through difficult times. Again, this analogy has difficulties. Everyone who works in a hospice comes from a different family. Each of those families has different dynamics. Some families can be very conflictual. Bringing family-of-origin issues to work can create all sorts of difficulties and can interfere with the ability to do what one is there to do.

A more helpful metaphor for hospice as a work group is a community. In a functioning community, each member has a distinct role that is needed for the community to operate successfully. Each role complements others and creates a kind of interdependence. There can be overlap as people cover for each other if needed in performing tasks.

In hospice, the total care of the patient is dependent on the efforts of each caregiver. If anyone fails to do his or her part, there is an effect on all. For example, the care can be excellent for months, but if the on-call nurse fails to be there for the family when the patient dies, the family may remember only their disappointment at the end. The expression "It takes a village to raise a child" could also be modified to "It takes a community to care for a dying person."

Volunteer Issues

Hospice and palliative care in the United States began through the efforts of volunteers. Many professionals and laypeople gave of their time and talents to create a new way of caring for dying people. The fact that people give of themselves to care for others has powerful significance to those who receive the care. People experience care given by those paid to provide care differently than they experience the same care given by a volunteer.

This observation has great significance for the success of the palliative care movement. The extra dimension of caring provided by volunteers has always been one of the unique features of hospice care. It is also one of the features that has become hard to sustain. As funding for hospice care has increased, so have the paid staff needed to deliver the increased benefits of hospice care to an increasing number of people.

When hospices cared for a small number of patients at a time, volunteers could handle the load. Now there are hospice programs caring for thousands of patients at home on a given day. As volunteers nowadays are often people who also work, it is impossible for volunteers to be able to respond to all the needs of patients who depend on hospice for their care. Palliative care programs also use volunteers but sometimes to a lesser extent.

There are also some 5%–7% of U.S. hospices that are not Medicare certified and that continue to provide all their services for free. They are often quite successful in delivering compassionate care, which may include all the components of certified hospices without the bureaucratic limitations that certification can bring. Some of these programs work in concert with a local home health agency to deliver nursing care. This approach can be successful; however, it may also leave the patient and family without services and benefits that can be provided under the Medicare hospice benefit.

Another important dynamic here is that volunteers are less inclined to give when they know others are being paid to provide the same services. People in this society are very focused on remuneration and can be resentful if they feel they are being taken advantage of. Some volunteers give their time with the expectation that they will eventually be paid for their services when a position becomes available.

These issues have led to a situation where few volunteers are used in hospice in a professional capacity. The main role of the hospice volunteer in the United States is to be a support person who provides emotional support and practical assistance for the patient and family: to be a listener when a day has been hard, to be there to give respite so the family can get away to do errands, to drive to an appointment, or to help with the kids.

In the developing world, health care workers are a major part of palliative care delivery. These trained paraprofessional health care workers visit patients and are usually unpaid workers. The motivation for volunteering can be to give back to the community, as in the volunteers of the Network Neighborhood project for palliative care in Kerala, India; or to express the values of faith in the Evangelical Lutheran Church workers in Tanzania. Medical, nursing, and psychosocial professionals need to be involved and backing up these home-based care workers for this arrangement to be successful, but developed countries could learn that a great deal of palliative care can be delivered by such volunteer workers.

To the credit of the hospice movement, volunteers still play a very important role in caregiving, unlike other social movements begun by volunteers. A volunteer can be the most significant person to the dying patient. Volunteers often have more one-on-one time to spend with the patient and can become very close. They provide much of the hospitality of hospice.

Standards and Accreditation

Standards

At the beginning of the hospice movement, there were few standards for how a hospice program ought to function, beyond those characteristics listed in chapter 1. Various standards have been put forward for hospice services. At the present time, the most comprehensive standards available in the United States for hospice care are the NHPCO's (2006b) *Standards of Practice for a Hospice Program.* The quality partners initiative is NHPCO's national program to ensure all provided organizations deliver quality care to patients and families.

The NHPCO's standards (2006b) are based on the 10 components of the quality initiative:

- Patient- and family-centered care
- Ethical behavior and consumer rights
- Clinical excellence and safety
- Inclusion and access
- Organizational excellence
- Workforce excellence
- Standards
- Compliance with laws and regulations
- Stewardship and accountability
- Performance measurement

These standards were developed by the NHPCO Standards and Accreditation Committee to reflect the breadth and scope of state-of-the-art hospice care in the United States. The Standards and Accreditation Committee is made up of experienced hospice professionals from around the United States. Representatives of the hospice disciplines are included (nursing, social work, chaplaincy, education, medicine, management, and administration), and support is provided by NHPCO staff.

The standards are presented in a principal-standard-practice example format. Each chapter is introduced by principles that reflect a fundamental tenet of hospice care related to that chapter. Each standard is a norm that represents excellence in hospice practice. Practice examples are examples of ways to measure the standards. The NHPCO (2001) has also published a companion to the *Standards* titled *Hospice Service Guidelines and Definitions* that gives specific guidance on issues such as staffing ratios and guidelines for services offered. The NHPCO also has a standards self-assessment process for members that allows you to rate compliance with NHPCO standards and produce a report providing guidance on how to improve compliance. The standards in each chapter tie directly to the

NHPCO's quality initiative so that hospices can also ensure compliance with the quality initiative by meeting the standards.

The patient- and family-centered care chapter focuses on the need to treat the patient and family together as the unit of care and includes standards that address access to the provision of care 24 hours a day; standards to ensure continuity of care; standards related to the development, modification, and implementation of the interdisciplinary team care plan; and standards relating to the provision of bereavement follow-up programs and services.

The chapter on ethical behavior and consumer rights focuses on the importance of upholding high standards of ethical conduct and advocating for the rights of patients and their family caregivers. Standards in this section address involving patients and families in decision making, rights to confidentiality, addressing complaints, acknowledging both patient rights and responsibilities, addressing ethical dilemmas when they arise, and appropriate use of the bereaved in hospice volunteer activities.

The chapter on clinical excellence and safety addresses the importance of safety in the provision of hospice care and ties to the NHPCO outcomes pathway (NHO, 1997a). Standards in this chapter include both the treatment and prevention of distress based on the patient's desires and preferences for care; special attention to the pharmaceutical needs of patients and the safe handling of medications; appropriate management of diagnostic services; the safe provision of complementary and disease-modifying therapies, as appropriate; the identification of psychosocial concerns and the prevention of self-harm; proactively preventing problems with coordination when changing care settings; planning for environmental safety, security, and emergency preparedness; safe handling of infectious and hazardous materials; and implementation of infection control programs. Other areas addressed include fire safety, utility system management, safe handling of nutritional and pharmaceutical products, incident monitoring and reporting, medical equipment handling, and record keeping.

Under inclusion and access, the focus is on inclusiveness in communities served by ensuring that all people—regardless of race, ethnicity, color, religion, gender, disability, sexual orientation, age, disease, or other characteristics—receive services. Standards address the importance of periodic community needs assessments, sensitivity to cultural diversity, the provision of bereavement services to the larger community, and the provision of services that tie to the identified needs of the communities served.

The section on organizational excellence focuses on building a culture of quality and accountability within the organization that values collaboration and communication and ensures ethical business practices. Standards address the need to accurately represent services provided to the community, and the collection and dissemination of accurate data on organizational operation.

Workforce excellence addresses the need for an appropriate number of staff and volunteers to meet the unique needs of the patients and families the hospice serves. Standards also address the need for staff and volunteers to reflect the community's variety and diversity, hiring practices that are competency based and nondiscriminatory, initial training and ongoing in-service training and development, clear personnel policies, leadership development, competency assessment for clinical staff and volunteers, the use of specially trained caring volunteers, and ongoing supervision that is provided for all staff and volunteers.

The workforce excellence standards call for quality interdisciplinary care delivery, with provisions that call for active involvement of the medical director in the supervision of medical care, active involvement of the attending physician in the provision of care, nursing care that is delivered based on the initial and ongoing assessment of the patient and family's needs according to the plan of care, social work services that are also based on initial and ongoing assessments and the plan of care, other professional and paraprofessional services such as therapies or home health aide services, spiritual care and services, and volunteers used in a variety of roles.

The standards chapter calls on hospice programs to utilize the NHPCO standards (2006b) or another framework like the National Consensus Project's *Clinical Practice Guidelines for Quality Palliative Care* (2008) to guide operations and care. Further, this chapter calls for ongoing self-assessment and performance improvement. The section on compliance with laws and regulations addresses compliance with applicable laws, regulations, and professional standards of practice implementing systems and processes that prevent fraud and abuse.

Stewardship and accountability standards concern the effective operation of the governing body; strategic planning and resource management; fiscal and fiduciary responsibility; assessment of leadership performance; administrator authority and responsibility; administrative policies that define the roles and responsibilities of the governing body, administration, and the interdisciplinary team; protection of information against loss, theft, or destruction; and maintenance of confidentiality.

The final chapter on performance measurement addresses collecting, analyzing, and actively using performance measurement data to foster quality assessment and performance improvement in all areas of care and services.

One of the current problems in the U.S. hospice community is the lack of consistency among hospices as to compliance with standards. The NHPCO standards are professional association standards. A member of the NHPCO is expected to meet the standards, but there is no means of enforcement. Too few hospices conduct self-assessment, let alone report their results. Another approach to standards compliance is to seek voluntary accreditation. Accreditation is a useful way to gain acknowledgment for standards compliance, though it is not a guarantee of quality palliative care.

For palliative care providers, a set of consensus standards has been produced (National Consensus Project, 2008) that were developed by the leading palliative care organizations in the United States: the NHPCO, the American Academy of Hospice and Palliative Medicine (AAHPM), the Hospice and Palliative Nurses Association (HPNA), and the Center to Advance Palliative Care (CAPC). These consensus guidelines describe how palliative care should be provided, especially outside of formal hospice programs.

Accreditation

In 1984, the Joint Commission on Accreditation of Hospitals (JCAHO) established an accreditation program for hospices. The accreditation standards were developed with extensive input from the hospice community. In 1990, the JCAHO discontinued the program. Of the approximately 550 hospices accredited by the JCAHO during that period, only about 50 community- or home health agency-based hospices made the voluntary decision to become accredited. The remainder are hospital-based programs that had to be accredited because of their hospital ownership.

The bulk of the hospice community did not support the program with their participation. Many programs said that they already had to meet Medicare guidelines and questioned the value of accreditation. As a result, the JCAHO was losing money and had pressure from the hospitals to discontinue the program.

In 1995, the JCAHO decided to again offer accreditation to hospices. This time, it would be as a part of the home health accreditation program. Many hospices pushed for a separate program. It was felt that making hospice a part of the home health program would reinforce the erroneous conclusion that home health and hospice were synonymous. Nonetheless, the JCAHO went ahead with the program. Hospitals and home health agencies with hospice programs are generally required to be surveyed.

Also, the Community Health Accreditation Program (CHAP) has had a hospice accreditation program for many years. In 1999, CHAP was the first accrediting body to gain deeming authority to accredit hospices at the same time as granting Medicare Hospice certification. Many of the CHAP accreditation standards are based on NHPCO standards. A third program for hospice accreditation is also available. The Accreditation Commission for Home Care (ACHC) also provides accreditation for home health and hospice (see the resources at end of this chapter).

Examples of Problems in Management

What follows are some examples of real problems seen in starting and running hospice programs. It is hoped that the reader will use them as instructive examples to be avoided in the course of operating any organization.

A hospice program was started by a group of people, including a physician, who all volunteered their time. Funding was sought, and a nonprofit board of directors was formed. The physician became the medical director as well as chairman of the board. A group of community people were invited to be members of the board, including another local physician. In the course of developing programs and hiring staff, the director, who was inexperienced in management, was asked to hire as a nurse manager the former wife of one of the board members.

Time passed, and the program grew. The nurse manager was ineffective in coordinating the clinical program, and the other staff began to complain to the director. The director tried to help the nurse manager to improve but was rebuffed. He began contemplating dismissal of the nurse manager and went to the medical director to discuss it. The medical director was against the idea.

The director went to a psychotherapist who had been hired to provide support to the patients as well as the staff and learned that the clinical manager and the medical director were having an affair. The director confronted the medical director about this but got no response. The director, realizing his predicament, decided it was probably best to leave the organization. Soon after this, at the chairman's suggestion, the board privately suggested that the director resign.

This example shows how dangerous it can be to confuse roles between the board and staff and how important it is to avoid dual relationships. Boards must avoid unethical self-serving actions. It is also a reminder that emotional entanglements can become a minefield in any organization.

The next example involves leadership style. A new hospice director was hired to run a community-based hospice that was a small, volunteer-based program. This director had a background in business and began working to establish the program on a sound financial footing. She gained Medicare certification for the program and greatly expanded the service area.

As funds came in, the program grew and more staff were hired. Each year, the fund balance grew and the organization saw a significant net profit. To maintain this level of financial performance, the director required the staff to justify all expenses. If a patient was hospitalized, the nurse case manager would be grilled about why this was needed (sometimes in front of coworkers). Any unusual expenses were questioned, and sometimes physicians were told they could not order tests or certain medications.

A rift grew between the office staff and the clinical staff. The office staff felt they were most important because they kept things organized and financed.

The clinical staff felt they were most important because without them, there would be no hospice care. They resented the emphasis on finances and the intrusions into their clinical judgment. They wanted some appreciation rather than just criticism for things that they could not control.

The director felt she had enemies on the staff and sought to get rid of some individual staff. Finally, the situation came to a head, and most of the clinical staff resigned. The director decided the situation was too stressful and also resigned. The organization was left without leadership and with a demoralized staff.

Hospices are often started by charismatic leaders without the skills to build an organization. At this point, boards often bring in someone with a business background who succeeds in creating the necessary structure but who lacks the vision or values to carry the organization forward. It is relatively easy to set up a business structure. What is needed are leaders who can inspire the staff to grow and move forward with the organization.

We turn now from specific hospice management issues to some of the more general problems hospices face in our health care system. The Medicare Hospice Benefit has shaped much of the movement in the United States. We will explore the impact of the MHB on hospice, as well as associated problems.

Recommended Reading

Collins, J. (1994). *Built to last: Successful habits of visionary companies.* New York: Harper Business.

Collins, J. (2001). *Good to great: Why some companies make the leap … and others don't.* New York: Harper Business.

DePree, M. (1989). *Leadership is an art.* New York: Dell.

DePree, M. (1992). *Leadership jazz.* New York: Dell.

Web Resources

Accreditation Commission for Home Care: http://www.achc.org

Community Health Accreditation Program: http://www.chapinc.org

Joint Commission: http://www.jointcommission.org

National Hospice and Palliative Care Organization Quality Initiative: http://www.nhpco.org/quality

National Hospice and Palliative Care Organization Regulatory and Compliance Center: http://www.nhpco.org/regulatory

Promoting Excellence in End-of-Life Care: http://www.promotingexcellence.org

CHAPTER 8

Hospice and Palliative Care in the U.S. Health Care System

> What tormented Ivan Illich most was the deception, the lie, which
> for some reason they all accepted, that he was not dying but was sim-
> ply ill, and that he only need keep quiet and undergo a treatment and
> then something good would result.

> **—Leo Tolstoy, *The Death of Ivan Illyich***

Death in the United States

In the 1800s and early 1900s in Sweden, just-married couples would visit the church graveyard to pick out a spot to bury their children who would not survive. High infant and childhood mortality was a fact of life, and few lived to a ripe old age. Thanks to advances in modern medicine, people can now look forward to an average life expectancy in the 70s. Although they may live longer, however, they may not enjoy the support of extended family that their ancestors did.

Today the family is barely able to take care of itself, let alone elderly infirm relatives. Most families, if intact, lack the ability to provide full- or part-time elder care. It is the norm for both husband and wife to work outside the home. The sense of bonding and acceptance of responsibility for parents seen in earlier generations is noticeably lacking in today's society. The proliferation of skilled nursing facilities for care of elderly and infirm persons is a testament to the breakdown in family and social structure.

In a Gallup Poll (discussed in National Hospice Organization, 1992), Americans were asked where they would want to be cared for if they faced a terminal illness. Nine out of 10 people said they preferred to be cared for and to die in their own homes, and 3 out of 4 were very interested in hospice care when it was described to them. However, 22% of those who were interested in the services hospice programs provide said, when presented with the word *hospice*, that they were unlikely to choose it because they were unfamiliar with it. By 2006, the majority of the public was aware of the word *hospice*, and most now know that it is covered by insurance.

There have been approximately 2.4 million people who die each year in the United States in recent years. There are many who will not use hospice or palliative care prior to death. These include all the obvious sudden deaths from accidents, suicide, homicide, sudden cardiac failure, and strokes, but also from non-HIV infectious diseases, and from acute conditions that occur in people who were otherwise healthy prior to their illness and death. These groups represent approximately 32% of all deaths (Connor, 1999). The remaining 68% or roughly 70% of deaths are from cancer, chronic organ failure, frailty, or dementia. These are the deaths that can most benefit from palliative and hospice care.

The prospect of health care reform is not unlikely in the United States. Both political parties are advocating for change. We need a system of health care like other major industrial countries that can guarantee that all citizens will receive health care especially at the end of life. It is unclear what impact something like universal health care would have on hospice. Likely, such a change would be a good development for care of the dying and might accelerate acceptance of palliative care.

The Medicare Hospice Benefit

In the 1970s, American hospices were mainly organizations that survived on grants, donations, and volunteers. Professional nursing services were often provided by a local home health agency, if at all. Some hospices provided free nursing services or got licensed as home health agencies to receive reimbursement for home health. Emotional, spiritual, and practical support continued to be provided by volunteers.

Volunteer services by professionals were hard to sustain. As money was raised, there was pressure to pay for professional services. When one professional got paid, others were reluctant to donate their services. When professionals from other organizations were involved, it was difficult for hospice to be in control of the care delivered. Gradually, U.S. hospices had to find a way to finance their multidisciplinary operation.

In the United Kingdom, hospice care was provided by professionals from the start; there was less emphasis on lay volunteering. Funding came primarily from philanthropic sources. Nearly all care was delivered in an inpatient setting. Supporters could see bricks, mortar, and how care was being delivered. The UK National Health Service only pays for about 38% of community hospice expenses.

In the United States, care was being delivered in the patient's home. Initial foundation and grant support was decreasing as hospices were no longer the new thing. Hospice leaders saw that for hospice care to grow and for comprehensive services to be delivered, there had to be an ongoing source of financial support. Because the health care system was funded through insurance reimbursement and most hospice patients were elderly and covered under the Medicare program, it made the most sense to develop a hospice Medicare benefit.

A national task force was formed to develop a model benefit proposal. The Health Care Finance Administration (HCFA) conducted a demonstration project to study the feasibility of reimbursing hospice care. Based on the results of that project, in 1982, Congress created a Medicare benefit for hospice care. The National Hospice Organization (NHO) became a forum for debate on the pros and cons of government support for hospice care. Some believed that becoming part of the reimbursed system of health care would ruin the U.S. hospice movement. Others saw it as the movement's means for success.

Those who worried about creation of a hospice benefit feared that it would introduce bureaucracy into the movement. Limiting admission to 6 months seemed an arbitrary restriction. They realized that hospices would have to become professional organizations with all the accompanying structures and documentation. There was a fear that volunteers, who were the mainstay of the movement, would be shoved aside by professionals. Some felt that hospice care should not be paid for, and that to introduce payment would contaminate the purity of providing selfless service to dying patients.

Others believed that hospice care would never become part of the health care system or be able to serve significant numbers of dying people without a reimbursement system. They argued that current hospice services lacked the professionalism and resources needed to deliver comprehensive services. This argument has largely been settled. Today over 93% of U.S. hospices are Medicare certified, and the Medicare Hospice Benefit is responsible for the phenomenal expansion of hospice care in the United States.

Medicare Certification

Medicare Hospice Benefit regulations require a hospice to become certified before receiving reimbursement. Usually a state surveyor will visit the hospice to determine if all the "conditions of participation" in the program were met. These conditions include arrangements for a physician medical director, an administrator, and a patient care coordinator. The hospice had to employ all "core" members of the hospice team, including nurses, social workers, medical director, and counselors. Bereavement follow-up with the families served had to be provided for at least 1 year. Hospice could either directly provide or contract for home health aides/homemakers; physical, speech, and occupational therapists; and inpatient care for symptom management and respite. In addition, the program has to provide for medical supplies, durable medical equipment, and medications. All these services have to be delivered if they were reasonable and necessary for the palliation and management of the terminal illness. Medical and nursing services, and other team services as needed, had to be available 24 hours a day, 7 days a week.

To qualify for the Medicare Hospice Benefit, a patient must be terminally ill with a life expectancy of 6 months or less if the illness runs its normal course. The patient must reside in the hospice's defined service area and must agree to receive palliative rather than curative care. The hospice is prohibited from providing curative care as part of its interdisciplinary team plan of care. A consent form is signed by the patient acknowledging that he or she is aware of forgoing other Medicare benefits for the terminal condition, and chooses to receive palliative care.

Hospices have to keep records, perform assessments, and develop and update plans of care. These updates are to occur at least every other week. Hospices have to provide education and in-service training for staff and volunteers. Volunteer activities have to comprise at least 5% of all clinical services, and cost-effectiveness had to be documented. The program had to conduct quality assurance activities and comply with all laws and regulations.

In May 2008, the 25-year-old Medicare hospice conditions of participation were republished with significant revisions designed to emphasize the importance of patient rights and improvement in quality care (Centers for Medicaid and Medicare Services [CMS], 2008). Major new requirements for Medicare-certified hospices include the following:

- The provision of a model statement of patients' rights that includes the right to effective pain control
- Strengthened provisions for comprehensive patient and family assessments done in a timely manner

- Requirements for interdisciplinary care planning and coordination of services
- A major emphasis on quality assessment and performance improvement
- Strengthening requirements concerning the organizational environment including:
  - Clinical records
  - Drugs and administration
  - Inpatient care
  - New requirements for delivering hospice care in the nursing facility
  - Personnel qualifications including criminal background checks for all staff and volunteers

Levels of Care

Four levels of care are covered under the Medicare Hospice Benefit. Routine home care is the benefit if the patient is at home or in a nursing facility and receiving routine services. Continuous home care can be provided during periods of crisis. Anywhere from 8 to 24 hours of mostly skilled care can usually be paid for if it would keep the patient out of the hospital. The third level of care is inpatient respite. This is up to 5 days of inpatient care in a Medicare-certified acute or skilled nursing facility for the purpose of giving the patient's caregivers a rest. The fourth level of care is general inpatient care, which again is provided in Medicare facilities and is for active management of distressing symptoms of terminal illness.

The patient is entitled to two hospice benefit periods of 90 days, and an unlimited number of 60-day benefit periods. At the end of each period, the patient must be recertified as terminally ill. Upon admission the patient is required to sign an election statement signifying that she or he chooses hospice care for management of the terminal illness in place of regular Medicare benefits. The hospice must also obtain the signatures of the patient's attending physician and the hospice medical director certifying that the patient has 6 months or less to live if the illness runs its normal course.

Growth

The growth of the patient population served by hospices in the past 25 years has been phenomenal. In 1985, when NHO did the first hospice census, 158,000 patients were served. The latest census conducted in 2007 revealed that 1,400,000 were served. Figure 8.1 illustrates the growth in hospice patient admissions. Average growth in patients served has been 16% since 2000.

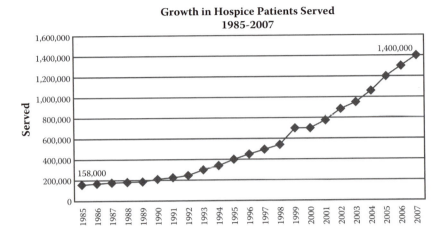

Figure 8.1 Growth in U.S. Hospice Patients Served

In the 30-some years since the first hospice program began in the United States, there has been a rapid proliferation of program development. In 2008, the National Hospice and Palliative Care Organization (NHPCO) identified over 4,700 operating or planned sites where hospice programs were delivering care in all 50 states and Puerto Rico. Average annual growth of new hospices has surged in the past 8 years.

In 1994, 14.8% of all people who died in the United States from all causes were under the care of hospice programs. By 2008 that number had increased to two in five, or almost 40% of all deaths from all causes. In 1994, 36% of those who died of cancer received hospice care. In 2002 the percentage of cancer deaths in hospice increased to 65% (Connor, Elwert, Spence, & Christakis, 2007). In 1994, 31% of people with HIV/AIDS who died in the United States received hospice care. Thanks to highly active antiretroviral therapies, the percentage of hospice patients with HIV/AIDS is now 1%.

Hospice care was predominantly delivered to cancer patients in the early days. The NHPCO challenged U.S. hospices to expand to serve all patients with life threatening illnesses. Gradually the percentage of patients with noncancer diagnoses has increased. The percentage of noncancer patients served has grown to overtake the proportion of cancer patients. In 2007, almost 59% of hospice patients had nonmalignant diseases (go to http://www.nhpco.org/statistics [NHPCO, n.d.-b] for the latest data on hospice use in the United States). Breakdown of hospice admissions by primary diagnosis is as follows:

Cancer	41.3%
All noncancer diagnoses	58.7%
Heart disease	11.8%
Debility unspecified	11.2%
Dementia	10.1%
Lung disease	7.9%
Stroke or coma	3.8%
Kidney disease	2.6%
Liver disease	2.0%
Nonamyotrophic lateral sclerosis (non-ALS) motor neuron	1.9%
HIV/AIDS	1.0%
Amyotrophic lateral sclerosis	0.4%
Other	6.5%

Focused Medical Review

Until 1993, hospices received little scrutiny from Medicare. There was a perception that hospices were unique providers that did not need to undergo the frequent audits other providers were put through. A couple of hospice programs in Puerto Rico were found to be signing up people for the hospice benefit who were not terminally ill. These incidents of apparent fraud caused HCFA to reconsider this position and to suggest that intermediaries conduct audits to determine if hospices had unusually long lengths of stay.

Some of the Medicare intermediaries did look at hospice lengths of stay and discovered that a number of hospice patients remained on the benefit for unusually long periods. These were usually patients with noncancerous terminal illnesses such as emphysema, congestive heart failure, or Alzheimer's disease. These are diseases that are especially difficult to prognosticate about. A heart patient may appear very close to death and in a few weeks be relatively stable. Many of these patients can go through a rollercoaster trajectory, coming near to death and bouncing back to baseline. In comparison, malignant diseases have a much more predictable course.

The Office of Inspector General (OIG) and the intermediaries have also grown concerned that there is some potential for abuse under the hospice benefit. Along with home health agencies and durable medical equipment suppliers, there is little oversight of what is actually being provided to Medicare recipients at home. The vast majority of hospice providers are reputable organizations that want to improve care of dying patients.

However, there may be some who want to use hospice's good name to profit excessively.

Other areas of focus that undergo government review include the following:

- Engaging in marketing strategies that offer incomplete information about Medicare entitlement under the hospice benefit to induce patients to elect hospice
- Encouraging hospice beneficiaries to temporarily revoke their election of hospice during a period when costly services, which should be covered by the hospice plan of care, are needed for the hospice to avoid the obligation to pay for such services
- Failure of hospices to notify prospective patients or their representatives that they will no longer be entitled to curative treatment if they elect hospice
- Refusal by or failure of hospices to provide or arrange for needed care

Hospice Care in Nursing Facilities

There is also continuing concern about how the hospice benefit is provided to people in nursing homes. In some settings, there may be an inducement for the nursing home to refer patients to hospice and a duplication of services. If a hospice provides fewer services to a patient who is in a nursing home than they would provide to a patient at a personal residence, there could be a problem. The Department of Health and Human Services (HHS) OIG is examining the appropriateness of hospice payment for patients who reside in nursing facilities (NFs) that may result in a reduction in reimbursement for hospice care in nursing homes. Clearly, no one in the hospice movement wants providers who cut corners in patient care to increase profits.

Hospice care in nursing facilities has been challenged for some time. In 1997, the HHS OIG claimed that hospice patients in nursing facilities had unusually long lengths of service. A study was commissioned by the Assistant Secretary for Planning and Evaluation (ASPE) and was awarded to Brown University. A series of studies were produced (Gage et al., 2008) and are available at the ASPE website (http://www.aspe.gov).

These studies revealed a positive picture of the impact of hospice in nursing facilities. The most dramatic finding was that in facilities that had working contracts with hospices, the rate of transfer to and death in acute care hospitals was greatly diminished. Not only was the rate of hospital transfer much lower for hospice patients, but it also extended as a spillover effect to all patients in the facility.

Length of service (LOS) for hospice patients in nursing facilities was not found to be much larger than national averages, and the methods used by the HHS OIG to calculate LOS were not correctly applied, resulting in a longer than actual LOS for hospice patients. In addition, the Brown studies found many other positive benefits for hospice patients in nursing facilities.

- Hospice enrollment is associated with a 93% increased likelihood that patients in daily pain will have at least some attempt made at managing their pain.
- Hospice patients in NFs had superior pain assessments, and hospice patients in daily pain are twice as likely to receive strong pain relievers as are nonhospice residents in daily pain.
- Hospice enrollment is associated with an increased likelihood that patients with persistent depression and/or anxiety will receive medication for this condition, though the difference is not statistically significant.
- Hospice versus nonhospice residents are significantly less likely to be admitted to a hospital at 30, 60, 90, and 180 days. At 30 days, hospice patients are 70% less likely to be hospitalized than nonhospice patients.
- Lower proportions of hospice patients compared to nonhospice patients had invasive procedures such as physical restraints, IV feeding, or feeding tubes.
- Hospice involvement may reduce the presence of dyspnea (air hunger).
- The researchers noted a "spillover" effect in improved pain management and fewer acute hospitalizations in facilities that had high concentrations of hospice care. In NFs that had 9% or more of hospice patients, the nonhospice patients had fewer differences in the outcomes of pain assessment and treatment and acute hospitalization.

The Problem with Prognosis

Hospices are being asked to increase access to all dying patients at the same time as they are penalized if they make a wrong decision and admit someone who does not die on schedule. Hospices rely on the judgment of physicians to predict prognosis. After all, what is a terminal prognosis other than a physician's judgment that someone has an incurable condition that will shortly result in death? Medicare insists that hospices be accountable for their decisions to admit patients. They can no longer rely just on a physician's judgment. Some physicians and patients and hospices have reason to want to access hospice's array of services not just for terminally ill patients but also for chronically ill patients who were having trouble receiving services.

Hospices are specialists in the comfort and management of distressing symptoms. Hospice staff are less experienced in meeting the detailed requirements for medical documentation than the rest of the health care system. Hospice nurses might document that the patient is having a good day and feeling all right. This was taken as evidence that the patient must not be dying. Sometimes the paradoxical could occur. A hospice might have a patient with chronic obstructive pulmonary disease who was near death at admission. Over the course of a few months, the hospice provides the patient and family with tremendous emotional and physical support and oxygen. The result of this good care is that the patient improves. The hospice discharges the patient, and he proceeds to go downhill and dies. In this not-too-uncommon scenario, hospice becomes a kind of life support for a patient who otherwise cannot get good care in the health care system. After a while, the hospice becomes fearful of discharging such patients.

When polled, physicians say they value hospice for the emotional support given to families. When a physician has been caring for a chronically ill patient for many years, she or he gets attached. The doctor also gets to feeling overwhelmed by the patient's emotional needs. It is easy to give over such patients to hospice whether or not they are really close to death. Patients view the hospice benefit as appealing. Current Medicare patients can become pauperized by all the copays and lack of coverage they experience during a chronic illness.

Some hospices came to rely on these chronically ill patients for financial survival. These are the patients for whom the hospice usually received much more reimbursement than needed. Actual cost of care for these patients may be less than payment received. The hospice may feel it needs these patients to cover the expense of admitting all those patients who were only in hospice a short time and cost more than the hospice is paid.

In this conflicted and confusing environment, there has to be a more accurate way for hospices to decide which patients to admit and which might have to wait. When focused medical review of hospices began, the CMS realized that hospices were having a problem with accurate prognostication and that better tools were needed.

Prognostic Guidelines

The NHO (1995b, 1996a) was encouraged by the CMS (at the time, the Healthcare Finance Administration) to help develop guidelines that would assist the fiscal intermediaries and hospice providers to more accurately admit patients to the Medicare Hospice Benefit. As chair of the NHO Standards and Accreditation Committee at the time, I was asked to put together a group to develop such guidelines.

The first version of the guidelines was limited to general factors affecting prognosis and disease-specific factors for end-stage cardiac disease, end-stage pulmonary disease, and end-stage dementia. These three diagnoses covered the majority of patients admitted to hospices who were difficult to prognosticate about.

The *Medical Guidelines for Determining Prognosis in Selected Non-Cancer Diseases* (NHO, 1995b) was published by the NHO and sent to Medicare to use in claims and focused medical review. The second edition of the guidelines (NHO, 1996a) expanded the diseases covered (cardiac and pulmonary disease and dementia) to include HIV disease, liver disease, renal disease, stroke and coma, and amyotrophic lateral sclerosis.

The *Medical Guidelines* were just that, guidelines. They proposed questions a competent clinician ought to consider when making a prognostic determination. They were not intended to be *criteria* for eligibility for hospice. However, the *Guidelines* were modified to be in a yes-no format so that nurse claims reviewers could review hospice medical records to decide if a hospice claim should be paid. The *Guidelines* then became local medical review policies (now local coverage decisions) used by the intermediaries to review claims. If the patient met these *criteria*, the claim would be paid. If they did not meet the *criteria*, they could still be paid but only if the hospice documented why the patient was terminally ill anyway.

No one knew if the guidelines would bring about a reduction in the number of patients served by hospices or an increase. The authors hoped that use of the guidelines would result in an increase in admission of appropriate patients to hospice. The initial result of the publication of the *Guidelines* was an increase in the number of patients with noncancer diagnoses being admitted to hospices, a trend that has grown with time.

The NHPCO and CMS agreed that the *Guidelines* would need to be modified as necessary as new research was published. Since the publication of the *Guidelines*, a number of researchers have attempted to measure their predictive validity and have found that they do not predict death within 6 months with accuracy. Schonwetter et al. (2003) found that the Medicare review policies for dementia patients did not predict death within 6 months. Increased age, anorexia, and poor functional status were the best predictors of mortality. Mitchell et al. (2004) used the nursing home minimum data set data to look at the sensitivity and specificity of data elements and found 12 MDS data elements that helped predict 6-month mortality better than existing Medicare criteria. McClusky and Houseman (2004) compared criteria originally developed by the amyotrophic lateral sclerosis (ALS) group at Columbia University with Medicare criteria for ALS and found that the Columbia criteria were much better than Medicare criteria for predicting 6-month mortality.

Clearly, much more needs to be done to improve the accuracy of determining prognosis in these chronic and life-limiting illnesses. More research and better measurement tools are needed. It may also be necessary to change the requirement for hospice admission from one that is based on a 6-month prognosis to a more needs- or disease severity-based system. However, the 6-month prognostic criteria will remain in place until another method to qualify hospice patients for service is developed.

Reification of Hospice

In a lecture by the sociologist David Clark (1995), Max Weber's theory on the development of religion and the life course of a social movement was used to examine the genesis of the hospice movement. Weber used the religious metaphor to characterize how social movements progress from sect to denomination to church.

In the sect phase, the current world is rejected. Charismatic leaders produce key writings. For the hospice movement, people like Cicely Saunders, Elisabeth Kübler-Ross, Herman Feifel, Robert Fulton, and John Hinton are examples of leaders who rejected society's taboo on discussion of death well before it became popular to do so. Classic books such as *On Death and Dying* (Kübler-Ross, 1969), *The Meaning of Death* (Feifel, 1959), *Death and Identity* (Fulton, 1965), and *Dying* (Hinton, 1972) gave hospice pioneers a kind of permission to push the boundaries of what was permissible.

Hospice in the United States entered the denominational phase in about 1983 with the creation of the Hospice Medicare Benefit. About this time, the movement started compromising with the world and began attempting to be respectable. The NHPCO began to grow, and the Joint Commission on Accreditation of Hospitals (JCAHO) started developing its accreditation program. New services began to proliferate.

It may be that hospice has now reached the church stage in that it has become a mainstream part of the U.S. health care system. There are now a number of hospice companies that are traded on the New York Stock Exchange. In the United Kingdom, hospice and palliative care do seem to be legitimate and have become part of the medical establishment. Some there are in favor of dropping the term *hospice* for *palliative care*. In the United States, hospice is widely respected but still not embraced by the leaders of the medical establishment. Work in palliative care is gaining some respect but is still not thought to be at the cutting edge of science.

Although hospice in the United States is still viewed as new, it does seem to be viewed by many in the euthanasia debate as one of the more conservative elements. Hospice does not seem to be willing to take as many of the risks it used to routinely face. A possible measure of the onset of entropy was suggested by David Clark (1995), who said that when "regurgitive conferences" begin to emerge, a new social phenomenon may be stagnating.

All social institutions undergo a process of reification. That is to say, they gradually form boundaries and rules that define both what the institution is and what it is not. This is a process that gives the entity both definition and clarity while hardening it into something that is much more difficult to change. Where hospices, and now palliative care programs, were initially fluid and creative in their responses to the needs of dying patients in their communities, they are now concerned more with survival, consistency of care, and efficiencies of management.

Arrogance of Hospice

Those who work in hospice care view their field as unique. No other health care provider is seen as quite as dedicated or caring or in tune with its patients' needs. Some in the field believe that hospice care is a model for the interdisciplinary delivery of care to all medical patients. Clinical experts in the field have made overarching statements about hospice's ability to manage all symptoms of the dying process and that no patient has to ever die in pain. The problem, from hospices' perspective, is that not all patients are allowed to access hospice care. If they were, dying would always be a satisfactory and potentially rewarding experience.

Although hospice care has been shown to improve the quality of care for dying patients and their families, it is not for everyone. And although hospices have pioneered the best in palliative care procedures, there are some patients whose symptoms defy all interventions. Yes, patients can be sedated if their symptoms are too unbearable, but is this the same thing as a good death? Hospices must recognize and come to grips with their limitations if they are to improve and be truly integrated into the existing health care system. They must also accept the role of being a niche in the system and realize that hospice care may not be the model for all health care delivery systems.

The interdisciplinary care model is a breakthrough in the treatment of patients with complex medical problems. For an acute emergency room patient, however, the need is for decisive physician-directed intervention. For the patient with a single ailment, primary care will ordinarily suffice. The health care system cannot afford to attend to the medical, emotional, and spiritual needs of all patients all the time.

At a time when the health care system is finally becoming interested in end-of-life care, the hospice movement's response is that it is the answer. Just give all these patients to hospice and there will not be a problem. This attitude does not help others to learn more about care for the dying. Also, *hospice*, as defined by the Medicare Hospice

Benefit, is not for all people facing death. Hospices need to share what they have learned about caring for the dying with the rest of the health care system for major changes to occur in the care of all the dying. The palliative care movement has been more effective in bringing the competencies of palliative care to the attention of the larger health care system. The hospice community seems to believe that end-of-life care belongs to hospice. There are many others who have a legitimate interest in the care of the dying and who need to be partners with hospice in developing a working system that meets the needs of those nearing the end of life.

What is needed is a health care system that provides needed services all along the continuum of care for patients with life-threatening illnesses; care that is appropriate for the stage of illness and the needs and goals of the patient and his or her family. There is an appropriate time for using all aspects of health care from acute care, to day care to home care to long-term care to hospice care. To achieve this integrated health care system that is designed to provide the right amounts of care at the right times we will need changes in the reimbursement systems that drive provider behavior. If we redesign the health care system so that providers are rewarded for ensuring that the patient is cared for by the right provider at the right point, there will still be plenty of opportunity for all providers to prosper.

What we have now is a system that rewards over use of health services and the wrong mix of services at the wrong times. We have an acute care system that is struggling to meet the needs of patients with chronic care needs. We have physician providers who are rewarded for overtreatment and overspecialization rather than continuity of care. We have a long-term care facility system that is encouraged to send patients back to acute care unnecessarily. We have a home health system that should be working collaboratively with hospice providers. No one wants to lose their piece of the reimbursement pie, but what is needed is a system that works for the needs of the patients and families, not the provider community.

The tendency toward arrogance is often reinforced by families who are in awe of the hospice workers' abilities to help them face death. Time after time, families tell the hospice staff and volunteers that they could not have survived the experience without hospice. After a while, staff and volunteers begin to believe that they really must be rather special.

It certainly is rewarding when the people one serves express appreciation; however, there is a danger here. Some in hospice work tend to have a need for such praise. When it is not forthcoming, there can be disappointment, and for those families incapable of appreciation, there can be disdain. After all, remember that it is not hospice workers' needs that are important here. Hospice can do its best work when there is honest humility in the care provided. It is more therapeutic for hospice to take a backseat to the family's role in caregiving.

Many families need very little from hospice other than empowering them to provide care and to communicate openly. Lao T'su (in Blakney, 1955) spoke wisely when he said,

> A leader is best when people barely know he exists,
> not so good when people obey and acclaim him,
> worst when they despise him.
> Fail to honor people, they fail to honor you.
> But of a good leader, who talks little
> when his work is done, his aim fulfilled,
> They will all say, we did this ourselves.

The bulk of the work of caring for dying patients is done by the family. Hospice provides them with the crucial training and support they need to accomplish this. It is really the family who deserve the credit and praise. It is more therapeutic to direct the attention to them as they will have less difficulty in bereavement if they believe their work made a difference in how their loved one died (Connor, 1996a).

Hospice patients face some of the most complicated medical management problems found in the health care system. However, as a managed care provider there is a disincentive to use outside consulting resources. It is not uncommon for hospice patients to have complex wound or stoma care requirements, yet there are very few hospices that have access to an enterostomal therapist. Hospice program philosophy stresses high-touch, low-tech care. Patients and families do better with less complex treatment options. However, there are some patients whose symptom management could be greatly enhanced through high-tech interventions.

The hospice community varies considerably in its medical sophistication. On one extreme are programs that refuse to do any "intrusive" interventions, such as IV fluids. On the other extreme are hospices that set no limits on the types of treatments administered, including total parenteral nutrition, resuscitation, or experimental chemotherapy.

The difficulties here are both philosophical and pragmatic. Hospice promotes the principle of autonomy. Patients have the right to choose whichever treatments they wish. However, when hospice disagrees with these choices, there is a problem. Hospice care is palliative care, yet how far can the notion of palliation be stretched? Many oncologists believe that nearly all the care they provide is palliative in that it will not cure the patient. Yet does it promote relief from distressing symptoms? Sometimes yes, and sometimes no.

Arrogance comes into play when hospice or the palliative care service thinks it knows what is best for the patient. People make choices for many complex reasons, both conscious and unconscious. The patient's goals are the patient's goals. The best hospice can do is help to understand and articulate them. Well-developed hospice programs try to do this around the time of entry into the program to avoid confusion. However, people are entitled to change their minds, and they often do.

Greatly limiting the choices patients can have in hospice leads to reduced access to hospice care. Removing all limitations to treatment in hospice leads to hospice care that is indistinguishable from care provided in the rest of the health care system. Hospice can bring its knowledge of how best to manage care at the end of life to patients, families, and physicians, but it has to accept their decisions and goals as right even if it disagrees.

Quality of Care

Is hospice care better than traditional care? Can quality of living or dying be measured? What are the measurable outcomes of hospice care? These and other questions are now finally beginning to be addressed. Much of what has been described as unique to hospice care is difficult to measure.

The vast majority of hospices in the United States do not conduct research. Most programs are small and lack the expertise necessary to carry out research protocols. More important, there is a general reluctance to involve patients in any activities that might burden patients and families in unusually stressful circumstances. The privacy of patients and families is carefully guarded.

On top of this, there is an unwillingness to consider using randomization when studying hospice care. It would be unethical for some patients to be denied access to hospice so that the effects of hospice could be studied. Because the randomized controlled design is the gold standard in science, it is very difficult for nonrandomized results to be accepted as definitive. There are, however, opportunities to do randomized trials of palliative care interventions when there is true equipoise as to their benefit.

The health care system is moving toward agreed-on systems for measuring quality of care. The JCAHO has developed a system for providers to submit performance data. The CMS has developed a number of publicly reported outcome measures for Medicare providers so that consumers can compare outcomes for nursing facilities, home health care providers, and others. The NHPCO has developed a large project to collect standardized data for family evaluation of care and for pain control (see chapter 12). At present, there is no agreed-on way of addressing other symptoms, let alone psychological or spiritual services.

Lack of Research

The hospice movement is now more than 40 years old. Many books have been written, and there are a number of journals being published that have created a body of literature for hospice and palliative care. What remains striking is the lack of targeted funding for the field of palliative care in the United States.

There was a state-of-the-science conference at the National Institutes of Health in December 2004 that identified the major gaps in knowledge for palliative care, but no strategic program of requests for proposals has been issued (Lorenz et al., 2005). The Lorenz review identified 24,423 total citations, of which 911 comprised the final set used for an evidence report. This very large, diverse body of literature reflected the tremendous growth of the field of end-of-life care over the last decade.

A number of efforts to stimulate research in the field of hospice and palliative care have been attempted. The Project on Death in America of the Open Society Institute funded a variety of projects to look at end-of-life care and also funded a large group of scholars. The Robert Wood Johnson Foundation funded over $100 million in projects to improve understanding of end-of-life care and initiated a campaign to try to engage the public in demanding better end-of-life care through education and awareness building. The fruits of that project are now part of the Caring Connections program of the NHPCO (see Appendix 2, "Organizational Resources").

Both the Project on Death in America and the Robert Wood Johnson Foundation program to address the need for better end-of-life care have been discontinued. Their legacy is a much larger group of committed researchers and programs; however, most of the problems with end-of-life care in the United States remain, and there is inadequate funding for sustaining the research effort.

Physician Involvement

The hospice movement was founded by physicians and other health care providers who were dissatisfied with the way dying patients were cared for. Today, the success of a particular hospice largely rests with how it is viewed by the medical community. Most physicians begin with a bias toward continued disease treatment.

The Hippocratic Oath, emotional involvement with the patient, and medical economics all push against acknowledging that a disease is incurable. Recommending hospice care means having to openly acknowledge that the physician has been unable to cure the disease. This seems like a failure to many physicians who are sworn to work toward curing the patient. In addition, doctors become emotionally involved with many patients. When the patient becomes seriously ill, they focus more attention and concern on their welfare. Failure of medical therapeutics becomes a personal failure. It is human to feel they have let the patient down.

On top of all this are financial considerations. In the U.S. physicians are paid based on active diagnosis and treatment, the more medical care delivered, the more payment the physician receives. Many specialists, lacking the intensity of emotional involvement with the patient of the primary care physician, have a powerful financial incentive to continue treating the patient even when cure is unlikely. The movement toward managed health care changes this formula by eliminating the incentive to overtreat.

How does hospice fit into all this? Some physicians view hospice as a great relief to the burden of supporting the patient emotionally; others see hospice as a symbol of their failure or as a competitor. These attitudes determine how local physicians will choose to use or not use a particular hospice program. It is possible for a hospice to change these perceptions, but it will require the right kind of education and experience. Education provided by other physicians is most effective, and positive experience working with the hospice is critical. If the physician hears from other respected colleagues that the program has helped and from patients and families that have been well served, some of the most ardent critics can be won over.

All of this occurs in the context of a health care system that does not value palliative care. Most physicians view the important work of medicine as efforts to cure or control the major diseases. Genetic research, transplantation, and pharmaceutical advancement are the areas of appeal for scientists and physicians.

The magic of overcoming humankind's perennial ills is appealing enough, but added to this are enormous financial incentives. The newest treatments, equipment, and specialist expertise are often the most rewarded. The health care system in the United States is fundamentally a business, and a profitable one at that.

In contrast, the relief of suffering comes in a poor second, if that. Yet is this lack of interest and funding for palliative care appropriate given reality in the health care system? Each year in the United States, approximately 560,000 people die of malignant disease. Of these, a large percentage will experience severe pain. All will likely experience distress related to their disease or treatment. Add to this approximately 1,300,000 patients who die each year from other chronic conditions such as chronic obstructive pulmonary disease, heart disease, kidney or liver failure, dementias, motor neuron diseases, and the like.

Should vast sums continue to be provided to fund research into curative treatment and the investigation of treatment aimed at relief of suffering be neglected? At least some significant funding should be directed toward the science of palliative medicine.

A growing number of countries are recognizing hospice and palliative medicine as a specialty or subspecialty. After many years of advocacy, the American Board of Medical Specialties has approved hospice and palliative medicine as a subspecialty in the United States. The most prominent specialties that have agreed to allow subspecialization in hospice and palliative medicine include internal medicine and family medicine. Some who were approved by the now discontinued American Board of Hospice and Palliative Medicine will be allowed to take the new boards; however, soon new physicians wishing to add hospice and palliative medicine as a subspecialization will have to complete a 2-year fellowship program. We can only hope that enough physicians will be interested enough in the field to qualify as a subspecialist in the field.

Profit and Nonprofit Hospice

Modern hospice care began in the United Kingdom as a charitable enterprise. The Polish patient who left 500 pounds to Dame Saunders to start St. Christopher's Hospice near London did so as a charitable gesture. For the most part, hospice care in the United Kingdom continues to be funded by philanthropic support.

In the United States, early hospices were all begun as not-for-profit organizations. There was no funding other than donations and volunteer labor. The first hospice to change over to for-profit status was Hospice Inc. in Florida. They observed that for hospice to grow, capital was needed. They felt the best way to attract capital was to allow investment. It is important to note that the average hospice is still quite small (with an median daily census of fewer than 52 patients). Hospice Inc. changed its name to VITAS to emphasize a commitment to a broader range of care to patients at the end of life.

Should hospices remain charities? This is a complex issue. The not-for-profit hospice has the following positive aspects. It does not have stockholders to satisfy and make a profit for. It is more reliant on and part of the community it serves. Charitable hospices tend to provide more services for their communities (e.g., support groups, counseling and bereavement follow-up, education programs, trauma services, and camps). They tend to make more use of volunteers and to respond to local unique needs.

The downside of nonprofits is their relative lack of efficiency and organization. There is a tendency to stay with the familiar and to resist growth. There is little financial incentive to grow, and with increased size come challenges that many managers are not prepared to respond to. The result is often that difficult populations are not served.

For-profit hospices have found a foothold in areas where significant populations have gone unserved. If the existing hospice does not respond quickly when hospital discharge planners need help with the disposition of an inpatient, they will give their business to someone who will.

Potential advantages of for-profit hospices include a tendency to be more efficient and able to change. They are more likely to be bigger as they do not owe their allegiance to a particular community. Having more capital available, they may develop or provide a wider range of programs (e.g., inpatient, nursing facilities, pharmacy, home health, and residential care).

Drawbacks to for-profit hospice care can be conflict of value over the true mission of the organization, inability to develop viable volunteer services, and a tendency to focus on core income-producing services instead of the actual needs of the population.

Some say that there is really no difference between for-profit and not-for-profit organizations in that they both actually strive to produce a profit. The only difference is how the profit is used. Some not-for-profit organizations have done better at producing higher net incomes than for-profit corporations.

The for-profit versus not-for-profit difference may ultimately be less critical. The most important issue is the true purpose of the organization. If the purpose of the hospice is to effectively meet the needs and exceed the expectations of as many dying patients and their families as possible, then it is doing its job. If it is not, then it should move aside.

Case Illustration

George

George was a 68-year-old patient with chronic obstructive pulmonary disease who was admitted to hospice in bad condition. He was continuously short of breath and could not ambulate or do personal care without assistance. He lived with a daughter who worked and could not stay with him. Our plan of care included assisting with personal care, nursing support, counseling, home equipment, and 24-hour support. After a few months, George seemed to be improved. He was breathing easier and had more energy. We continued to work with him, and he was quite open about preparing emotionally for death.

This situation continued for more than a year, and hospice personnel began to wonder if George was really terminally ill. We had his physician assess him, and we all concluded that he had improved but remained with an uncertain prognosis. After a few more months, we came to believe that George could continue like this indefinitely. We began to make arrangements to discharge him from the hospice program. We had ample time to say goodbye and made alternate arrangements to help with his personal care.

Everyone tried to make the best of the situation, but George was sad. It seemed as if he felt he had failed us in some way. The family was instructed to call us if his situation changed, and we stopped coming. Everyone wondered how George would do, and his nurse called a few times to check.

A few months passed, and one day we had a call from his daughter: George was much worse, and could we come out? His nurse went right out and found George to be close to death. Hospice services were resumed, and staff helped care for him over the next 2 days. He died peacefully in his bed at home.

Afterward, everyone felt awful. We felt somehow we had contributed to his death by discontinuing services. In some ways, hospice became a kind of life support for George. The constant attention to his physical health and emotional well-being had kept him going. Without hospice, he felt he was a burden to his family. This is one of the paradoxes of hospice care; with good care, many patients can actually live longer than they might otherwise have (Connor, Pyenson, Fitch, & Spence, 2007).

The business of hospice care is difficult enough. Added to this is society's disavowal of death. In the next chapter, the denial of death that is ingrained in today's culture is examined.

CHAPTER **9**

Society and Denial

Death is a very dull, dreary affair, and my advice to you is to have nothing whatsoever to do with it.

—W. Somerset Maughan

I'm not afraid to die. I just don't want to be there when it happens.

—Woody Allen

The effectiveness of hospice in helping patients and families face death is profoundly affected by their ability to face reality. Each patient and family comes to this ordeal with differing amounts of inner resources. Families vary enormously in their coping ability. Some can face adversity with tremendous strength, and others collapse or fall apart. Some refuse to believe the diagnosis will result in their death and fight to the bitter end; others fight for a while but tire and give in to their deaths.

The dynamics of hope and denial are a universal part of the experience of facing death. All people want to hope for the best and believe that they will be the 1 out of 20 who makes it. It is a normal and healthy part of the reaction to news of a life-threatening illness to refuse to believe that it is really happening. A person thinks, *There must have been a mistake, the reports got mixed up, it just can't be me, this only happens to other people!*

After enough time has passed, it begins to sink in: *This really is happening—I could die of this disease.* This process does not happen the same way for everyone. Some persist in the belief that a mistake was made or minimize the seriousness of the situation. Why is it that so many people rail against the inevitable? Why do they have so much trouble accepting the reality that they can die?

Are We a Death-Denying Culture?

Throughout history, man has attempted in many ways to defeat death. The ancient Egyptians saw death as a journey to a new land. The dead person was buried with provisions to aid in the long journey. The physical body was carefully preserved so it would stay intact. Valuable items were left in the tomb so that one's station in this life could be maintained in the next. All this was in the vain belief that death was not really death.

Most religions attempt to reassure people that there is continuity to life and that death is not the end of one's individual existence. Modern medicine views death as the enemy to be defeated no matter what the cost. There is an implicit message that life can and should be prolonged no matter what the consequences. In the past 50 years, there has been so much progress in the treatment and cure of disease that society has come to see death as an unwanted, unnatural consequence and as someone's fault.

In this same time span, death has gone from being a part of the fabric of life at home to a far-removed event that happens in hospitals and institutions. Youth is worshipped, and old age and death are banished. People protect their children from death by making them stay home from funerals and use euphemisms for death such as *passing away, resting,* or *gone away.*

When someone does die, it has to be because someone made a mistake somewhere. It must be someone's fault—the doctor or the hospital or the ambulance or the insurance company. This society is the most litigious in the world. U.S. citizens file twice as many lawsuits per capita as do people in other industrialized countries. People refuse to accept that sometimes death just happens in spite of everyone's best efforts.

However, we do need to remember that there are many who do die in our health care system because of mistakes. The study (Institute of Medicine, 2000) on the hazards of our health care system estimated, some say modestly, that there are about 100,000 preventable deaths annually in our health care system.

It is still universal practice in hospitals that all patients must be resuscitated in the absence of a do-not-resuscitate (DNR) order. Of course, most people would want all efforts to be made to save them if they had a reversible condition. This is more the exception than the rule in acute hospitals, however. Those resuscitated are predominately chronically and terminally ill people who will not recover in spite of the resuscitation attempt. For all patients 60 years and older, only 10–17% survive after arrest; and for those with a chronic condition and poor prognosis, the survival rate is 0–5% (Murphy et al., 1994).

The United States is both a death-denying and death-obsessed culture. Our people are obsessed with unnatural death but avoid natural death. The media are saturated with unnatural death. Violence, mayhem, and destruction are the staples of television, movies, and fiction. People lose interest in anything that lacks violent or romantic content.

In contrast, it is rare to find entertainment that addresses natural dying. When a show does attempt to deal with the subject, it is usually considered too serious or depressing. Surprisingly, some of these efforts have left strong impressions. People recoil from reminders that they must experience their own personal death. It is easier to distance themselves from death when it is happening to someone else, especially someone they dislike.

The growth of the hospice movement is greatly affected by the tendency to want to avoid facing the reality of an incurable condition. Hospices in the United States have been set up in such a way that patients must renounce further attempts at curative treatment. They must acknowledge being informed of the diagnosis and prognosis and make the shift to palliative care. In spite of all the wonderful services and support that hospices have to offer, this is a difficult thing to face. By forcing people to face reality and their own denial, hospices may have limited their ability to serve those most in need of help.

Theories of Denial

The idea of denial originated in the early writings of Sigmund Freud (1924). He introduced the term *disavowal*, meaning a refusal of reality. He originally thought of this as a symptom of psychosis but later came to view it as a mechanism of defense (Freud, 1940). Anna Freud (1948) saw denial as a necessary component of all defensive operations. Psychoanalytic thinkers view denial as the result of intrapsychic conflict. For a terminally ill person, the external threat of death can cause a person to feel in danger of being overwhelmed with anxiety. An individual who lacks higher functioning defenses resorts to the more primitive use of denial to survive emotionally (see Sjoback, 1973, for a more thorough account of the development of the psychoanalytic concept of denial).

Other writers have viewed denial as a more adaptive coping process (Beilin, 1981; Beissler, 1979; Dansak & Cordes, 1978–1979; Haan, 1965; Hackett & Cassem, 1970) or as a helpful strategy in the early stages of response to cancer (Detwiler, 1981; Falek & Britton, 1974; Kübler-Ross, 1969; Weisman, 1972).

Other researchers have seen both negative and positive functions for denial in seriously ill and elderly people. Becker (1973) attempted to explain the inability to deal with death through Otto Rank's depth psychology of heroism and its failure. A hero faces death without denial. This society has failed to incorporate the values of the hero.

Weisman (1972) proposed three degrees of denial. First-order denial is obvious denial of the main facts of the illness: "Who, me? I don't have cancer!" Second-order denial is denial of the significance or implications of the illness: "Sure, I have cancer, but it's no big deal." Third-order denial is refusal to believe the illness will result in death: "Yeah, I have cancer and it's serious, but I'm not going to die." Such people will believe that they can remain in their incapacitated state indefinitely.

Breznitz (1983) expanded on Weisman's (1972) three degrees by proposing seven different kinds of denial. They are each related to a different stage in the processing of threatening information. They are denial of:

- Information
- Threatening information
- Personal relevance
- Urgency
- Vulnerability
- Effect
- Affect relevance

In Breznitz's view, the more denial used, the more reality distortion is present.

A significant association between denial and preservation of significant relationships was observed by an associate of Weisman's named Hackett. Hackett (Hackett & Weisman, 1964, 1969) observed how denial arose within the social sphere. Hackett proposed a scale (Hackett & Cassem, 1974) that classified deniers into three groups: mild, moderate, and major. Those in the major category would never acknowledge a fear of death, whereas those in the mild category were readily fearful and lacked consistent defenses against their anxiety. Most were classified in the moderate category. Hackett noted, however, that the criteria were never precise.

From the field of stress and coping, Richard Lazarus has contributed a great deal to the literature on the use of denial. Lazarus and Golden (1981) suggested that age is an important factor in response to terminal illness and that older people tend to use denial less. They suggested the term *denial like processes* to show that what may appear to be denial is not what one thinks it is. They concluded that "denial like processes can have both beneficial and harmful consequences depending on the timing, circumstances, and pervasiveness" (p. 305). Lazarus and Golden's concept of cognitive appraisal helps researchers understand that people will vary greatly in their reactions depending on how they evaluate the significance of the threat to their well-being. This can help researchers understand the variety of emotional responses seen in those facing death.

Another author (Taylor, 1989) explored the adaptive use of positive illusions. These are the sometimes self-deceptive ways people help get themselves through difficult crises. "Repression and denial alter reality whereas illusions simply interpret it in the best possible light."

Denial and Acceptance

Denial and acceptance are usually thought of as two points on a continuum of how people respond to dying. Denial is the least adaptive response, and acceptance is the most adaptive. This is certainly an oversimplification of a very complex dynamic.

Elisabeth Kübler-Ross (1969) put forward one of the first theories to explain how people respond to the knowledge of impending death. Her stage theory begins with denial, which functions as a psychic shock absorber that gradually gives way to anger at the reality of the situation. This is followed by bargaining with God to live and, when this does not work, depression at one's helplessness. Finally, the person reaches acceptance, which is characterized by a turning away from life and giving in to death. Kübler-Ross's observations were never intended to be cast in stone or to be taken as the only way people face death; however, people tend to want to simplify difficult subjects and have misinterpreted her work.

A number of authors have criticized the whole notion of stage theories of dying (see chapter 4). One's response to the knowledge of impending death is not linear. It is distinguished by vacillations in emotional and cognitive response. The most common response is ambivalence. The person simultaneously hopes for a cure while he or she wishes for release. People want either to beat the disease and return to their previous existence or to have it over with. It seems that being in the limbo of neither living nor dying is the least tolerable. Avery Weisman (1972) referred to this state as "middle knowledge," or the chronic living–dying interval. In spite of the popularity of Kübler-Ross's (1969) model, there really is no well-recognized or empirically valid succession of emotional responses that is typical of people facing death.

In spite of this, there are some people who seem to face death with clarity and openness. They seem to accept the fact that they are dying and see no need to struggle over it. This sometimes occurs after unpleasant initial reactions or may just as likely be their reaction from the beginning of their knowledge that death is near. It is difficult to know why some people face death with an inner peace and others fall into fear or avoidance.

When acceptance is seen in a dying person, it has variously been described as a kind of peace that came upon the person or a withdrawing from life and worldly things. It is a less-than-common response that caps an exceptional life. It is not the resignation often seen in someone who asks, "What else can I do?" or says, "I want to die and get it over with." Resignation is a kind of learned helplessness. The anger, attempts at control, and other responses have not changed the relentless course of the disease. It is no longer possible to maintain denial in the face of decline. At least enough time has passed to gather the strength to face reality.

One might see acceptance in resignation. Being able to face the reality of one's death without being overwhelmed emotionally is a considerable accomplishment. But there is something different about the quality of acceptance. It is more than just giving up and turning away. It is perhaps a curiosity about what lays ahead, a sense of completion, a feeling that one's life has been accomplished and one's work has been done. It is to be in awe of the inevitable miracle about to happen. It is a profound understanding that life goes on without one and that everything will be all right; one is not essential to the continued functioning of the rest of life.

Interpersonal and Intrapsychic Denial

When one thinks of denial in the face of death, one thinks of a person who cannot face reality. One assumes that the person is so devastated that he or she must resort to a primitive defense that blocks out the obvious reality. The person's persistent denial is evidence of serious psychological disturbance, an almost psychotic refusal to face reality that will have serious consequences.

Although this may sometimes be the case, it is probably the exception rather than the rule. It has been suggested that what is usually thought of as denial is more often a conscious decision to present a more optimistic picture. This is done in the belief that it will preserve interpersonal relationships that are necessary for coping. People are afraid that if they speak truthfully about how they feel, it will drive their loved ones away. Unfortunately, the opposite is usually the case; when people do not talk openly about their fears and feelings, those around them are uncomfortable and tend to become more distant.

The notion that most denial is based on interpersonal relations is consistent with experience in hospice and has been documented in the literature (Connor, 1992). Denial may be used for a number of relational reasons. People may wish to protect their loved ones from the distress they may imagine their loved ones will suffer if they must confront the reality of their dying. They may feel guilt over their condition and the distress it causes others. A dying person may fear abandonment by those closest to him or her if dying is discussed openly.

In contrast to denial for interpersonal reasons is denial for intrapsychic reasons. This is denial used as a defense to decrease anxiety. When inner resources for coping are limited and individuals feel in danger of being overwhelmed, they may resort to this more primitive defense. For them, the possibility of death is too much to face; it just is not happening.

If there is a continuum of intrapsychic to interpersonal denial, then people will fall at different points along the way. Some will be firmly at the intrapsychic position, and others will be focused on the interpersonal dimension. Most may be at some point in between. Many need some time to muster the adaptive coping abilities needed to more squarely face the reality of the situation. Those who are closer to the interpersonal position may need some help to overcome their fears or beliefs. Clinicians who see patients as being in denial are challenged by whether they should intervene psychosocially.

Conventional therapeutic wisdom has said one should not interfere with the use of a psychological defense. It seems accurate to say that someone who is marginally coping and needs to use denial to survive emotionally should be left to his or her use of denial with only supportive interventions. However, those whose denial is rooted in their interpersonal lives often respond well to psychosocial interventions that help to open channels of communication.

Intervention

Psychosocial intervention with a dying patient who appears to be using denial can be fraught with difficulties. The clinician has to be exquisitely sensitive to how the patient is coping with the illness and to his or her changing emotional needs. What is needed is the ability to pace intervention to the patient's readiness to face reality.

It is usually best to find out what a patient believes about the illness. If the patient is convinced that he or she is not dying in spite of being told the facts, trying to convince him or her otherwise would be countertherapeutic. As in any therapeutic relationship, it is necessary to form a relationship first and to develop trust. With time, it may be possible to assess whether their refusal to deal with reality is based on their limited coping resources or their fears of abandonment.

For patients described as intrapsychic deniers, it is best to avoid interventions directed at helping them face the reality of their dying. Supportive interventions that bolster their defenses are best. For those whose denial is more interpersonal, interventions that lead to increased communication with those they love are best. For those who are not yet ready to face reality but who have the ability to cope, it may be best to both bolster their defenses while gradually helping them to face reality. Figure 9.1 describes this concept.

One of the beliefs that is attendant to being seriously ill is that one has to maintain a positive attitude at all times or face a worsening of one's condition. Although positive thinking can help in the recovery process, it

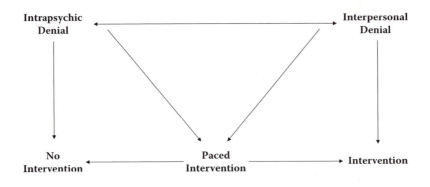

Figure 9.1 Connor's Psychosocial Intervention Model

can pose dangers for someone who is terminally ill. Underlying this belief is the unspoken notion that if you can affect the outcome of your illness, then perhaps you were part of what caused it in the first place. This can lead to feelings of guilt and self-blame for not being strong enough to overcome the illness. It is also a way in which people may distance themselves from a dying person's feelings. They may not want to have to deal with the sadness of facing the fact that the person is dying, so they tell the person not to talk "that way" or admonish them if they want to talk about painful feelings. When people tell the dying person not to feel the way they feel or to talk about their fears, it is a fundamental discounting of them as a person. Lazarus (1985) referred to this as trivializing the distress of the dying person.

The following case shows how it can be possible to maintain hope while facing the reality of death.

Case Illustration

John

John was a 38-year-old engineer with two young daughters who was dying of metastatic melanoma. He had taken a year off with his family to sail around the Caribbean. In the past year, he returned and was working on an important breakthrough in his field. Once diagnosed, he joined a wellness group and started treatment. He was certain that he would beat the disease.

He was referred to hospice after his wife reported that he was too weak to get out of bed. At the hospice intake session, he said that he was certain that he would not die and just needed to regain his strength. His wife was realistic and needed much support. She was concerned about her two daughters, who were very close to John, and how they would react to his death. Her mother had just arrived to help but was still grieving over the death of her husband less than a year earlier.

We agreed that the best approach was to continue to support John's hope but to gradually work on his ability to face the current reality. In conversations with John, it became apparent that he was single-mindedly focused on the wellness philosophy. He believed that if his will were strong enough, he could beat the cancer. To help him with this, we enlisted the aid of his wellness group's facilitator. She was a marriage and family counselor who was quite cooperative and understanding about the situation.

John placed a great deal of faith in her, and when she came to say that the end was near and that he had done all that was possible to help in his healing, he was able to begin facing the possibility of his death. We continued to support John's need for hope but helped him to allow for the possibility that he could die soon. We appealed to his paternal side to encourage him to talk with his daughters about his life and the possibility that he might not always be there.

John never regained his strength, nor was he able to deal with his painful guilt over having triggered his disease during the Caribbean sailing trip. He had ignored the changes in his skin that preceded the diagnosis. He did remain comfortable up to the end and died at home with his family. His young daughters were able to say goodbye to him before he died and helped with his care. His wife and mother-in-law received emotional and bereavement support and were able to help each other. This case illustrates the importance of meeting a person where the person is in his or her readiness to hear painful information and then pacing psychosocial intervention to the person's willingness to face reality.

From denial, I now turn to the important issue of assisted suicide and euthanasia. In the next chapter, hospices' role in the debate over the right to die is explored.

CHAPTER **10**

A Right to Die?

If your time ain't come, not even a doctor can kill you.

—American Proverbs

Euthanasia and assisted dying are currently among the most hotly debated topics of our time. A growing number of states in the United States have held referendums on whether physicians should be allowed to provide terminally ill patients with the means to die, and at this writing only Oregon and Washington States have done so. State legislatures have attempted to make physician-assisted suicide a distinctly illegal act. U.S. courts have tended to oppose laws banning suicide and, in some federal districts (the Second and Ninth), have recognized a right to suicide.

In the Ninth Circuit case *Washington v. Glucksberg* (1997 WL 348094, 65 USLW 4669), the court challenged Washington State's ban on assisted suicide, asserting that there is a liberty interest protected by our Constitution that protects the right of a mentally competent terminally ill adult to choose PAS. They argued that citizens should be able to control the time and manner of their death.

In the Second Circuit case *Vacco v. Quill* (1997 WL 348037, 65 USLW 4695), the court reviewed a decision that struck down New York State's statute prohibiting assisted suicide on the basis that it violated constitutional guarantees of equal protection. The Second Circuit argued that there was no difference between a terminally ill person who had a legal right to withdraw or forgo life support and a gravely ill person seeking to hasten death by suicide.

The U.S. Supreme Court overturned both of these decisions and ruled that there is no constitutional right to assisted suicide. In the Washington

157

case, it cited the enduring themes of our philosophical, legal, and cultural heritage, and the state's rational interest in preserving life, preventing suicide, protecting vulnerable people, protecting the integrity of the medical profession, and protecting family members. In the *Vacco* case, it noted that there is a fundamental distinction between withdrawing life support and affirmative acts that cause death.

The Supreme Court also established in the *Vacco* case that states have the right to allow or disallow assisted suicide and that the federal government cannot prohibit physician-assisted suicide by disallowing the use of controlled substances (Gonzales v. Oregon, 2006).

Physicians in the Netherlands have had the ability to assist patients to die for years. Although not completely legal, physicians are allowed to end patients' lives if they follow prescribed guidelines, including patient consent and receipt of a second physician's opinion. Concern has been expressed that these guidelines are ignored with no consequences to the physician.

In the United States, there has been a quiet but not uncommon practice in the medical profession of "medicating the patient out." Some physicians have done this for years in private without any safeguards. Reports of medical professionals' involvement in acts that have terminated life have revealed that a significant percentage of registered nurses have participated in or had knowledge of patients being euthanized by their physicians. This has been done in an effort to relieve the patient's, or often the family's, distress. However, there may be some confusion here with regard to the use of terminal sedation which is used to relieve symptoms, not to euthanize patients.

There is also a vocal and polarized argument between those who oppose any form of euthanasia and those who seek to legalize it. Most vocal was pathologist Jack Kevorkian, who has made it his mission to provide people with the information on how to end life. He has been supported by public interest groups and by many of the general public in the United States. Jailed in connection with a publicly broadcasted assisted suicide, he has agreed to stop publicly participating in assisted suicide. Public support for PAS may stem from the health care system's difficulty in managing death.

On the other side of this debate are groups that argue for the sanctity of all human life. These groups are often aligned with religious organizations and the antiabortion movement. They argue that any liberalization of current restrictions on euthanasia will lead to further and further pressures for patients to die. They pose a "slippery slope" argument that once laws and restrictions begin to be relaxed, pressure will build to eliminate all restrictions on euthanasia or assisted suicide.

There are also disability rights groups such as Not Dead Yet that decry the devaluation of disabled or differently abled persons. There is a growing suspicion that advance directives may be used to prematurely end the lives of disabled people who are less valued by society. It is indeed true that the able community harbors many prejudices against the disabled that they have little awareness of.

Ethicists take a variety of positions in this debate. It is well recognized that if death results from a physician's efforts to control pain or other symptoms, it is not Assisted Suicide (AS). However, giving a lethal dose that is far more than needed to control symptoms is AS. The key issue is intent. It is also now well established that patients or their surrogates have a right to refuse or withdraw from treatment, including those that can continue life, such as ventilatory support or artificially provided fluid and nutrition.

The fundamental arguments regarding AS involve one's basic ethical position. Some take the deontological or moralistic position that AS is fundamentally wrong. Others take a more pragmatic position that one must weigh the benefits and burdens of the situation to find what is right for the patient facing death. These are different basic positions that are hard to reconcile.

What has been notably absent in this debate is the role of hospice care. Hospices offer a middle ground in this argument. Instead of premature death, hospice offers relief from the symptoms and conditions that drive terminally ill people to consider suicide.

Hospice's Role in the Case of Terri Schiavo

Ms. Terri Schiavo's story is now well-known to most. She was a young woman suffering from a likely eating disorder who had a heart attack resulting in severe brain damage. She was cared for for many years by a husband who became a nursing professional while caring for her. Ms. Schiavo's husband, acting as her surrogate health care decision maker, petitioned the court to allow her feeding tube to be removed, saying that Terri had expressed to him that she would not want to be kept alive if severely brain damaged. The court agreed, but Ms. Schiavo's parents objected and the case continued in the courts for years until her husband prevailed and her feeding tube was finally removed, resulting in her death. The story was sensationalized by the press, and both U.S. Congress and the then-current presidential administration became involved in what are now thought to have been inappropriate ways. The case became a cause célèbre for groups that oppose abortion and have expressed a growing concern for the development of a "culture of death" in the United States.

There are several issues with regard to hospice's involvement that may be helpful to include. Ms. Schiavo was referred to the hospice in Florida after her husband first obtained a court order to have her feeding tube removed. She qualified for hospice at that time as her prognosis without tube feeding was short. Shortly after hospice admission, her parents were able to obtain a stay on the court order permitting feeding tube removal.

Hospice's position on the situation was that the patient had been admitted to their inpatient facility and should not be abandoned while the court sorted things out. No one could have foreseen that it would take so many years to resolve the case.

It is generally held that a spouse, if available, is best able to act as a surrogate decision maker for a patient who is unable to express his or her wishes. The concept of substitute judgment is based on who would best know the mind of the person and could make a decision consistent with the person's values, wishes, and goals. Ultimately, the court ended up siding with the husband over the parents, who had a different and parental relationship with their daughter.

There were many individuals who claimed that Ms. Schiavo demonstrated some degree of cognitive ability, in spite of numerous competent medical examiners who determined that Ms. Schiavo was in a persistent vegetative state. At its core, the accusation against hospice is that it participated in an act of euthanasia by omission by facilitating the starvation of a woman who was disabled, not in a vegetative state. Certainly, some members of her family wanted to see signs of cognitive ability in Ms. Schiavo and wanted her to recover her cognitive abilities. However, we know that patients clearly in a vegetative state will never recover the ability to have conscious thought. Their responses are reflex and not evidence of consciousness. Ultimately, the diagnosis of a persistent vegetative state was confirmed on autopsy, when medical examiners discovered that Ms. Schiavo's brain had atrophied to less than half its normal size.

One has to ask the ultimate question of what constitutes life. Is it the ability to breathe air and pump blood? Or is life defined by the ability to experience consciousness? If we cannot experience any degree of conscious awareness, then are we alive? Most of us would say that if we have no awareness, then we are not alive and would not want our bodies to be kept alive under such circumstances.

The case of Terri Schiavo is not unique. There are an increasing number of supposed cases where hospices are being accused of being complicit in causing the deaths of disabled persons who have conscious awareness. While every hospice must be on guard to ensure that such patients are not admitted, such accusations continue and are the result of well-meaning family members who want desperately to believe their loved one will recover in spite of overwhelming evidence to the contrary.

There is some irony in the belief that the provision of artificial nutrition and hydration, to persons without any hope of recovery of consciousness, is not a medical treatment and is ordinary care. Is this not playing God by insisting on continuing physical existence when the person has effectively died? The NHPCO has taken an official position supporting patients' rights to choose treatment or nontreatment but opposing the legalization of assisted suicide as unwise public policy. Hospices do not want to hasten or prolong anyone's death. Hospice's role in these difficult situations is to ensure that their patients receive the best care possible and die with comfort and dignity. In spite of the claims that Terri Schiavo suffered greatly from dehydration when her physical body died, those with her reported that her death was comfortable and peaceful.

The Hospice Solution

The desire for euthanasia may be fueled by fear—fear of actual or imagined distress. Those with terminal illnesses, and some with painful chronic illnesses, consider suicide to escape unbearable distress or loss of control. When that distress is relieved, thoughts of suicide may recede. Pain is a common distress feared by seriously ill persons. Because hospices are adept at controlling pain, the memory and fear of pain recede with good control.

Of course, there are many other types of distress associated with dying. Besides other physical symptoms, there is distress at being dependent on others for care, distress over unresolved relationships with others, fear of losing control and loss of dignity, and fear of oblivion, to name a few. Hospice as an interdisciplinary system of care looks to address any source of distress in patients and their families.

Being dependent on others can be as much a blessing as a curse. Hospices often redefine the opportunity for family members to care for a patient as an opportunity to give back to someone. Our parents cared for us when we were young, and now we can care for them. Our spouse has been our life-long partner, and providing care is a way of giving thanks as well as a helpful memory during the grieving process (Connor & Adams, 2003). More research is needed on the impact of caregiving. While hospice caregiving can have positive outcomes, research on the health impact of caregiving on caregivers reveals that there are many complex factors and unknowns and that prolonged caregiving leads to health risks (Schulz, Boerner, & Hebert, 2008).

The opportunity to resolve hurt relationships is one of the most powerful reasons to avoid premature death. Hospice workers often help to heal these relationships before a person dies. Reminding family members that this may be their last opportunity to say, "I'm sorry," "I love you," or "I forgive you" often gives them permission to make things right. The best death is one that leaves relationships whole.

Modern life is full of anxiety. People try to handle it by attempting to control events. When a terminal illness strikes, one cannot control the outcome. Richard Lazarus (1966) defined the difference between problem- and emotion-focused coping. Problem-focused coping is what people do when there is a problem that needs to be solved: the car breaks down, or one has to figure out how to beat a competitor. When faced with a terminal illness, people often try to use problem-focused coping but get frustrated when it does not work and feel helpless.

What they then do is turn to emotion-focused coping. They mediate their internal reactions and adapt to the situation. Some of these reactions are more adaptive than others. Hospice workers help people to understand they are facing a loss of control and to find other things they can realistically control.

Some people hate the idea of losing their independence, having their body image change, or losing roles that are important to their self-esteem. There is not a great deal that anyone can do about these losses except to help people to grieve and come to some accommodation to a new reality.

The impending loss of the self and fear of the unknown are also difficult to address. For those with a belief system that includes a continued existence after death, there may be less anxiety, and spiritual support helps them to overcome their doubts. According to Hayes and Hendrix (2008), for those who have resolved themselves that there is no afterlife, there may be less anxiety. Those who are unsure (agnostic) may be most likely to be in conflict over the impending oblivion. Psychotherapy continues to lack a conceptual framework for inclusion of religious issues (Hayes & Hendrix). Personal meaning making may be the most important way to stimulate psychological meaning making when working with the bereaved.

An additional problem for those facing death is the likelihood that clinical depression could color attitudes and decisions about continuing life. Faced with the stereotype that death is always painful and full of indignity and being vulnerable to depression over feeling helpless, some contemplate suicide as a way out.

Rather than encouraging a hasty end to life, it makes more sense to find out what the source of distress is and then respond to it. It would be very unusual for dying people to want euthanasia when their symptoms are controlled, they are not depressed, and they feel supported by those around them. This is exactly what hospices strive for in the care of their patients.

Unbearable Suffering and Sedation

There are a small number of patients whose suffering cannot be controlled without impairment of consciousness. This may be due to severe neuropathic pain, extreme disfigurement, or circumstances that cannot be resolved. For patients with pain that cannot be controlled without impairment of consciousness, the prevailing opinion is that barbiturate sedation is appropriate. The level of sedation should be enough to produce unconsciousness but not death. This terminal sedation should be infrequent and would most commonly occur during the final stages of the illness. The

American Medical Association (AMA, 2008) has approved a statement on sedation to unconsciousness for some terminally ill.

All efforts to control pain by other means will have to have been attempted prior to using sedation. For severe neuropathic pain, this may include use of coanalgesics, very large doses of opioids, nerve blocks, and so forth. Sedation is a last resort but will remove the perception of pain. The patient would usually not be expected to regain consciousness, though this should be discussed prior to initiation, and death would be expected usually within days, depending on the patient's condition.

Other rare situations where patients are faced with potentially unbearable circumstances include extreme disfigurement. This can include patients with large fungating lesions, head and neck tumors growing out of orifices, and widespread Kaposi's sarcoma. In these cases, efforts are made to control problems with sight and odor. Bandaging and use of chlorophyll or charcoal may help. The issue of severe existential suffering remains controversial, but sedation may be indicated in some cases.

Suffering is a subjective experience. What constitutes suffering for one may be easily tolerable for another. As with pain, it is whatever the patient perceives it to be. It is often surprising that a patient may be able to cope with something that someone else might find unbearable. What can be taken from this is that there is always something that can be done in situations of extreme suffering that may diminish the patient's desire for euthanasia.

The Problem with Assisted Suicide and Euthanasia

Euthanasia is, in this context, the taking of life. Treatments accurately aimed at relieving symptoms that result in death are not euthanasia. Neither is the withdrawal of artificial life support or treatments that postpone a death that would otherwise occur naturally. Either the physician or another takes the patient's life or the patient takes his or her own life by suicide. This does not constitute murder when it has been requested by the patient.

As previously discussed, it is much more effective to deal with the fears and problems that drive the patient to want an early death than it is to provide the patient with the means to suicide. The decision to seek AS is a complex one. Decisions are often colored by interpersonal dynamics. Patients may feel compelled to seek the end to relieve the burden they feel they have become on their family.

Hospice care can help relieve this burden in most cases. There are some families, however, who are ill prepared to cope and need more than can be provided even through hospice. In these situations, alternate caregiving arrangements need to be made to provide for the patient's needs through either privately hired in-home care or a residential or nursing care facility.

A documentary in the Netherlands intended to show the positive side of the Dutch euthanasia policy. In the film, a terminally ill patient was interviewed. During the interview, the patient hardly spoke. His wife did all the talking and conveyed how difficult his illness had been. The patient consented to euthanasia, but it was clear from the couple's interaction that he was anything but a willing subject. In spite of a belief in the primacy of patient autonomy, health care workers forget how much all health care decisions are made in the context of a family system.

Patients make their treatment decisions with the family's reactions in mind. A treatment that the patient does not want may be accepted because the family wants the patient to fight. The patient does not want to disappoint loved ones. If treatment is refused, the family may feel the patient wants to end his or her life because he or she does not love them and would just as soon be dead. In the same way, patients may come to believe the family is tired of caring for them or that everyone would be better off if they were gone. Fear of dependency is more common than even fear of pain.

In addition to family, health care providers and society exert subtle or overt pressure on patients to consent to excessive disease-oriented therapy. Other patients may be similarly pressured to consent to euthanasia if it is legalized. These unspoken dynamics are very powerful and can greatly influence decisions about euthanasia.

Hospice and palliative care programs, as well as other healthcare providers, are increasingly finding it useful to utilize bioethics committees to provide support to patients and families in making difficult decisions about the end-of-life.

The state of Oregon has been an interesting laboratory for the study of what happens when assisted suicide is legalized. Actually, many of the things that were predicted if AS became legal have not come to pass. However, Linda Ganzini and colleagues at Oregon Health Sciences University have studied the characteristics of individuals who request and go through with assisted suicide. The one predominant personality trait seen by hospice workers in this population is a strong desire for control (Ganzini et al., 2002). This desire for control has been extreme in some cases, including a patient who insisted on being resuscitated in the hospital in order to be able to take her lethal medication when discharged home.

Other problems with euthanasia include determining who is terminally ill, who will administer fatal doses, where does one draw the line, and the problem of clinical depression. At present, it is rather difficult to determine how long anyone will live. The SUPPORT Investigators (1995) study previously mentioned developed a complex algorithm for determining probability of death for patients grouped with seven types of terminal conditions. One of the study authors, Joanne Lynn, commented that any method for determining prognosis that had a .50 or greater probability of accuracy was probably as good as one can get at this time.

The NHPCO has been working on the problem of determining prognosis in terminally ill patients since 1994. Guidelines are continually being revised to help in identifying patients who are likely to die within 6 months. These guidelines are based on what is found in the current literature. Probably the best that can be said is that the science of prognostication is still in its infancy.

As there is no hard science to determine when someone is terminally ill, how is a person to decide if he or she qualifies for AS? Current referendum efforts limit euthanasia to those who are terminally ill. Many of the patients who were seen by Jack Kevorkian were not terminally ill. They may have had an incurable condition that caused them distress, but many were not terminally ill by the usual current definition of less than 6 months of life if the illness runs its normal course. So should the definition be expanded to all who have chronic illnesses? This could open a floodgate of potential patients who may request or be pressured to accept AS.

Many patients who request AS are too debilitated to actually take a lethal dose. They must have someone's help to accomplish termination of life. This poses a dilemma. Physicians often do not want to administer death. It is fairly easy to write a prescription to give to a patient. It is much harder to give the lethal dose. Family members have the same problem. They do not want to have the memory of actually being responsible for ending their loved one's life. So who will provide assistance in the act of ending the patient's life?

I have said that the boundary of terminal illness is vague. So where does one draw the line? A report from the Netherlands (Pijnenborg, van der Maas, van Delden, & Looman, 1993) showed that there have been a growing number of cases of involuntary euthanasia (0.8% of all deaths). The number of cases may be much higher than recorded due to underreporting. In these cases, the physician has determined without consent that the patient's life should be ended. The physician may believe that the patient is suffering and it would be the humane thing to do. Physicians are supposed to get another physician's assent, but often this is done by another colleague who has never seen the patient.

What is troubling about these cases is their frequency and the lack of any oversight. In 1990, based on an anonymous physician survey, approximately 1,000 people received involuntary euthanasia in the Netherlands. In 41% of these cases, the physician had no information on the patient's wishes. Although the fears of those who use the slippery slope argument may be exaggerated, there is serious cause for concern that making euthanasia available will lead to abuses. In addition, it has been reported that as many as 25% of those undergoing AS in the Netherlands are initially unsuccessful (Hendin, Rutenfrancs, & Zylich, 1997). This raises the specter of a painful, dysphoric, lingering death rather than the smooth transition sought by patients.

One of the symptoms of clinical depression is a tendency toward suicidal ideation, and depressed people are more apt to commit suicide. When depression is properly treated, suicidal tendencies are diminished. Terminally and chronically ill people are vulnerable to clinical depression, which often goes untreated. Some assume that the illness is cause to be depressed and that treatment is unnecessary.

This goes back to the old exogenous versus endogenous distinction in depression. It used to be assumed that depression caused by external factors (exogenous) did not respond to treatment, whereas internally produced depression (endogenous) did. This distinction is no longer considered relevant, though those with vegetative signs of depression (psychomotor retardation, sleep disturbance, etc.) tend to respond better to pharmacotherapy.

There is real danger in allowing depressed patients to go through with suicide without treatment. The same is true for all other treatable forms of distress. Rather than ending life, it makes more sense to treat the underlying cause of the distress.

Society's Role

Public opinion polls have shown that the majority of Americans favor legalizing AS. This opinion seems to derive from the collective social belief that people ought to have as much freedom as possible and that the government is interfering in our lives too much. The courts have supported this position by declaring laws against AS unconstitutional.

Attempts to legalize AS in the United States have not fared well. The only states that have successfully passed and implemented AS are Oregon and Washington. Many other states are experimenting with the legalization of AS and other options such as mandatory notification of options for the terminally ill that was passed in California. This leaves an ambiguous gray area—which is possibly where AS is best left.

Many national organizations have expressed strong opposition to AS. The American Medical Association along with the NHPCO have declared opposition to legalization of AS. NHPCO has also asked hospices to serve all terminally ill patients, even those who desire AS.

Should AS be legalized and recognized in many states, hospices would be put in a particularly difficult position. Should any of their patients wish to avail themselves of AS, the hospice would find itself in a dilemma. Would they support patients in ending their lives in the manner they choose, or would they try to dissuade them? Certainly all hospices would want to address any treatable distress so the patient would have no reason for AS. If, however, the patient still insisted on AS, what would the hospice do?

Some hospice programs are addressing the issue proactively. A few have taken the position that they would discharge the patient from the hospice. They take the position that this is like the patient who insists on receiving curative treatment and leaves hospice. Hospice neither hastens nor postpones death. It also seems like abandoning the patient at a crucial moment. Patients may choose to leave hospice, but to discharge the patient does not seem therapeutic. Yet what is a hospice to do if it is adamantly opposed to AS?

Other programs support the philosophical position that patient choice is the most important value in this discussion. Even if they oppose AS, they support the patient's right to decide for him or herself. If the hospice decides it will continue to serve the patient who insists on AS, then comes the difficult decision regarding what role hospice will play. Should they actively assist the patient in arranging AS? Can they stand back and allow AS to go forward without any role?

As with any ethical dilemma, there are few hard-and-fast rules. Each case may have to be addressed in a dialogue with the patient and family. Hospice will have to negotiate its role in AS with the same sensitivity it uses to handle other difficult psychosocial issues. What is right for one patient may not work for another. NHPCO has encouraged hospices to address this issue proactively and to support patients' legal and reasoned decisions to choose AS. Most of the patients in Oregon who have choosen AS have been served by hospices.

Case Illustration

Dr. K.

Dr. K. was one of the early leaders in the hospice community. He was a founding medical director of a hospice and a strong proponent of symptom control and hospice care. Over the years, he became more cynical about hospice's ability to relieve distress. When his wife died following a stroke precipitated from a simple surgery, he became quite bitter about health care in general. He was depressed and wished his life would end. He had long been a proponent of legalizing euthanasia and AS.

About 18 months after his wife's lingering death, Dr. K. was diagnosed with widely metastatic cancer with an unknown primary. His surgeon did an open-and-close laparotomy. He advised Dr. K. to get his affairs in order. A few months before this, Dr. K. had fallen in love again and was living with his girlfriend. After returning home, he was referred to hospice. During the hospice intake discussion, he said, "The moment my pain is too uncomfortable, I plan to kill myself, and if you have a problem with that, leave right now."

Hospice services were initiated, and Dr. K. insisted on being in control. Over the course of his last 6 weeks, hospice staff provided nursing and emotional and spiritual support. He decided to marry his girlfriend, and the hospice chaplain performed the service in his home. Equipment was brought in, and medication provided. The family was taught how to provide care. A full bottle of sleeping pills remained in the headboard of his bed. In one conversation, he stated his desire to make his death a statement for euthanasia by writing an article about his suicide and publishing it posthumously. His main worry was for his wife and the possibility of getting his family in legal trouble if they were to help him end his life.

In the following days, he continued to decline but remained comfortable. As his death neared, those close to him gathered around him. The day before his death, I visited and said my goodbye. He was unable to speak, but he held my hand and smiled. The full bottle of pills lay nearby. Somehow I knew he never reached the point where his distress was bad enough for him to end his own life.

In the next chapter, the unique aspects of hospice care are explored.

Recommended Reading

Colby, B. (2007). *Long goodbye: The deaths of Nancy Cruzan.* Carlsbad, CA: Hay House.

Foley, K., & Hendin H. (2004). *The case against assisted suicide: For the right to end-of-life care.* Baltimore: Johns Hopkins University Press.

Hastings Center. (1987). *Guidelines on the termination of life sustaining treatment and the care of the dying.* New York: Author.

Morgan, J. D. (1996). *Ethical issues in the care of the dying and bereaved aged.* Amityville, NY: Baywood.

Quill, T., Battin, P., & Pabst Battin, M. (2004). *Physician-assisted dying: The case for palliative care and patient choice.* Baltimore: Johns Hopkins University Press.

CHAPTER 11

How Palliative Care Is Unique in the Health Care System

A life is not important except in its impact on other lives.

—Rachel Robinson, wife of Jackie Robinson

Many view palliative and hospice care as just another health care service that is not particularly unique. The individual services provided can by and large be delivered by other providers. Most dying patients are cared for by other providers throughout the health care system. So why do those associated with hospice and palliative care consider them to be unique?

True Teamwork

This book has discussed types of team functioning and hospices' interdisciplinary approach. When this works at its best, it is a remarkable process. Team meetings enhance a sense of community within hospice. Each member of the team is valued as an essential contributor to the process of helping patients and their families to achieve a good death.

In many multidisciplinary health care teams, the physician dominates the discussion and there is clearly a hierarchical structure. The contributions of those further up in the hierarchy are given greater value and credence. When the hospice interdisciplinary team is working well, there is no hierarchy. Each team member's contribution is valued on the basis of its relevance to understanding the unique process the patient and family are facing.

At another level, the palliative care hospice team functioning is a kind of support group for those faced with caring for dying patients. They are able to share the joys and sorrows experienced in day-to-day care. When they are wrestling with a difficult problem, they can go to the brain trust of the team and help find a solution. The rest of the team serves as a witness to the work of each team member. A nurse can describe how the dying process went and be acknowledged for the patient's having a good death. If things did not go well, the team can help to gain perspective on how this came to pass.

Interaction in hospice or palliative care team meetings at their best is collaborative. The primary aim is to develop a team sense of who the patient and family are and how they can best be served by hospice. In a typical team meeting, new admissions are discussed in detail. A medical history is given by the nurse case manager, followed by a psychosocial and spiritual assessment from the social worker and chaplain. Current problems are identified, and plans for intervention are developed.

At these meetings, there is also discussion of deaths since the last meeting, problem cases, and any updates on stable patients. The flavor of discussion is planning for the best care and coordination of who will take the lead in meeting particular needs. Each member of the team is acknowledged and valued for his or her contribution. This is not to say that people are not challenged. There can be spirited discussion of important issues of how best to provide care as well as identification of problems that require policy or practice changes in the agency.

Prevention

Palliative care's effectiveness in controlling the distress of those who are terminally ill is directly related to its focus on prevention. Any symptom is easier to manage if you prevent it from happening in the first place. Using pain as an example, say a hospice admits a patient whose pain is out of control. The experience operates as reinforcing feedback. The more the pain remains out of control, the less confidence the patient has that his or her pain can be controlled.

Through aggressive palliative care, hospice is able to control the patient's pain, usually within a short period of time. Medication is dosed so that the level of analgesic in the blood is high enough to prevent the pain's return. After a while, the memory and fear of the pain is diminished so much so that less medication may be needed. The same approach works with other symptoms as well.

Hospice and palliative care workers know where the pitfalls are when facing death. After working with so many people who have died, these professionals develop a sense of the common psychosocial challenges facing the dying. Each dying person faces these challenges in a different way. Palliative caregivers help patients and their families to face difficult decisions about care. They educate about the different treatments available and the benefits and burdens of each. Hospice team members help the patient formulate goals for care at the end of life. These goals will determine how the patient is treated. Areas addressed include use of antibiotics, blood transfusions, oxygen, respirators, cardiopulmonary resuscitation, dialysis, chemotherapy, radiation therapy, ambulance transport, IV therapies, tube feedings, and hospitalization.

Depending on state laws, team members help see that advanced directives and other legal protections are in place to ensure the patient's wishes are obeyed and the patient is protected from unwanted treatment. It is usually appropriate to also help the patient and family make or finalize arrangements for funeral services. Dealing with all these difficult questions ahead of time is definitely a preventative service. When these issues are left unresolved, there can be a great deal of turmoil in the family about what to do. When plans are made, everyone can relax more by knowing what the patient wants.

Deinstitutionalization

Over the past 50 years, health care has been delivered more and more in institutional settings. Following World War II, there was a major push to ensure that hospitals were available to all citizens in the United States. These hospitals became the center point for delivery of health care. As medical technology advanced, so too did the services based in hospitals. As the population has aged and hospitals have had to specialize in the care of the sickest patients, the nursing home industry has developed into an enormous institution for the ongoing care of elderly and disabled persons.

As a society, people have come to both love and fear these institutions. They insist that acute care services be immediately available for any illness and demand that these services be effective in handling all medical problems. When a medical problem cannot be solved, the institution often continues to make the attempt and the patient must endure a juggernaut of treatments, tests, and procedures.

When all these efforts fail, the patient either is left to die in a sterile hospital environment or is transferred to a nursing facility, there to wait out a death sentence while being cared for by strangers. All people have strong feelings about spending their last days helpless, in the hands of overworked and underpaid caregivers. There are, of course, many excellent nursing facilities and hospitals where staff are very caring and allow patients to express their unique humanity. The point is that they are still institutions where one is a patient and must conform to the environment. They are not one's home where the person is ultimately in control, surrounded by the memories and collection of a lifetime. In one's home, you can listen to the music you like, you can get that book you want, and you can decide what to eat and when to eat it. You can laugh or cry or belch without fear of upsetting the next person.

So it is no wonder that there has been a gradual rebellion against the institutionalization of health care. The hospice movement is in fact part of a consumer movement. People do not want health care at the convenience of health care providers. They want care that is directed to their needs as an individual. They want care that allows them to remain as independent and human as possible. They want care that is provided where they live; if they have to be cared for in a facility, they want few rules and to be treated as an individual. It is not surprising that one of the first things Dr. Saunders envisioned at St. Christopher's Hospice was a different set of house rules for her patients. There would be 24-hour-a-day visiting. Patients would be allowed to bring their own things into the room to make it more homelike. Children would be allowed and encouraged to visit. Patients would always be treated with kindness, respect, and courtesy. There would be a large number of staff to care for the patients. The afternoon tea tray would be brought around.

In the United States' inpatient hospices, the same philosophy pervades. There are some lovely freestanding hospice facilities where patients are cared for. They get food when they want it, served by family or to family. Accommodations are provided for family to sleep over in the patient's room. There may be a sound system and videotapes. Rooms are decorated to be more homelike. Patients will get their bath when they prefer it. Length of stay will be determined by how well their symptoms are managed rather than their diagnosis-related group (DRG) or diagnosis.

Likewise, inpatient palliative care programs are growing throughout the United States. Most provide consult teams to help the treating physician and the patient and family to clarify goals, achieve good pain and symptom management, and receive needed psychosocial and spiritual support. Often, this results in the patient expressing a desire to go home, and when appropriate, a handoff to a hospice provider is preferable. Some inpatient palliative care programs have excellent inpatient facilities like hospice, with homelike amenities and interdisciplinary services. Some nursing facilities are following this lead with the creation of greenhouses, small homelike facilities rather than large impersonal facilities.

Care in the acute hospital setting has become enormously expensive. Care in the home has emerged as a much more cost-effective alternative. It makes more sense to use some resources to maintain a patient at home than to have to spend a lot to provide for all their needs in a facility. Once patients enter a health care facility, they are the responsibility of the institution. Extended family are moved aside and discouraged from taking responsibility. Sure, they are encouraged to visit, but they are usually not allowed to deliver any care. This is not the case in hospice and palliative care facilities, where active involvement in delivering care is strongly encouraged and is critical in training the family to continue meeting the patient's care needs at home.

Home health care is provided by a number of providers in the United States. Home health agencies, homemaker services, home infusion companies, durable medical equipment providers, and private duty nursing pools all provide services to patients at home. They most often deliver care to patients who are recovering from an illness and help rehabilitate them to the point where they are able to care for themselves. Current home health agency payment rules encourage patients to be admitted, and the agency is rewarded if they can complete the care in as short a period as possible. Home health agencies also provide health services in the home to chronically ill patients whose prognosis is uncertain. These patients may use home health care to be able to leave the hospital early or to prevent readmission. Home health agencies also care for terminally ill patients but are less effective at meeting their total needs than hospice programs.

In the United States, home health care has not been set up to effectively prevent hospitalization and institutionalization. When the patient is in a crisis, home health agencies must contact the physician, who routinely has the patient sent to a hospital emergency room. From there, the patient is usually given an extensive diagnostic workup and is admitted. In many parts of the United States, the home health service is not available 24 hours a day, and patients in crisis must seek out an emergency room themselves.

In contrast, hospices usually plan ahead for these crises. Orders are given ahead of time for managing exacerbations. Medical staff are always available 24 hours a day to go to the home if necessary. The emergency room is routinely avoided. If admission is needed, a direct admission is preferred. As the goals of care are agreed on, there are no true emergencies in the usual sense. The goal is management of the symptoms. Practically anything that can be done in the hospital for a hospice patient can be done in the home as well.

Hospice's success in keeping patients at home and out of institutions is due in large part to its focus on family involvement in caregiving. The patient's attachment network (family) actually does the largest share of the patient care. The simple secret is that families usually require only permission to do what is necessary to keep the patient at home. Health care providers sometimes prefer to keep family caregivers in the dark about how to take care of the patient. This may be done out of a misguided concern that they might harm the patient or as a way of ensuring their own job security.

Whatever the motive, there is every reason to teach families as much as possible about caregiving. Their education must always be tempered by an understanding of each individual's capacity for learning as well as his or her emotional history with the patient. Nonetheless, hospices have found that even families with limited capabilities are able to do a great deal of nursing care. It requires giving them permission to care so often denied when the patient is in an institution.

Once families are empowered to provide care, they are usually eager to learn the specifics of how to transfer, feed, toilet, do mouth care and skin care for, and give medication to their family member. This does great things to alleviate feelings of helplessness and anxiety and helps ease the grief process. It also makes the difference between being able to be cared for at home rather than in an institution.

Hospice and Palliative Care Workers

Is there something unique about the people who work in hospice and palliative care, or are they just like other health care providers? For the most part, they are like other health care workers, except they too have been given permission to act in a different way toward their patients. The tradition of hospice caregiving calls them to bring their whole selves to the work they do. Some of this difference can be heard in the words of the patients and families served by hospices. Over and over, they say things like "There is no way Mom could have died at home without hospice," "I don't know how I could have done it without you," or "The love and caring I received was overwhelming; we thank you with all our hearts, we will never forget what you did for us, you all are part of our family now."

Why is it that hospices receive such accolades from those they serve? It is likely because of the dedication of the staff and volunteers who view their work as more than a job. Hospices certainly have their share of difficult employees, but the kind of person who chooses to work in a hospice is often seeking to express more than just a set of job skills. Most have had many years of experience in the health care field and have been frustrated in not being allowed to express true caring.

Health care workers usually have a vision of what it is like to be a caregiver. This vision goes something like this: I will help people who are in real need to be comforted or cured and will feel satisfied that my efforts make a real difference in the lives of people I come to care about. After working in a health care institution, these workers come to experience a different reality: I am overwhelmed by the needs of so many whom I can neither help nor get to know as people. Nurses spend their time running from IV to IV, and social workers spend their time handling paperwork without ever getting to do the counseling they expected to do.

Work in hospice offers these idealists an opportunity to do what they came into health care to do. They actually get to help people and get to make a difference that they can see. This may be an oversimplification, but it works. Hospices encourage staff and volunteers to get to know their patients and to become somewhat involved with them emotionally. This involvement does carry risks, but the rewards can be worth it.

Dr. Dale Larson (1993), a psychologist from Santa Clara University who trains hospice and palliative care workers, has described the concept *accurate empathy* to demonstrate how hospice workers can be effective in helping without burning out. Imagine a continuum on which one end is the caregiver who is totally empathetic. This caregiver is so involved with the dying patient and family that she or he moves in and becomes part of the family. This is a very painful place to be and cannot be done very long. On the other end is the detached professional who keeps a professional distance and never gets involved with a patient. This person does not get much satisfaction from the work and feels bad about him or herself.

Hospice workers tend to start out as the hot empathetic person who bonds with the patient and family. After experiencing a deep sense of loss when patients die, they tend to pull away from getting so close, to protect themselves. This leaves them feeling cold and unsatisfied, so they go back to the close hot end of the continuum. After a while, they begin to feel like a yo-yo and cannot be very effective.

To survive in palliative care, one must first have a strong sense of empathy for the patient. One learns that if you get too involved, you become ineffective. So good hospice caregivers find a balance where they are able to show their caring without becoming too invested or enmeshed emotionally with those they care for.

This healthy caring is one of the things that families find special about hospice. They are used to cold impersonal caregivers and may feel burdened by those who want to get too close or do everything for them. Caregivers who lift the family up by encouraging their involvement in patient care and praising the work they do are most appreciated.

Psychosocial and Spiritual Care

When hospice or palliative care is suggested, it is often because it is believed that hospice can provide more emotional and spiritual support than can be found elsewhere. This is often true. Health care is still quite segmented. Mental health services are segregated from medical care, and spiritual care is not really considered part of the health care system at all. Hospices are the only providers that have integrated these components into a comprehensive program. Psychological care and social support are integral parts of palliative care. Chaplaincy and spiritual support are part of the assessment and caregiving process in any hospice. The bereavement follow-up services provided by hospices are also unique.

Psychosocial services can only be paid for in the health care system if the person has a mental disorder. In hospice this is unnecessary, as all patients and families are eligible to receive counseling. Their circumstances qualify them to receive this care. Good hospice programs provide as much counseling as requested and needed. Every patient and family ordinarily has a social worker assigned to visit as needed to help everyone prepare emotionally for the impending loss. There is usually a crisis response at the time of death to increase the amount of psychosocial support provided.

The provision of spiritual or pastoral care is a neglected part of the health care continuum. Beyond providing chaplains to visit patients while in the hospital, there are few pastoral care services in health care. In hospice, a significant amount of attention is given to ensuring that patients receive the spiritual support they need. Most hospices have chaplaincy staff that are available to visit patients at home, and all are required to address spiritual needs through coordination with community clergy. Including spiritual or transcendent needs in the hospice plan of care is essential to having a truly interdisciplinary program. Addressing these needs is critical to achieving quality of life for many dying patients. Spiritual care is for many patients the most important aspect of care, as it is focused on their most important fears and opportunities for growth.

The provision of bereavement services may be the most unique aspect of hospice care. No other provider has established an in-depth response to the needs of grieving people. The mental health system considers bereavement a legitimate focus of treatment but has done little to develop services for the bereaved as bereavement is not yet considered a disorder and therefore is not reimbursable (see chapter 5 for further discussion on this point). While the bereavement services provided by hospice vary, hospices are in the forefront of creating services specifically designed for populations of grieving people, including grief camps for children, specialized support groups for different types of loss, expressive therapies for adults and children, and death notification support, to name a few.

Beyond Symptom Management

Most people view the experience of facing death as an unpleasant reality in which the best one can hope for is the absence of pain and distress. Hospice workers have discovered after many years of caring for those near death that there is also the possibility that the end of life can be a time of growth and positive feelings.

Many dying patients have reported that as death approached, a number of opportunities are presented. They are confronted with a finite measure of remaining life, and this can bring about a focusing of the mind. A change in perspective occurs such that unimportant issues are ignored and things that matter to the patient take the foreground.

This is only possible if the symptoms of the terminal illness are controlled. Without relief from pain or other distressing physical symptoms, the patient cannot attend to other concerns. Once freed from physical distress, the patient is able to attend to psychological, emotional, interpersonal, social, and transcendent or spiritual matters.

Developmental Landmarks and Tasks for the End of Life

One of the foremost proponents for the view that the end of life holds opportunities for growth is Dr. Ira Byock. Byock has lectured widely and written about these opportunities to international audiences. A hospice physician since 1978, he has learned what he knows of this from the experiences shared by many of his dying patients. Byock has developed a working typology for helping people understand these opportunities for growth.

Byock (1997) promoted the notion of "dying well," the desired outcome for those facing death. By this, he meant a continuation of the lifelong developmental process. This process continues during the time of approaching death and actually may accelerate. Byock's 10 major developmental landmarks and tasks are as follows.

Sense of Completion with Worldly Affairs: Transfer of
Fiscal, Legal, and Formal Social Responsibilities

The patient gets his or her affairs in order. A will is done, funeral arrangements are made, and social responsibilities are terminated.

Sense of Completion in Relationships with Community:
Closure of Multiple Social Relationships (Employment,
Commerce, Organizational, and Congregational)

Components include expressions of regret, forgiveness, acceptance, and gratitude, and appreciation—leave taking, the saying of goodbye. This task involves the advance transfer of any business responsibilities to others. It may mean arranging for a family member to take over running the business or liquidation of partnerships. One may have to resign from organizations or discontinue attendance at meetings. As illness progresses, attendance at church, temple, mosque, or synagogue is disrupted; it is hoped that the clergy is available to continue providing support.

Along with this process of withdrawal, there are many opportunities to share regret at being unable to continue. There is also often an outpouring of support and gratitude to be received. The process of leaving can be a time of acknowledgment from others that might not otherwise occur.

Sense of Meaning about One's Individual Life: Life Review—the Telling of One's Stories; Transmission of Knowledge and Wisdom

The opportunity to review one's life before death is a transformative process. The process of stepping out of your life to review it can have a profound effect. Every life has some important milestones and major events. These can be as basic as the birth of children, service in the community or military, or a career of considerable significance, such as heroic action, invention, or other creative activity.

Hospice workers often recommend a review of one's life as a therapeutic activity with persons facing death. When written or taped, it can be suggested as a gift to the family who are left behind. This oral life history includes many stories from the person's life. In addition to recounting the important milestones in one's life, it is an opportunity to convey a person's philosophy about life and one's personal wisdom about life. It is especially helpful for a person with young children to leave this as a legacy to live on in the lives of those left behind.

Experienced Love of Self: Self-Acknowledgment and Self-Forgiveness

Often people are their own worst enemies and harshest critics. The time before dying can be an opportunity (perhaps for the first time) to genuinely appreciate oneself and to forgive oneself for those things one regrets doing.

Experienced Love of Others: Acceptance of Worthiness

For those with poor self-esteem, the admiration and love of others are always sought but rarely embraced. Most of us feel unworthy at times. As death approaches, people may allow themselves to feel the love others have for them.

Sense of Completion in Relationships with Family and Friends: Reconciliation, Fullness of Communication, and Closure in Each of One's Important Relationships

Component tasks include expressions of regret, forgiveness and acceptance, expressions of gratitude and appreciation, acceptance of gratitude and appreciation, expressions of affection, and leave taking (the saying of goodbye).

The opportunity to say goodbye to the people who form one's immediate attachment network can be profoundly moving. In saying goodbye, people allow for the expression of many powerful and healing emotions. Corrective emotional experiences can occur that can transform a lifetime of emotional pain into feelings of relief and release. In the presence of death, people have permission to show emotions and to say things they otherwise would not. This creates the opportunity for closure as well as the possibility of deep feelings of love and well-being.

Acceptance of the Finality of Life, of One's Existence as an Individual

This includes acknowledgment of the totality of personal loss represented by one's dying and experience of personal pain of existential loss, expression of the depth of personal tragedy that dying represents, decathexis (emotional withdrawal) from worldly affairs and cathexis (emotional connection) with an enduring construct, and acceptance of dependency.

Death is the loss of one's self. Each dying person must face this on a personal level and grieve over what is to be lost. It is at this juncture that people can pull away from life and withdraw. Rather than being a negative retreat, however, it can be a time for feeling connected to whatever enduring construct for continuation one feels.

Sense of a New Self (Personhood) beyond Personal Loss

Out of this personal grief process comes a new sense of self that is the essence of personhood. Once a person strips away all that he or she has come to think of as him or herself (profession, roles, learned behaviors), what is left is that part that has not changed throughout his or her life. This essential unchanging part is truly who one is.

Sense of Meaning about Life in General

This includes achieving a sense of awe, recognizing a transcendent realm, and developing and achieving a sense of comfort with chaos.

At this point in the developmental process, the dying person has completed saying goodbye, has grieved for the loss of self, and has gotten to the core of him or herself. From this may come an opportunity to transcend the self and to see life in a different way. Each experience may seem fresh and meaningful. Instead of trying to control life, one may find comfort with the way things are, an understanding that life goes on with or without one and that things will be all right.

Surrender to the Transcendent, to the Unknown: Letting Go

So often with those near death, there is a hesitation about leaving life. People hold on to those they love or are not sure of their faith or ready to face the unknown. Hospice workers often have to coach the family to get them to tell the dying person that it is all right to leave, that they will be fine. A final task is being able to let go and to embrace or surrender to whatever is next. It is allowing oneself to step off the precipice and go on.

Dealing with the preceding developmental issues can lead to the possibility that dying may be a time for a heightened sense of well-being. This may not always be a pleasant feeling. The struggle of growth can be painful but leads to a greater sense of mastery and integration.

Rather than only focusing on the negative, problem-oriented aspects of the dying process, clinicians need to be receptive to the possibilities of growth. Even though clinicians are used to being limited in the health care system to only working on problems, hospice and palliative care is one of the few examples of a milieu where helping the patient to grow is acceptable.

There is no prohibition from funding sources against including intervention that results in personal growth. Other health care services like medicine and mental health can only receive reimbursement for treating disorders. In hospice, once you have a terminal illness with the requisite prognosis, you are entitled to psychosocial and spiritual support that can go beyond the treatment of problems or disorders. This can only be done if the hospice or palliative care program recognizes this as a legitimate area of concern and need.

Hospice and palliative care workers should be cautioned that imposing expectations that the dying person should grow during this period can be unhelpful. There is a fine but important line between suggesting possibilities for growth that the person may not have considered and pushing the idea of developmental changes that the patient is neither interested in nor capable of attaining.

It is also important that all areas of suffering be addressed as the person goes through this time. To try to skip emotional pain on the way to developing a transcendent perspective is like trying to ignore physical pain to focus on psychological concerns. The dying person cannot deal with emotional issues with a body aching from bone metastases. Nor can the dying person develop a new sense of self when surrounded by unresolved interpersonal conflicts.

This chapter has examined what differentiates hospice as a health care provider in a general sense. The next chapter examines more specific measures of effectiveness.

CHAPTER 12

How Good Are Hospice and Palliative Care?

Statistics are like a bikini. What they reveal is suggestive, but what they conceal is vital.

—Aaron Levenstein

Hospice care may have some unique attributes in the health care system, but is palliative care better than "traditional" or mainstream care of the dying patient? What proof is there that it is as good as its proponents claim? Hospices have not been especially good at collecting data or doing research. Most hospices lack the funding or expertise to carry out research. Even so, some efforts are being made to take a hard look at the care being delivered and its impact on both the patients and families served and the system it affects.

Results of Studies of Hospice and Palliative Care Effectiveness

It is interesting that most studies of effectiveness to date have looked at cost-effectiveness rather than clinical outcomes. Cost-effectiveness has been a major variable in studies in an effort to preserve funding and expand coverage for hospice care. The results of these studies are equivocal in that some researchers have found no cost savings, and others have noted substantial savings. An early study of hospice care (Kane, Wales, Bernstein, Leibowitz, & Kaplan, 1984) done entirely in the Veterans Administration health care system found no significant difference in treatment costs or satisfaction with care between hospice and conventional care patients.

Critics of this study questioned some of the measures used and noted that the intervention (hospice care provided in the Veterans Administration system) may not have been characteristic of care provided by other hospice providers. The study was also done before the implementation of the Hospice Medicare Benefit, which enhanced the services hospices could offer. It was, however, the only large randomized trial to be conducted on hospice versus no-hospice care.

Random assignment (participants are assigned to either a treatment or control group on the basis of a table of random numbers) has been greatly resisted by hospice investigators. There is already a widespread belief in the value and efficacy of hospice care. To deny someone access to this care in order to study its effectiveness is viewed as unethical by some researchers.

A national hospice study was funded by the old Health Care Finance Administration to analyze hospices' cost effectiveness. Results revealed that home care-based hospice programs' treatment costs were lower than the costs of conventional care regardless of length of stay (Mor, Greer, & Kastenbaum, 1988). Hospital-based hospice programs' treatment costs were less than conventional-care costs only for patients with lengths of stay in hospice of less than 2 months. Although compelling, there remain questions about whether selection bias may have influenced these results, as randomization was not practicable.

Results of the first 3 years of experience under the Hospice Medicare Benefit have been widely reported. According to Medicare Part A data, $1.26 was saved for every dollar spent on hospice care. However, questions have again been raised about whether these savings are overstated as a result of persistent selection effects (Birenbaum & Kidder, 1992). Were those using hospice less likely to use more expensive services before death, or were they perhaps healthier than other dying patients?

In an effort to address some of these selection questions, the NHPCO commissioned an independent study of the Medicare data (NHPCO, 1995). The health care research company Lewin VH1 analyzed data on 191,545 Medicare recipients who died between July 1 and December 31, 1992. Costs for all services were analyzed during the last 12 months of life. The study included 39,719 recipients who were hospice users. A comparison group of 123,323 patients who did not receive any hospice care was carefully matched for age, sex, and disease. This larger group was matched with the hospice group to determine population differences.

Results of this study demonstrated that on average Medicare beneficiaries with cancer who enrolled in a hospice program cost Medicare $2,737 less than comparable nonusers. For every dollar spent on hospice care, Medicare saved $1.52. This study was limited to only cancer patients and has also been criticized for lack of an effort to control for selection bias.

Savings were affected by length of stay in hospice. The greatest savings were for patients served for a two-month period. Savings decreased for each continuing month of service, but there were still gains at 12 months of hospice care. As the median length of stay in U.S. hospices has been reported to be 20 days (NHPCO, 2008a), it would seem that it would be beneficial for patients to be admitted to hospice sooner than at present. It is also fair to question hospice patients who continue to be in the program for lengthy periods, although there are few of these (<15%).

Several more recent studies of hospice's impact on the Medicare program have been undertaken. Campbell and colleagues examined hospice impact on Medicare costs in the last year of life and attempted to control for selection bias (Campbell, Lynn, Louis, & Shugarman, 2004). While cost savings for cancer patients were observed, hospice patients with noncancer diagnoses were sometimes found to cost the Medicare program more than those who didn't use hospice. Hospice care, overall, was found to cost 4% more than care for patients who do not use hospice. It is unclear for this study how effective the propensity adjustments were to account for hospice care. Since only administrative data was used, there was no way to adjust for things such as education level, which could have been a very significant variable.

Another study (Pyenson, Connor, Fitch, & Kinzbrunner, 2004) attempted to overcome selection bias using an actuarial methodology by matching patients in the Medicare 5% sample based on clinical claims indicating advanced illness and then following them downstream, not looking back from death. The results showed that among 16 diagnostic cohorts, those using hospice cost less and appeared to survive longer.

A study looking at managed care, site of death, and hospice expenditures during the last year of life was done by Ezekiel Emanuel and colleagues (2002). Similarly, they found good savings for cancer patients but unclear results for noncancer hospice patients. Overall, they found savings attributable to hospice use.

Don Taylor at Duke University (Taylor, Ostermann, Van Houtven, Tulsky, & Steinhauser, 2007) also studied the question of hospice impact on Medicare costs at the end of life and used a more sophisticated methodology to overcome selection bias. Instead of looking at all costs in the last year of life, he matched hospice and nonhospice patients on a wide range of factors, including, most importantly, the amount of time in hospice. His study found average savings of $2,309 for hospice users.

In spite of the studies that have been undertaken, there is still no consensus about the cost impact of the hospice program on Medicare among policy makers and industry analysts. Lack of random controlled trial research continues to be a concern, as does the overall cost of hospice care and its very comprehensiveness. It may also be unfair and unwise to promote hospice as a way to reduce health care expenditures. No other providers are held to such a standard. Hospice and palliative care are not that inexpensive to provide, and we certainly don't want palliative care that is weak or substandard.

One thing seems clear from the preponderance of research on this question. Hospice care achieves its best financial impact on the system when it is of moderate duration of about 2 months. Long-stay patients erode the cost savings hospices achieve by reducing the frequency of unnecessary diagnostics and hospitalizations. However, short hospice patients stays may be more important in eroding the benefits of hospice care. If a patient is admitted to hospice in the last week of life, the opportunity to prevent an unnecessary hospitalization is missed and hospice costs may be additive. Reduction in short hospice stays seems to represent the most important opportunity to achieve better value.

Still more studies are needed to demonstrate that the cost-effectiveness of hospice care is not just due to the nature of the people who choose it. Beyond the issue of cost, though, more attention must be paid to the quality and outcome of the care provided. As with most of health care, there continues to be a lack of evidence base linking palliative intervention to desirable outcomes. Managed care continues in its zeal to reduce costs, but purchasers of health care also demand that satisfaction with and perception of services delivered must be high and good objective outcomes must be achieved.

Quality Management

Hospice and palliative care providers want to operate effectively. As one of the newest health care providers, they do not have a history of bureaucratic operation. With little outside scrutiny, hospices have been fairly free to be creative in how they function. This has resulted in some very complex business operations and some that lack even basic structures. Hospices that are part of a hospital system or a home health agency have tended to adopt the policy, procedure, and protocol systems of their parent organizations. Those that are community based and freestanding have usually undergone an evolution from very unstructured volunteer-intensive operations to a gradual transition to formal business operations.

In freestanding programs, there is a point of transition when the program reaches a certain size. The informal structure begins to fall apart, and management is changed. Community-based boards or hospice owners usually hire a nonhospice person with a background in business to introduce the internal structure needed to manage continued growth.

Beyond the basic business tools of having a billing and financial operations department, up-to-date personnel policies, criteria-based job descriptions and evaluation process, management information systems, and so forth, it is helpful to develop a systematic approach to delivering quality care and a continuous approach to improving performance.

Hospice programs are still in the process of transitioning from the older quality assurance (QA) programs to a quality assessment and performance improvement (QAPI) approach. QA emphasizes structure and process. A lot of effort focuses on ensuring that all the right forms are filled out and in the chart. A lot of data are collected that describe the services provided. A lot of rechecking is needed to make sure things were done and done according to policy or procedure. The processes of care were examined to see, for instance, whether a care plan was completed with enough individualization to reflect the patient's actual needs. In QA, there is also a focus on proving that the care provided is just fine and not much focus on finding problems or opportunities to improve.

What was often missing in the QA approach was any look at what was actually happening to the patient or the organization. As the QAPI transition occurs, there is an effort to look at the outcomes of care and to design more effective processes. Process redesign techniques have been borrowed from the business world, which has been using total quality management or continuous quality improvement for many years.

Every hospice or palliative care program needs to adopt a process that cycles clinical and operational improvements based on data collected on the care delivered and program operations. Some common improvement cycles include the Plan Do Check Act (PDCA) system that plans changes to care or operations, implements these changes, and then checks on whether the change was effective in improving the problem or opportunity to improve. Finally, based on that feedback, the change is implemented as part of care and the cycle continues to repeat.

The structure needed for a hospice can be found by using existing standards such as the NHPCO's (2006b) *Standards of Practice for a Hospice Program* or accreditation guidelines put out by the JCAHO or the Community Healthcare Accreditation Program (CHAP). There are also additional conditions of participation that need to be met for Medicare certification in the United States (see Chapter 8).

Internal and External Evaluation

A hospice can develop its own process for internal evaluation, and this should be done at least annually. A helpful guideline for this can be found at the NHPCO website (NHPCO, 2008c), where members can perform an online standards self-assessment using the Quality Partners Self-Assessments. For a hospice program to survive in the current health care climate, it is essential that the program continually strive to reinvent itself and to learn from its experiences how to survive and thrive in its environment.

As important as internal growth and change are, it is how a hospice or palliative care service is externally evaluated that determines its success or failure. These are really two sides to the same coin and have to be looked at together. If an external evaluation such as a complaint about care is received, it may trigger closer scrutiny of an internal activity. Ultimately, all external feedback ought to affect internal operations, and vice versa.

One long-standing external evaluation practice involves use of satisfaction or patient experience of care surveys. Patient perception or experience of care is preferred over satisfaction as a construct. Satisfaction surveys are very leniency biased and tend to not give actionable information on how to improve care. Like all health care providers, hospices want feedback from those who use their services. A variety of instruments have been developed to measure experience with care. Most are directed at the family or primary caregiver and have been sent after the death. Some of these surveys often use a Likert-type 1–5 format with 1 being *very dissatisfied* and 5 being *very satisfied*. Other questions ask if the person received the right amount of care or information. Individual hospice programs or data vendors collect these data, and they can be very useful in internal evaluation.

Patient and Family Evaluation of Hospice Care

The NHPCO has partnered with researchers at Brown University's Center for Gerontology and Healthcare Research to develop a postdeath experience of care survey that is being used by over 1,200 hospice programs throughout the United States (Connor, Teno, Spence, & Smith, 2005). This tool, called the Family Evaluation of Hospice Care (FEHC), is a 61-question instrument (48 evaluation and 13 demographic questions) that is based on a patient-focused family-centered conceptual model. The FEHC has 4 domains that measure (1) how well care was coordinated; (2) how effective the hospice was in attending to family needs for spiritual and emotional support; (3) how effectively the family was kept informed on what they needed to know to care for the patient as death approached; and (4) how well they were informed about how to manage symptoms such as pain and shortness of breath. In addition, families provided surrogate evaluation of how effective the patient's symptoms were managed including pain, shortness of breath, anxiety, and/or sadness.

The FEHC also asks numerous questions about aspects of care including after-hours availability, personal care, being treated with respect, and having one's treatment choices honored. Some questions are rated 0–10, but most ask for specific information on whether they had the right amount of care or received it in a timely manner to allow for more actionable analysis. A comprehensive benchmarking report is provided quarterly to participating hospices that gives state and national comparisons with significance testing to look for results that are significantly above or below comparative data. There are also comparisons for size of program and type of program.

Results from the FEHC are used to identify problem areas or simply opportunities for improvement. It is still necessary for the hospice to follow a performance improvement process to institute a change in practice and to then reevaluate whether the changes made had a desirable result. For example, one of the FEHC questions asks if the family member thought the patient was referred to hospice too soon, at the right time, or too late. About 12% of hospice patients are perceived to have been referred too late. For these families, almost twice as many problems are noted on the FEHC (Teno et al., 2007). Some hospice providers have tried to reduce the number of hospice patients who are referred too late to hospice.

Hospices are moving toward a system of externally collected patient and family evaluation data. In this arrangement, the hospice contracts with an outside firm to collect the data. The family sends the survey to this research firm. The firm analyzes the results and sends feedback to the individual hospice. Results include the individual hospice's report along with a comparison of how they did in comparison to other programs using this service. Such externally collected data are much more convincing to insurers and others interested in knowing how well the hospice is performing.

Family evaluation of care after some time has passed is important information and tends to be reliable feedback. Many times, people will not tell their health care providers what they really feel while they are in treatment for fear that it could negatively affect the care they receive (Strasser & Davis, 1991). Unfortunately, if there is a problem it may be a long time before the hospice finds out about it. Hospices also want to know how the ultimate consumer, the patient, feels about the care provided. Unfortunately, so many hospice patients are referred close to death that the great majority will have died or lost the ability to communicate once enough time has passed for them to have enough experience with hospice to evaluate.

A patient evaluation of hospice and palliative care survey process is being developed through the NHPCO to obtain concurrent data on patients' experiences in hospice. Some of the methods being tried to elicit useful feedback from patients include asking for forced-choice ratings and forced negative evaluations and using outside evaluators who preserve patient confidentiality. Domains for the patient evaluation include physical comfort, emotional and psychological comfort, spiritual and existential needs met, communication and interaction with staff, self-determination, coordination of care, and an overall assessment of care.

In addition, there are a number of efforts to expand the measurement options for hospice and palliative care providers. The Centers for Medicare and Medicaid Services (CMS) have commissioned an assessment of available indicators of quality palliative care and are looking to develop a set of recommended measures for providers to use and to eventually be part of a public reporting system for hospice outcomes, similar to other web-based reporting systems like Nursing Home Compare and Home Health Compare.

Health care measures for accountability or for quality improvement are now frequently reviewed by the U.S. National Quality Forum (NQF). The NQF is a private but quasi-governmental organization that reviews existing measures of health care quality. A carefully designed process of review is followed to establish standards for measurement. By using this process, defined in the National Technology Transfer Act, government is obliged to accept the measures approved by NQF unless an objection is filed in the Federal Register. To gain NQF approval, a measure must be found acceptable to all constituent NQF membership groups, including the consumer council, provider council, researcher council, and payer council. This way all stakeholders, not just the providers themselves, have to be in agreement. The NHPCO FEHC has been approved by the NQF as a measure for cancer patients. The FEHC is also used to measure hospice care in the Agency for Research and Quality's national reports on health care quality and health care disparity.

A hospice or palliative care service wanting additional external evaluation can do this a number of ways. It can seek an independent evaluation, or it can seek external accreditation from recognized organizations such as JCAHO or the Community Healthcare Accreditation Program. A number of independent consultants are available to evaluate a hospice's operation. These are usually organizational consultants who can evaluate how well a program is operating on the basis of whatever criteria the hospice and the consultant agree on. The quality of the information generated can vary greatly, and hospices should use caution in selecting an external consultant.

To some extent, becoming Medicare certified to provide hospice care is a form of external evaluation. To qualify for certification, the hospice must comply with all regulations pertaining to providing the Medicare Hospice Benefit. The state usually checks the operation periodically to make sure all requirements are met. If any are not met, a deficiency exists, and a plan of correction must be developed.

The main form of external evaluation is through accreditation. A hospice voluntarily requests accreditation and is surveyed by staff from the accreditation agency. The survey involves sending a lot of information in advance to the accrediting body. A site visit is arranged, and a number of specialists are sent to visit the program. During the site visit, staff are interviewed, patients are visited, and records and policies are reviewed. At the conclusion of the visit, major findings are presented in a summation conference. The final results of the survey are prepared and sent to the hospice. Any recommendations made by the surveyors are included. A significant recommendation must be addressed for the hospice to be accredited. This is done either through a written response or, if it is a more serious issue, through a return survey. Once accredited, the hospice must be resurveyed at least every 3 years.

Outcomes of Hospice Care

There is an increasing emphasis on measuring the outcomes of hospice care. There is still a lot of confusion over the definition of an outcome and there are different types of outcomes. One of the ways of categorizing outcomes comes from the OASIS Project (Center for Health Research, Denver, Colorado), which gives three types: end result, instrumental, and utilization.

An end-result outcome is something experienced by the patient. An instrumental outcome has to do with the effectiveness of the intervention provided or care delivered. A utilization outcome has to do with how much care was accessed or needed. For health care providers, instrumental outcomes are particularly important in that if done most effectively there will be a positive impact on both end results and utilization.

Ultimately, the most important outcome is the end result. An end-result outcome is a change in the health status of the patient over two points in time. Changes in health status can be physiological, functional, cognitive, emotional, or behavioral. They may or may not be related to the care that was delivered.

A health care provider wants to find out if the outcome was related to the interventions delivered. Certain changes are part of the natural course of the illness (i.e., dying patients will usually get weaker as illness progresses). Some risk adjustment may be needed to control for deterioration and other characteristics.

Hospices try to measure outcomes a number of ways. Most important, they regularly ask the patient to rate how she or he is feeling. Effectiveness of symptom management is critical to the provision of quality care. Because pain or other forms of distress are what the patient says they are, it is accurate to have the patient do the rating. These ratings are among the best ways to begin to look at the outcomes of the care being delivered.

A 0–10 rating scale is commonly used to measure distress, with 0 being the complete absence of distress and 10 representing the worst imaginable distress. This approach can be used with physical as well as psychological symptoms. In a test of multiple ratings taken from multiple patients by 11 hospices, average pain scores in the last 30 days of life while in hospice ranged from .51 to 4.1. The average for all programs was 1.67 (National Hospice Organization [NHO], 1995b).

Unfortunately with a median length of service of 20 days and 30.8% of patients being served for 7 days or less (NHPCO, 2008), obtaining verbal ratings from patients is quite challenging as communication ability is greatly diminished as death approaches. In a study of over 1,300 hospice patients (NHPCO, n.d.) at only 46% of assessment intervals were patients able to give verbal reports at both. This study looked at the effectiveness of pain control episodes and found that 82% of paired pain assessments resulted in acceptable outcome defined by pain level below 4 on the 0–10 scale or reduction of at least 2 levels.

Attempts to measure psychosocial and spiritual care outcomes have been particularly difficult to do successfully. Simply measuring levels of distress is descriptive, but there are too many variables to understand the information. For example, in one informal study (Connor, 1996b), social workers asked patients and family members to rate their anxiety levels on a scale ranging from 0 to 10. Results showed that families were most anxious and that the levels tended to increase as death neared.

Population data varied widely, and rater differences were difficult to control. Some experienced social workers seemed to get higher distress levels from their families. This may have been due to their ability to get family members to open up more about their feelings and fears rather than measuring their ineffectiveness at managing anxiety.

Such problems are not unique to hospice. The mental health system also has much difficulty in measuring outcomes. Bereavement care poses similar challenges. Some of the principal measurable outcomes for the bereaved are mortality, morbidity, and use of health care resources. Spiritual care may offer an even greater challenge. There are no empirical measures of spiritual growth currently in use.

For those intangible aspects of care, some have used the presence or absence of certain self-statements indicating psychosocial or spiritual resolution, absence of interpersonal conflict, or presence of inner peace; much more work needs to be done on measurement of such internal processes or states. Researchers could also make greater use of qualitative indices rather than always looking for quantitative measures.

Studies such as these begin to give researchers a way to see how well hospices actually do in the task of managing the dying process. Carefully collected data on symptom control will help to show how good hospices are, and these can be compared with data on care provided outside the hospice venue. One of the only studies comparing evaluation of care near the end of life in various venues was done by Teno et al. (2004). This mortality follow-back study asked next of kin to evaluate care received at the end of life in hospitals, nursing facilities, home health agencies, and hospices. Results were mixed, but only in hospice was care evaluated as excellent by over 70% of respondents. In all other settings, excellent ratings were below 50%. Also needed are reliable data on a hospice's impact on the quality of life of its patients. Hospices rate measurement of quality of life as their number one research interest (NHO, 1997b).

Quality of Life

Quality of life is an elusive construct that has been hard to measure. There is not a universally agreed-on definition for quality of life. Most would agree that quality of life has two fundamental components, multidimensionality and subjectivity (Cella, 1994). It is multidimensional in that it includes a broad range of domains of experience, including the following:

- Psychological functioning
- Social functioning
- Physical functioning
- Family well-being
- Side effects and symptoms
- Sexuality and intimacy
- Treatment satisfaction
- Transcendent concerns

It is also fundamentally subjective in that it can only be understood from the patient's perspective. Efforts to estimate quality of life by rating overt behavior fail because they neglect the underlying cognitive processes that mediate a person's perception of quality of life. These include perception of the illness, perception of treatment, expectations of self, and cognitive appraisal of the situation.

Quality of life may best be understood as the gap between one's ideal standard for each of the domains of experience and one's actual experience. One's quality of life is higher to the extent that these standards are being met (Calman, 1984). Each patient has a different sense of what quality of life means, and it changes over time and across situations. There has been an explosion of research into quality of life in the last 20 years. Literally hundreds of instruments and measurement strategies have been put forward. In many ways, quality of life has come to be defined by the tools that have been developed to measure it.

Most early attempts to measure quality of life have relied heavily on measuring the patient's functional ability (Karnofsky, 1949; Zubrod et al., 1960). If the patient could perform activities of daily living, it was assumed that there was good quality of life. Research into patients' perceptions of quality of life has revealed that functional ability does not contribute very much to one's sense of quality of life.

Others have devised single-item estimates of subjective well-being or appraisal of quality of life (Bernheim & Buyse, 1984; Gough, Furnival,

Schilder, & Grove, 1983). Single-item measures may help give an overall idea of the patient's level, but they lack dimensions and clinical utility.

Some have argued that global quality of life is too large a construct for understanding patients, and that researchers need to focus on measuring health-related quality of life (Guyatt, Feeny, & Patrick, 1993; Padilla, 1992). However, if research focuses exclusively on health concerns, it may ignore the dimensions of patients' experience that are most important to their quality of life.

Some suggest that quality-of-life instruments are best if designed for specific diseases (Cella, Lee-Riordan, & Siberman, 1990), and some have developed instruments specifically for use in palliative care (Mount & Cohen, 1997). These efforts help to target the issues that are most likely to affect particular patients; however, they must be able to address those dimensions of experience that affect quality of life in all people.

One of the approaches to measuring quality of life that is specific to palliative care (Byock & Merriman, 1998) is the Missoula/VITAS Quality of Life Scale (MVQOL). The MVQOL attempts to measure five dimensions of the patient's experience (symptoms, functional ability, interpersonal relations, well-being, and transcendent). It is a 25-question instrument that can be administered to cognitively intact patients (a 15-question version has also been developed).

One of the most important things about the MVQOL is that in answering the initial questions, the patient determines the relative importance of each of these five dimensions of experience to his or her quality of life. This addition makes the MVQOL unique. The remaining questions measure the patient's perception of quality of life in each area and how much it varies from a baseline. The resulting scores can be helpful to clinicians in designing interventions. In fact, instruments like the MVQOL may be more useful as clinical tools rather than being used for accountability or outcome measurement.

If the patient's quality of life is derived from his or her sense of connection with others (interpersonal), then hospice caregivers can help to make sure the patient feels well supported by the extended family. If the patient is focused on the transcendent, it is important to explore the patient's spiritual life and help ensure that any unresolved issues are addressed.

Quality of life remains a difficult construct to measure. It is a very useful tool to use clinically, but it is such a subjective experience influenced by many different factors that it may or may not have anything to do with the palliative care received. Specific elements found to be important to patients at the end of life can be measured, but the QOL construct is just too overarching to be used as a primary outcome for hospice and palliative care. Better to measure how patients and families evaluate palliative care's impact on the care they received.

Quality Improvement

Hospice programs have been trying to assess the quality of their services since the hospice movement began. Palliative care program are also taking a more evidence-based approach. When the Medicare Hospice Benefit was created, it required hospices to assess quality. Efforts to systematically evaluate quality probably began in the United States with the implementation of the JCAHO accreditation program for hospice. Programs were required to implement and document their efforts at QA.

QA standards required the program to measure quality by monitoring important aspects of care, as well as high-volume or problem-prone activities. The emphasis was on identifying problems and making changes to programs or operations that would correct the situation. Programs were also required to evaluate their problem-solving interventions to ensure effectiveness.

Individual hospice programs designed monitoring activities and measured their performance at regular intervals. As each program measured quality in its own way, there were no mechanisms to compare results from one program to another. These monitoring results were examined for trends, and programs would strive to improve their performance on the measures chosen.

Medicare and JCAHO suggested certain areas of monitoring such as nursing care and one other discipline or stress management. By and large, it was up to the program to design monitors. The program could measure a structure, a process, or an outcome. JCAHO encouraged programs to work toward outcome measurement, though there was confusion about what an outcome was.

A considerable amount of monitoring activity in hospice has been directed at structure and medical records. Programs want to ensure that their records are complete and to prove that components of the program are in place. This usually pleases state surveyors from licensure and certification, although it does little to improve care.

Monitoring in hospice includes looking at important processes and outcomes of care. Many processes are vital to achieving good outcomes. For example, the process for assessing pain is critical to achieving the outcome of pain control. Other monitors used in hospice include, for example, effectiveness in controlling infections and decubitii, or shortness of breath; ability to manage emotional distress; ability to complete advanced directives; and accuracy in assessing bereavement risk.

There has also been a push for change to the new QAPI philosophy. The emphasis has shifted from problem identification to designing systems and processes for quality. The thinking here is why wait for problems to develop—design your care so that problems are prevented. This comes from the total quality management, continuous quality improvement movement in industry that was successfully embraced by the Japanese.

The transition of total quality management from industry to health care has not been smooth. Health care does not exactly run assembly lines, although some patients feel that way at times. Still, the continuous quality assessment and performance improvement emphasis does seem to be an improvement over the old QA QI system, which did not seem to improve much of what was done. QAPI is also focused on looking for opportunities for improvement. When a process or aspect of operations seems less than smooth, an improvement group is formed rather than monitoring it to describe what perhaps is already known.

These groups are made up of people who are familiar with the area being studied. The first thing to do is to gain a detailed understanding of the processes involved. The group creates a process map by means of one of a number of tools. After mapping out all the steps and decision points involved, it sometimes becomes apparent how to improve the process. Once the changes are agreed on, the group also has to plan for how to change the process and how to effectively implement the change without creating new problems.

Once the change is carried out, it is necessary to evaluate whether the change has in fact improved the operation. Usually there is an agreed-on measure that will allow comparison of the old method with the new. QAPI requires good information. In fact, accurate information is the lifeblood of good QAPI. However, the right information must be collected. Many hospices are coming to realize how limited their information systems are. At present, NHPCO's benchmarking reports provide hospices with the information needed to have the quality assessment (QA) portion of the QAPI equation. They must act to carry out the performance improvenent (PI) part of the equation.

The NHPCO research committee is actively engaged in trying to establish specifications for electronic medical record systems used in hospice programs. The difficulty is that many hospices customize their data collection in ways that limit their ability to compare results from one hospice to another. It is critical that data collected and reported be "apples to apples." Hospices report their results in the aggregate at the agency level. Much more accurate data can be compiled from patient-level data collection that may soon be possible with the widespread use of electronic patient medical records. Data can be reported as a kind of patient registry to include information gathered at the time of admission, at each patient contact, and at death or discharge. Such data can help paint an accurate picture of who the hospice and palliative care population is, how much care is being received, and ultimately how good the quality of this care is. This will eventually make comparative provider reports much easier to create and to use.

Such a hospice "report card" could include a wide variety of measures on clinical care as well as organizational performance, and rather than having to wait months for results it could have almost real-time data. It is no longer good enough to look at what happened 6 weeks ago. Hospice needs to know what happened yesterday.

Common measures could include the following:

- Pain control data
- Data on other measures of safety (falls, medication errors, and so forth)
- Demographic data on patients served
- Information on location of death
- Use of inpatient facilities
- Perception of the quality of care
- Cost per day
- Visit frequency and duration by discipline
- Length of stay data
- Ratios that measure visit frequency, bereavement contact, and on-call response

Pathways

NHPCO Pathway

A model for treating the whole patient and family can be found from work done by the NHPCO's Standards and Accreditation Committee (*A Pathway for Patients and Families Facing Terminal Illness*; NHO, 1997a). In seeking to understand the outcomes of hospice care, this model helps providers understand how hospice care can operate so effectively. This conceptual model attempts to create a common language for providers that can be used to understand and describe the enormous territory hospices deal with in caring for dying patients and their families.

Most pathways in health care have been developed to help improve the efficiency of health care delivery. Health care workers want to get patients in and out of the hospital as quickly as possible with the best outcome. They do not want them to return with the same problem. These pathways are usually centered on particular diseases. If the patient has congestive heart failure, here is how he or she should be treated during a hospitalization or home health stay. Here is how a patient coming into the hospital for a particular orthopedic surgical procedure should be handled.

Palliative care does not fit this model very well. Hospices deal with a variety of diagnoses with different trajectories and no easily determined end point. All have the condition of terminality, so a hospice pathway might best be described as a condition pathway (Figure 12.1). Each patient

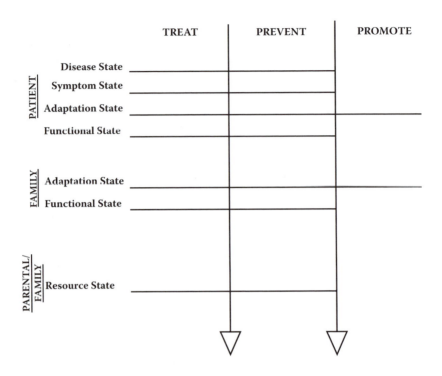

Figure 12.1 Hospice Patient–Family Grid

and family comes with different resources for coping with the experience and different needs. There is, however, a territory that must be understood for good palliative care to be delivered.

As the patient, the family, and the patient–family unit are assessed, hospice workers need to ensure that they are looking at all the dimensions of the patient's experience. This conceptual framework can help hospices ensure that they are looking at the whole patient–family system.

When hospice or palliative care programs intervene, they are treating, preventing, or promoting. By treating, they are eliminating or lessening a problem by using skilled assessment, education, and therapeutic intervention. By preventing, they avoid a possible problem through skilled assessment, education, and therapeutic intervention. By promoting, they are encouraging growth or a higher level of health through skilled assessment, education, and therapeutic intervention.

Much palliative care is preventative. Problems do not happen just because of good assessment, prophylactic intervention, and education. This conceptual model helps hospices to understand which areas of the patient's and/or family's experience they are dealing with. Dying is more than a medical event; it is also a life experience. Palliative care is more than medical treatment of pathology. It can also be a time of opportunity and growth. Much of the potential of palliative care is in promotion of health and growth at the end of life.

Using NHPCO's conceptual grid, palliative care achieves the best outcomes through an interdisciplinary assessment of the patient and family states. Each state has associated problems and opportunities associated with it. Patients experience dying in four different states: disease, symptoms, adaptation, and function. Figure 12.1 illustrates the states as experienced by both the patients and their families.

Although hospice does not attempt to cure the patient of his or her disease, it is important to understand where the disease is in terms of progression. They also have a responsibility to know when the disease may be improving so that appropriate treatment can be provided. It is also important to understand the effects of secondary diagnoses and comorbid factors that affect a patient's disease state.

The symptom state is the subjective manifestation of the disease state. The kinds of problems or conditions assessed range from sensory or neurological problems to nutritional problems, to fluid balance problems, to elimination problems, to integumentary problems, to cardiac or circulatory problems, to respiratory problems, to immunological problems.

In the adaptive state, hospice focuses on coping, grieving, and existential problems as well as opportunities for growth or higher levels of wellness. The functional state includes a person's physical, cognitive, or social capacity to communicate, learn, and carry out activities of daily living or care requirements. The kinds of issues addressed include physical mobility and compliance.

The family members are not terminally ill, so they do not experience the disease or symptom states. Hospices do need, however, to address their adaptive and functional states. The family's adaptive ability is their ability to emotionally, or spiritually, adjust to the changing environmental conditions or life circumstances. Issues addressed include problems in coping, grieving, and existential concerns as well as opportunities for growth through the experience. The family, too, has different levels of ability to participate functionally. Some may be able to assist in care, and others may not be able to comply with the demands of the situation. Some patients may have no caregiver.

The primary issue for the patient–family unit is their resource state. These are their environment, personal, and financial resources related to the provision of patient care and future family health. Issues addressed include safety, shelter, inadequate finances, lack of directives regarding care, unresolved estate, funeral plans, or finances, and legal or custody concerns.

Having a more complete assessment of the patient and family is critical to achieving the primary outcomes for those facing terminal illness. The NHPCO document (NHO, 1997a) gives three primary outcomes for the patient and family:

- Self-determined life closure
- Safe and comfortable dying
- Effective grieving

Within these three major areas, many specific measurable outcomes can be found. Ultimately, what hospices are trying to achieve is for persons anticipating their death from a life-threatening illness to remain safe and comfortable until death, supported in life closure as they conceive it by family caregivers, volunteers, and professional staff whose needs for education and counsel are appropriately met.

Other Pathways, Domain Sets, and Conceptual Models

In addition to the NHPCO pathway, a number of other models for care at the end of life have been described. In 2004 a national consensus project for quality palliative care was formed primarily to set clinical practice guidelines for quality palliative care (National Consensus Project, 2008). The consensus project was created by NHPCO, AAHPM, CAPC, and HPNA to help define broader palliative care in the United States, as hospice standards were already in place (NHPCO, 2006b).

The Consensus Project Guidelines were then brought to the National Quality Forum, which convened a panel in 2006 to review the field and to develop a national framework and set of preferred practices for palliative and hospice care quality (National Quality Forum, 2006). This framework and set of practices have now been used to help create a structure for the establishment of a set of indicators that may eventually be used to measure palliative care in various settings and may be used to help in public reporting as well as quality assessment and performance improvement.

The framework includes the following domains:

- Structure
- Process
- Physical
- Psychological and psychiatric
- Social
- Spiritual, religious, and existential
- Cultural

- Care of the imminently dying
- Ethical and legal
- Other

The CMS remains very interested in the development of quality measures for hospices and others that provide care at the end of life, and has engaged Quality Improvement Organizations (QIO) to help identify measures that could be recommended for use by providers. Eventually, the CMS will require some form of public reporting for hospices and others on the quality of end-of-life care. The NHPCO continues to help lead efforts to more effectively measure the quality of end-of-life care. See Teno and Connor (2009) for guidance on referring a patient to quality hospice and palliative care services.

Whether the hospice movement survives and thrives or becomes a footnote in the history of medicine may be determined by how well it is able to demonstrate the effectiveness of the care it provides.

In the next chapter, the rise of palliative care worldwide is explored.

CHAPTER **13**
Hospice and Palliative Care
Around the World

Go around and see what is being done and then see how your own circumstances can produce another version; there is need for diversity in this field.

—Dame Cicely Saunders, founder, St. Christopher's Hospice

The modern hospice and palliative care movement is now over 40 years old. What began at St. Christopher's Hospice has grown to an estimated 10,000 palliative care programs of one kind or another worldwide as of this writing. Generally, the term *palliative care* is used around the world to describe the specialized care provided to those facing life-limiting illness. In some counties, *hospice care* is the preferred term.

Geographic Spread of Palliative Care

In 2006, NHPCO and Help the Hospices commissioned the International Observatory for End-of-Life Care to conduct an analysis of palliative care development worldwide (NHPCO, 2008b). Building on a measurement model, they divided development into 4 types: (1) no evidence of palliative care development or interest; (2) interest in development of palliative care but no service provision; (3) palliative care services exist, but there are localized provision and a lack of integration into the main health care system; and (4) palliative care is provided to a significant portion of those in need and is integrated to some degree into major health care institutions.

Results from the study found that only half the world's countries have any direct provision of palliative care. Only 15% achieved the 4th category of approaching integration. In 35% of the world's countries, there is some provision of palliative care, but this could vary from merely one provider in the entire country to a number of providers but no inclusion in the health care system. The geographic areas of the world most lacking in palliative care include most of Africa, the Middle East, and many parts of Asia, Eastern and Central Europe, and Latin America (see Figure 13.1).

How Countries Develop Palliative Care

For palliative care to be integrated into a country's health care system, there needs to be a number of significant structures in place. These include a group of stakeholders or champions wishing to promote palliative care; standards for the provision of palliative care that define the scope of care delivery; a national body or association to promote palliative care; some acceptance of palliative care as an area of professional specialization for physicians, nurses, and others; the ability to access opioids and other essential palliative care medicines; training curricula in palliative care in the predominant language(s) used; centers of excellence for both didactic and hands-on training; and a payment stream to fund delivery of services.

The first step in developing palliative care in a country is to conduct a comprehensive needs assessment. The needs assessment should include an analysis of data on country-level mortality. What are the principal causes of death? What are the demographics of the country and those who need palliative care services? Who are the existing palliative care providers (if any), or who are the existing health care providers that could be skilled up to provide palliative care? What health care facilities exist generally, including hospitals, clinics, and home-based care providers? How many inpatient beds will be needed? What is the existing health care workforce, and how many palliative care-trained health care workers will be needed to meet the needs of the population needing palliative care?

Once a comprehensive needs assessment is completed, a stakeholders group should be formed if one does not yet exist. The stakeholders group should ideally include those in government that have authority for health care services and drug importation. Ideally, the stakeholders group could receive some type of mandate from the Ministry of Health (or equivalent) to develop recommendations for establishing or expanding palliative care in the country. One of the key early steps in palliative care development is the establishment of national standards for palliative care.

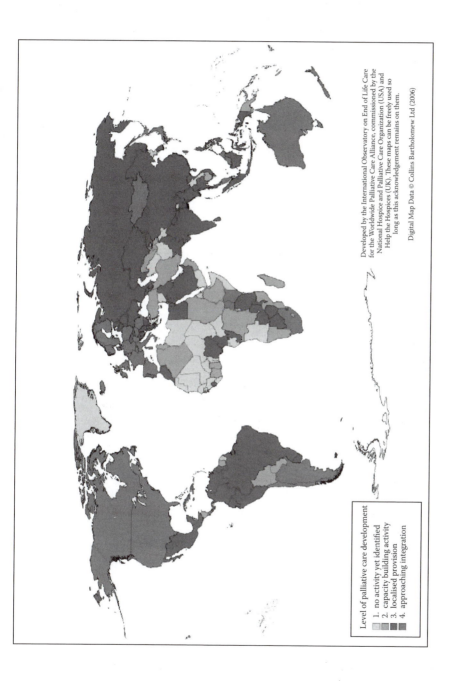

Level of palliative care development
1. no activity yet identified
2. capacity building activity
3. localised provision
4. approaching integration

Developed by the International Observatory on End of Life Care for the Worldwide Palliative Care Alliance, commissioned by the National Hospice and Palliative Care Organization (USA) and Help the Hospices (UK). These maps can be freely used so long as this acknowledgement remains on them.

Digital Map Data © Collins Bartholomew Ltd (2006)

Figure 13.1 Levels of Palliative Care Development: All Countries

Standards of Palliative Care

National palliative care standards are needed to define what palliative care is and what it is not. Advocating for palliative care requires the ability to define what a palliative program of care looks like and who receives care. Palliative care standards typically include the following:

- A history and introduction
- A definition of palliative care and the population served
- Standards that address the following areas:
  - Patients' rights and ethics
  - Interdisciplinary team composition, operations, and training
  - Home-based care
  - Inpatient care
  - Care in other settings
  - Care for special populations (children, homeless, prisoners, and so forth)
  - Medical records
  - Quality assessment and performance improvement
  - Management, administration, and governance or simply leadership
- Appendices and glossary

The NHPCO developed the first set of national palliative care standards in 1979 and has been refining standards for hospice programs ever since. The current NHPCO *Standards of Practice for Hospice Programs* is organized around the 10 components of the NHPCO Quality Initiative (NHPCO, 2006b):

1. Patient and family-centered care
2. Ethical behavior and consumer rights
3. Clinical excellence and safety
4. Inclusion and access
5. Organizational excellence
6. Workforce excellence
7. Standards
8. Compliance with laws and regulations
9. Stewardship and accountability
10. Performance measurement

Many countries have now sought to establish national palliative care standards. To view a listing of palliative care standards worldwide, go to http://www.nhpco.org/standards (NHPCO, n.d.-b).

Formation of National Palliative Care Organizations

As of this writing, there are over 79 known national palliative care associations in the world. To find contact information for national associations and palliative care providers by country, go to the Hospice Information Service (n.d.; http://www.hospiceinformation.info). National palliative care organizations can be thought of as being at 3 different stages of development. There are those that are just forming, those that have been formed and are trying to get more established and effective, and those that have been established for some time but want to become more sophisticated.

A palliative care association toolkit has been developed to help national palliative care associations to increase their ability to effectively operate. Go to http://www.nhpco.org/associationtoolkit (NHPCO, n.d.-a) for more information on this toolkit. In this website can be found the following types of resources:

- Resources for strategic planning
- Setting up an office and organization
- Core governance resources, including constitutions, policies and procedures, the role of trustees, management and administration, board role descriptions, committee use, resources for planning, and use of volunteers
- Membership issues
- Resources and fund development
- Communications
- Educational programming
- Public policy advocacy and lobbying
- Development of guidelines and standards
- Organizational growth and development
- Affiliate organizations
- Global outreach

Professional Specialization

Another key step in palliative care development in a country is the estab-lishment of palliative care as a recognized area of specialization in health care. The certification or recognition of palliative care as an area of pro-fessional specialization is beginning to gain recognition worldwide. The first country to approve palliative medicine was the United Kingdom in 1987. Since then, more and more countries are including palliative care as a specialty or subspecialty. In 2007 the American Board of Medical Specialties approved hospice and palliative care as an approved area for subspecialization by any of the existing medical specialties. Internal and family medicine have expressed the most interest.

Since hospice and palliative care is by definition an interdisciplinary field, it is appropriate that all related professions develop a process for recognizing competence. The core disciplines that should be included are medicine, nursing, social work, chaplaincy, counseling, and psychology. Additionally, consideration should be given to the disciplines of physiotherapy, speech pathology, occupational therapy, and expressive therapy.

Access to Essential Palliative Care Medicines

Palliative care without opioids and other essential medicines is not palliative care; it is supportive care. The World Health Organization (WHO) (Stjernwärd and Clark, 2003) has published a model for the development of palliative care. To achieve palliative care, it is necessary to have at minimum three big things.

1. Policy
2. Drug availability
3. Education

Engaging government in establishing policies that recognize palliative care in the health care system and create a framework for the availability of essential palliative care medicines including opioids or step 3 analgesics is a necessary requirement for the delivery of palliative care. Creating policy, however, is not enough. Essential palliative care medications must be not only available but also accessible. To be accessible, a secure supply chain must be created, and there must be adequate quantities of medication delivered to pharmacies, hospices, hospitals, and others authorized to dispense prescribed medications. The medications would also need to be accessible to those with limited financial resources through either insurance mechanisms or subsidy programs. Finally, there have to be adequate numbers of prescribers trained to prescribe and monitor these essential medications.

Medications essential to practicing palliative care are not limited to opioids. The International Association for Hospice and Palliative Care (IAHPC) and WHO have defined essential palliative care medications to include drugs from the following classes:

- Analgesics
- Antianxiety agents
- Anticonvulsants
- Antidepressants
- Antiemetics
- Laxatives

- Sedative hypnotics
- Steroids

Palliative Care Education and Curricula

It does little good to provide opioids and other essential medications if there are no health care professionals trained to prescribe them. The biggest problem facing the growth of palliative care in new venues is the lack of trained professionals and volunteers. Palliative care is still a new discipline in most of the world and there is still a lack of universally recognized curricula for the interdisciplinary professions. Medical and nursing schools still offer little content on palliative care, even though it is an essential component of any complete health care system and health care practitioners are more likely to need palliative care skills than, for example, obstetrics skills.

Some progress is being made in the development of curricula for the professions. The Education for Physicians in End-of-Life Care (EPEC) course was developed, and a specialized version has been developed for oncology (EPEC-O). A number of versions of the End-of-Life Nursing Education Course (ELNEC) have been developed, including one for pediatrics and one for international use. ELNEC has also been translated into many languages for teaching nursing professionals. The EPEC and ELNEC courses are valuable additions to providing a standardized training for health professionals; however, these are still generally basic introductory training programs for health professionals and are not intended to ensure competence and capacity to provide specialized care. They also lack the necessary bedside training components so necessary for demonstrating competent practice.

Most palliative care educators believe that more extensive training is required to achieve demonstrated competence in palliative care. For example, in Uganda nurses can be granted authority to prescribe opioids but only after completing a 9-month training conducted by Hospice Africa Uganda, based in Kampala. Also, we continue to lack effective curricula for psychosocial and spiritual professionals. Similar standardized training programs and teaching curricula are needed for social workers, psychologists, and chaplains.

There are some general standards for training lay volunteers. In the developed world, lay volunteers may do less than in the developing world. In general, the volunteer needs to be familiar with all major aspects of palliative care. NHPCO standards for volunteer training include the following topics:

1. The purpose and focus of hospice care
2. The important role of the volunteer in hospice care
3. The interdisciplinary team's function and responsibility
4. Roles of the various hospice team members
5. Concepts of death and dying
6. Communication skills
7. Patient and family rights and responsibilities
8. Care and comfort measures
9. Diseases and conditions experienced by hospice patients
10. Psychosocial and spiritual issues related to death and dying
11. Concept of the unit of care (i.e., the hospice patient, family, and caregiver)
12. Stress management
13. Infection control practices
14. Professional boundaries and patient–family boundaries
15. Staff, patient, and family safety issues
16. Ethics and hospice care
17. Grief and bereavement
18. Confidentiality
19. Reporting requirements related to patient changes, pain, and other symptoms
20. Other topics based on the hospice's unique mission and defined patient population
21. Specialized training, which is performed when volunteers provide care or services in facility-based care settings or with other specialty patient populations

Regulating and Funding the Provision of Palliative Care

Palliative care is established in the health care systems of very few countries. Even in the 35 countries where palliative care is approaching integration, there are only a handful that have well-established mechanisms for regulating and funding palliative care. In the United Kingdom, where modern hospice care was founded, the voluntary hospice sector only receives about 35% of its funding from the National Health Service. Yet if palliative care is to be made available to all who need it, there must be an economic engine to drive the provision of care. The argument for paying for palliative or hospice care is best made based on its value to patients and their families.

Many attempts have been made to show that hospice or palliative care is cost-effective and will reduce medical costs. While this may be true in some countries, it is a difficult argument to sustain. The basic argument is that palliative care is more appropriate care and often prevents unnecessary hospitalizations and futile care. In the developing world, where many receive little or no health care in the first place, palliative care would be mostly an added cost since there is not any expensive care to be substituted for. Even in developed countries, palliative care does have a cost and, particularly when provided for extended periods, could end up costing more than the care it prevents.

There is also a concern that palliative care not be promoted as a cheaper alternative to mainstream health care lest it be perceived that people are being denied care just to save some money. This is a slippery slope and is especially of concern to minorities and disenfranchised populations, who may perceive that the health care system has prevented them from receiving the usual standard of care to begin with.

As palliative care grows in an individual country, there is a need to ensure that the provision of care meets standards and is of sufficient quality. The public should be protected from substandard health care, and so some legal and regulatory structures need to be put in place. What may have been acceptable for a single pioneering nongovernmental organization (NGO) to provide will need to be codified as others establish services and when funds are being paid for care delivery.

There are a number of funding strategies that have been used to pay for the provision of palliative care. In chapter 8, the per diem payment system in the United States was described. In countries where universal health care exists, palliative care has sometimes been grafted into the existing inpatient, outpatient, and home-based care systems. In other countries, efforts have been made to provide payments that cover part of the cost of care. In most instances, payment systems are designed to discourage overuse of inpatient facilities. This can be done by providing some amount of coverage for home-based care through either visit reimbursement or per diem payment. Inpatient payment for an admission or per diem should be included but with an emphasis on short-term care for severe symptoms or end-stage care.

New Models of Palliative Care

The original model for hospice developed in the United Kingdom has proven to be quite malleable in various countries and cultures. It was based mainly on an inpatient model of hospice as a place. In the United States, hospice has become very much a home-based care model of palliative care for individuals and families delivered in the place they call home. In India, one of the emerging models is built on neighborhood involvement in palliative care. In Africa, some of the faith-based health care delivery systems are using congregational volunteers trained to be community health workers backed by professional staff. They have shown in India and Africa that a significant amount of palliative care can be provided by trained, supported, and supervised voluntary workers.

While the developing world has shown that a large amount of palliative care can be provided by nonprofessional health care workers, it remains critical that competent interdisciplinary professionals are available to back up such workers and provide ongoing supervision of care. In too many situations, home-based care has been developed without access to prescribers and essential medications, professional nursing intervention, and competent psychosocial and spiritual care. Without such interdisciplinary service, care is little more than supportive hand-holding. Still, lay health care workers can be the eyes and ears for the professionals and can be taught to deliver and teach essential caregiving skills that are extremely valuable to providing comfort and care.

One such program that has been remarkably successful in delivering palliative care is the Network Neighborhood Project in the Indian state of Kerala. In one district alone, over 2,000 trained voluntary health care workers, many of whom are professionals trained as teachers, social workers, and so forth, are backed up by 200 professional nurses and 12 physicians to serve one large area. This successful program is based on existing systems of neighborhood support where neighbors look out for the health and welfare of each other.

Worldwide Palliative Care Alliance

The Worldwide Palliative Care Alliance (WPCA) is a Global Action Network (GAN). GANs are a new kind of organization. Developed after the end of the cold war, they exist to address specific international problems that cross borders and are global in nature. Examples of the types of problems that GANs address include corruption, provision of water, climate change, corporate reporting and performance standards, sustainable fishing and forestry, youth employment, nutrition, HIV/AIDS, tuberculosis, and malaria. International palliative care development fits nicely into this construct.

The WPCA is an alliance of national and regional palliative care associations. Its purpose is to promote the development of palliative care in all countries and to be a voice for those faced with life-limiting illness and their families. The vision of the WPCA is a world with universal access to quality palliative care. The mission of the WPCA is to foster, promote, and influence the delivery of affordable, quality palliative care.

The WPCA has two primary foci. The first is to be an advocacy organization, and the second to promote national palliative care organizations. While each national organization can speak on behalf of patients and providers of palliative care in their home country, there has not been an organization that has spoken up for the need for palliative care in international venues such as the United Nations, World Health Organization, and so forth. Since the WPCA is a body that represents national bodies, it has an inherent legitimacy to speak internationally for palliative care.

The promotion and development of national and regional palliative care organizations involves the provision of support and communication to members of the WPCA. In addition to advocacy, international work groups have been formed to help advance quality and standards, education, research, pediatric palliative care, organizational development, funding, and policy. The WPCA was initiated by a group of national associations that met in The Hague to hold a summit of national organizations. At that first summit, national organizations discovered that there was much to be gained by working collaboratively and much to be learned from each other. Many were new and in need of some assistance in getting established.

In the next and final chapter, issues for the future of hospice and palliative care are explored.

Web Resources

African Palliative Care Association: http://www.apca.co.ug
> The African Palliative Care Association (APCA) is the association for providers and country associations in Africa. APCA supports palliative care development, standards development, monitoring and evaluation, education and training, policy and advocacy, and organizational development.

Asia Pacific Hospice Palliative Care Network: http://www.ahpn.org
> The Asia Pacific Hospice Palliative Care Network (APHN) is a regional association for providers, national associations, and individuals in the Asia Pacific region to promote hospice and palliative care; it is based in Singapore.

European Association for Palliative Care: http://www.eapcnet.org
> This is the association for palliative and hospice care professionals in European countries. The association holds biannual congresses for research and practice and advocates for palliative care in the European Union.

Hospice Information Service: http://www.hospiceinformation.info
> The Hospice Information Service, based at St. Christopher's Hospice, is the site for information on hospice care worldwide. The service can also be used to locate providers by country and general information on hospice care.

International Association for Hospice and Palliative Care: http://www.hospicecare.com
> The International Association for Hospice and Palliative Care (IAHPC) promotes communication, facilitates and provides education, and is an information resource for patients, professionals, health care providers, and policy makers around the world.

International Observatory for End-of-Life Care: http://www.eolc-observatory.net

A team of social scientists and clinicians at Lancaster University in the United Kingdom that collaborates with colleagues all around the world in an effort to provide research evidence to impact the development of hospice and palliative care. Country reports on palliative care development are available.

Worldwide Palliative Care Alliance: http://www.thewpca.org

The Worldwide Palliative Care Alliance (WPCA) is an alliance of national and regional palliative care organizations dedicated to global advocacy for palliative care and to supporting the development of national palliative care organizations worldwide.

CHAPTER **14**

The Future of Hospice and Palliative Care

The riders in a race do not stop when they reach the goal. There is a little finishing canter before coming to a standstill. There is time to hear the kind voices of friends and to say to oneself "the work is done."

—Oliver Wendell Holmes Sr.

There is a fair amount of angst within the palliative and hospice community about the future of the movement. Efforts focused on becoming more integrated within the health care system have made progress and there is heightened social interest in care at the end of life, yet there is still an undervaluing of palliative care as a valuable essential component in any health care system. Some have even referred to palliative care as second-class care.

This is reflected in the debate over use of the name *hospice*. There are some, in both Europe and North America, who would prefer to abandon the term. They feel it has become too self-limiting and that some negative connotations have become associated with it. These negative connotations boil down to the perception that *hospice = death*. The self-limiting concerns relate mainly to restrictions on timely access to hospice brought about by creation of the Hospice Medicare Benefit in the United States and a tendency in other countries for access to hospice to be limited by cultural factors or economic conditions.

In place of *hospice*, the broader term *palliative care* has been suggested. This is put forward to offer the advantage of being a broader frame; you do not have to be dying to get it. It is also more descriptive for what a hospice actually does. However, no matter what it is called, it is still something associated with dying.

The word *hospice* has offered some advantages. It is an ambiguous word. It allows the communicator an opportunity to explain what is meant. It is also a metaphorical term. Death is alluded to indirectly through the comparison of a way station on life's last journey. The name problem is a societal one that simply reflects the continuing lack of ability to integrate the reality of death into our cultural experience.

Who Are Hospice's Patients?

Who ought to receive hospice care? When ought they to receive it? What should they receive? These questions have only been partly answered. The broadest frame is that anyone dying ought to have the opportunity of using the services of a hospice.

Dying is usually a process, not an event. Therefore excluded from the hospice denominator are people who die unexpectedly in accidents or of undetected illnesses such as a sudden unexpected massive heart attack or stroke. Also excluded are those whose acute conditions have a likely chance of cure. A patient with an acute attack of appendicitis may die, but one would not want to admit the patient to hospice. One of the few sources of information on how ill people are prior to death is the national mortality follow-back survey that was last conducted in 1993 and included data from 22,957 death certificates. Next of kin interviews revealed that about 30% of the sample had no limitations on their activities of daily living just prior to death.

Many AIDS patients benefit from hospice care, but a hospice would not think of admitting a patient with a tropical infectious disease. Hospices may have to rethink how to handle a world where large numbers of people begin dying of new untreatable infectious diseases.

It is estimated is that somewhere around 70% of those who die in a given year are appropriate for hospice care (Connor, 1999). These are, of course, almost all of the cancer patients, those dying of other progressively fatal nonmalignant diseases like Lou Gehrig's disease, and many of those dying of progressive chronic illnesses, most of whom reach a point where they choose not to continue pursuing curative treatment.

In the United States, hospice currently cares for about 40% of all deaths (National Hospice and Palliative Care Organization [NHPCO], 2008). In the United Kingdom, hospices care for about 11% of all deaths. Although there are still large numbers of people who need hospice care and are not getting it, it is also unfair to say that the hospice movement is too small, marginal, or unavailable. At least 70% of all cancer patients dying in the United States receive hospice care before death. According to Medicare Billing records, only about 3% of counties in the United States do not have a hospice activity.

The defining issue as to who in this group receives hospice care and for how long is more and more determined by what sort of treatment they receive. For cancer patients, if the treatment is aimed at curing the disease or achieving a remission, they do not enter hospice. The same is true for most other conditions. If the aim is survival, then hospice is not considered an option. A significant number of patients are seeking survival, no matter how unlikely the odds, and never getting hospice.

If a person is seeking a cure, he or she does not just want symptoms managed. The person will settle for no less than a cure or at least an uncertain future. Once given the label of being terminally ill, a person's future has been determined; there is no mystery about it—the person is expected to die. Staying in the gray area at least gives the illusion that all options remain open.

This brings us back to a fundamental question about the nature of hospice care. Is it necessary for every patient to acknowledge the fact of their dying to be served by hospice? Can there not be room for some uncertainty and mystery as they face the abyss? This is perhaps where things have gone amiss in hospice's efforts to fit into the health care system and to help patients to face reality. Hospice has become too identified with death rather than life.

It has always been said that hospice is about living, not dying. Yet, U.S. hospices embraced the Hospice Medicare Benefit with its requirement of a 6-month prognosis for admission. This has put hospice in a box with regard to treatment choice. The patient has to choose to stop receiving anything but palliative treatment. This means that the whole spectrum of patients who want to keep some option of survival open have been excluded from hospice. Patients still have a choice, but if they are dying and choose something other than symptom management, they cannot have hospice.

Some in hospice have come to take the Medicare benefit to be the definition of hospice. This puts the cart before the horse. It is not uncommon to hear comments such as "He doesn't belong in hospice" when talking about a patient who wants to continue chemotherapy or "She is not hospice appropriate" when referring to a patient who cannot agree to a DNR order. Since each hospice gets to determine which treatments are palliative and which are curative, it is possible for some patients to continue some therapies that are disease-modifying or are placebo-like and allow some hope for remission or life prolongation.

People who are intent on a cure may not be appropriate for hospice, but there are many who struggle with letting go of hope for survival. They may feel pressure from their family to keep fighting. These people may be more in need of hospice support than those who are seemingly accepting of their terminal condition.

Children

Roughly 54,000 children die each year in the United States. Nearly half die from intentional or unintentional injuries. Nearly half also die in the first year of life. Only about 24% suffer and die from a complex chronic condition including cancer, genetic disorders and other relatively rare diseases of childhood (Feudtner & Connor, 2004). While there are much fewer deaths from childhood than adult illnesses, the impact of these deaths is very pronounced. The untimely death of a child affects people more profoundly than an elder who has lived life to an old age and more natural conclusion. However, to deny that children die can be viewed as a form of denial, since childhood death has always been an integral part of the human experience.

Most U.S. hospices provide care for some children. Less than half admit children regularly, while the other half does so selectively. There are also a small number of hospices that specialize in the care of children. Some hospices have developed pediatric hospice teams. The care of a dying child requires extraordinary sensitivity and specialized knowledge of palliative care. Children are not little adults.

There has also been a tendency to be more flexible about some of the admission criteria adults are held to. Many children come into hospice while still receiving aggressive treatments. Their need to maintain hope for improvement is better tolerated by hospice workers. Many psychosocial resources are brought to bear, including, in some cases, expressive or art therapy to help the patient or siblings in their expression of grief.

The main barrier to children's receipt of hospice care is lack of knowledge on the part of hospice and palliative care workers in how to care for children. There is a corresponding lack of knowledge of how to provide palliative care on the part of pediatric professionals. To address these concerns there have been some important programs developed. The Children's Project on Palliative/Hospice Services (ChiPPS) began under the auspices of NHPCO in 1998. This project aims to develop educational materials directed at hospice and palliative care workers to give them the knowledge and tools to care for children. Several influential publications have resulted from this project, including *The Compendium of Pediatric Palliative Care* (NHPCO, 2001), *The Education and Training Curriculum for Pediatric Palliative Care* (NHPCO, 2003), and *Caring for Kids: How to Start a Home Based Care Program* (NHPCO, 2006a).

A parallel project was conducted by the Education Development Center that resulted in creation of the Initiative for Pediatric Palliative Care (IPPC). The IPPC has resulted in the development of sophisticated teaching materials that are primarily directed to pediatric health care professionals in hospitals and other settings to provide training in pediatric palliative care.

Another important initiative is the International Children's Palliative Care Network, a network of all the pediatric palliative care projects around the globe. This organization is also a component of the Worldwide Palliative Care Alliance. The United Kingdom has probably the most well-developed pediatric palliative care services, with a network of children's hospices and services.

In general, dedicated pediatric palliative care services are like islands of excellence in the sea of children's health care in the United States. Several exceptional programs include the Minnesota Children's Hospitals and Clinics; the Essential Care Program in Buffalo, New York; Pediatric Palliative Care at Children's Hospital of Philadelphia; the pediatric palliative care program at Hospice of the Florida Suncoast, San Diego Hospice, and Palliative Care's Pediatric Palliative Care service; and the pediatric palliative care program at Hospice of the Western Reserve. A feature of pediatric palliative programs that are part of hospice programs is that they often do not use the name *hospice* and have a variety of mechanisms to serve children outside of hospice, usually with charitable funding for services.

Chronic Care

Health care in the United States is organized to provide primarily acute care services, whereas the greatest need is for chronic care. The system does not effectively meet the needs of those suffering from health care problems. It is estimated that 99 million persons in the United States have chronic conditions, of which 41 million have limitations owing to their conditions.

Only 5.3% of U.S. deaths in 2004 were from infectious diseases, including influenza and pneumonia, 4.7% were from accidents, and 2.1% from suicide and assault. Chronic diseases including cardiovascular disease were the cause in 33.5% of deaths, 23.1% of deaths were from cancer, and 5.1% from chronic respiratory disease. Diabetes, chronic liver disease, Alzheimer's, renal conditions, Parkinson's, and hypertension account for 10.6% of all deaths. The remaining 15.6% were from other causes. All together, chronic conditions account for 3 out of every 4 deaths (Robert Wood Johnson Foundation, 1996).

More than half (55%) of all emergency room visits are made by people with chronic conditions. Hospital care is predominately being provided to people with chronic conditions: 80% of all hospital days and 69% of all admissions are for chronic care. Virtually all home health care (96%) is given to chronically ill persons. People with chronic illness sometimes receive care that is more intensive, more specialized, and more expensive than they need or want.

Issues for the Future of Hospice and Palliative Care

Hospices need to be more adaptable in providing services to dying patients that are outside the boundaries of current practice.

If the patient does not qualify for a standard hospice benefit, there may be other ways of providing services. Many hospices are experimenting with "prehospice" programs that meet the physical, emotional, or spiritual needs of patients who have a life-threatening illness but may not have a 6-month prognosis. Services should be designed to meet the needs of special populations of patients facing the end of life. Hospices should be careful that the intent of providing these services is to meet a need rather than to provide free services as a way of inducing referrals. New advanced illness care, bridge, or transition programs, have also been proposed (Larson & Tobin, 2000) that stretch the boundaries of traditional hospice care.

Hospice has a great deal to offer the health care system in the management of terminal and chronic life-threatening illness particularly in residential settings. There could be a way for the boundary to be expanded so that appropriate services could be provided and reimbursed for hospice to manage a variety of seriously ill patients. For example, hospice could receive a small case management fee to help manage the care of patients with congestive heart disease, dementia, or pulmonary diseases over a long period of time. The fees paid could be considerably less than the current payment for treating these illnesses. Hospices could provide more daycare services.

The patient and family would be educated about home management of care and how to handle crises. Services could be provided during periods of exacerbation of illness. The 24-hours-a-day hospice on-call service would be available, and the aim would be to keep the patient stable at home instead of in the hospital. At the point where the disease progresses to the end stage, they could be admitted to the regular hospice service.

Hospitals are increasingly developing palliative care services that do not have a prognostic requirement. Hospices have also begun to provide specialist palliative care services as a way of reaching patients in need who do not want or do not qualify for hospice services. Most hospices in the United States now report that they provide some palliative care outside the Medicare Hospice Benefit.

In the United Kingdom, an effort is being made to promote three levels of palliative care to broaden the availability of services. The first level is the promotion of a palliative care approach within the general health care system. All practitioners ought to have a general knowledge of palliative principles. The second level is creation of consulting palliative care services that would be available to provide some interdisciplinary services within the health care system. This would be along the model developed at St. Luke's Hospital in New York. A consultation team would be available to see patients having symptom management problems, usually in a hospital setting.

The third level of palliative care would be a specialty interdisciplinary palliative care service. This would be the service that is currently provided by hospice facilities throughout the United Kingdom and a growing number of units in the National Health Service. It would offer the full range of hospice services on an inpatient basis and would include home visitation as well as day care services.

Hospices need to be more responsive to diverse cultural groups.
The hospice movement in the United States continues to serve a predominantly white population. There is a rich diversity in our society of different responses to death and dying. More effort is needed to understand these differences and to develop hospice services that respond to the unique interplay of culture and religion found throughout our society. Progress is being made in reaching the African American community. Research on the percentage of those accessing hospice in 2002 (Connor, Elwert, Spence, & Christakis, 2008) revealed that while 29% of all Caucasian patients received hospice care that year, only 22% of African Americans did. The greater the overall use of hospice in a given state, the less desparity in access was seen. This is an improvement over the early days of hospice but shows there is still some ways to go to achieve equal access. Even larger disparity exists for Asians and the Hispanic-Latino population that include many distinct national subgroups with very diverse cultures.

Hospices will need a different mix of resources to effectively care for more dying patients and have a greater impact on end-of-life care.
Some hospices do not admit certain patients because their need for care is more than the hospice can deliver. This may include some patients who live alone without primary care providers, and those with complex or devastating complications of illness. Many of these patients remain in the hospital and many are cared for by the growing number of hospital based palliative care services. Hospices need a way to provide around-the-clock care to selected patients to help them die at home. The continuous care provisions under the Hospice Medicare Benefit are too restrictive and are only available for brief periods of severe crisis. What families say they need are greater amounts of practical nursing assistance.

There are also concerns that the "one-size-fits-all" nature of the Medicare Hospice Benefit leaves opportunity for misuse of the benefit. It may be useful to have some modifications to the "per diems" that hospices receive to account for the differences in patient populations with different diagnoses, different levels of acuity, and different needs for treatments and services.

NHPCO is actively exploring the impact that changes to reimbursement could have. The central concern of CMS is whether the payment made to hospices is proportionate to the effort needed to meet the needs of the patients served. Some changes to the per diem are likely to deincentivize long-stay hospice patients. There is also concern that short-stay hospice patients are costing hospices much more than they are paid. Some combination of payment that accurately reimburses for short-stay patients and avoids overpaying for long-stay patients is likely to be implemented.

Palliative care programs will need reliable revenue streams to expand to meet the needs of all facing serious life-limiting illness.

Palliative care is the preferred term for care of patients with the various life-limiting illnesses around the world. Every health care system needs to find a way to finance the provision of palliative care. Palliative care is an essential component of health care in every country. Without palliative care, a health care system is inadequate. Every person alive will die and will experience a sudden or protracted death. The great majority of humanity will experience a protracted death. Each person who dies needs the simple grace of having access to professionals competent in managing suffering. Suffering is experienced at many levels including physical, psychological, interpersonal, emotional, practical, and spiritual. It is not enough to simply have good pain management. Every dying person will need caregivers who have the ability to understand and address the manifold human needs as death approaches.

To help determine how to best serve patients at various points in the end-of-life continuum, better prognostic tools are needed.

Hospices have relied on the judgment of community physicians and their own experiences to make decisions about whom to serve. This has led to a situation in which most patients are admitted far too late for effective treatment and some are admitted too soon.

Nicholas Christakis has documented the problems with determination of prognosis in his seminal book, *Death Foretold: Prophecy and Prognosis in Medical Care* (1999). This book helps us understand that the science of prognostication has diminished in the medical profession and that a renewed interest in this essential physician role needs greater attention. Ironically the better the physician knows the patient the more inaccurate the prognosis. There is a general tendency for physicians to overestimate survival, especially in patients they know well. It is relatively easier for a physician to give an objective prognosis to a patient that is not known personally to the physician.

Efforts to further the development and revision of *Medical Guidelines for Determining Prognosis in Selected Non-Cancer Diseases* (National Hospice

Organization [NHO], 1996a) should be supported. Additional research on prognosis needs to be funded and conducted; these initial prognostic guidelines were based on limited science but mostly on expert opinion. When they were written, it was understood that they would need continual revision as knowledge was added to the literature.

Unfortunately, there have been few studies that have contributed to our knowledge of prognosis in life-limiting illness since the original *Guidelines* were published. There are several published articles that demonstrate the lack of predictive validity of the original *Guidelines* as modified by CMS and the fiscal intermediaries to use in making local coverage decisions (Pantilat & Steimle, 2004; Schonwetter et al., 2003). Research on prognosis for dementia has advanced (Mitchell et al., 2004) and a study proposing new guidelines for hospice for patients with amyotrophic lateral sclerosis (McCluskey & Houseman, 2004) was used in an NHPCO monograph (NHPCO, 2007) to help hospices make better admission decisions for ALS patients.

NHPCO has developed an ongoing program to create disease specific resources for improving access to hospice care (http://www.nhpco.org/access). Disease specific resources are available as well as for children, the disabled, various ethnic groups, rural communities, and so forth.

Recognition of hospice and palliative medicine as a subspecialization in medicine is helping to improve acceptance of the developing body of knowledge about care of the dying.
The American Academy of Hospice and Palliative Medicine and the American Board of Hospice and Palliative Medicine were successful in 2006 in leading the effort to gain approval from the American Board for Medical Specialties (ABMS) for hospice and palliative medicine to be recognized as a subspecialty. Any recognized medical specialty can add hospice and palliative medicine as an area of subspecialization.

Beginning in 2008, cooperating boards within the ABMS offer a subspecialty certificate in hospice and palliative medicine. Cosponsoring boards include the American Boards of Internal Medicine, Anesthesiology, Family Medicine, Physical Medicine and Rehabilitation, Psychiatry and Neurology, Surgery, Pediatrics, Emergency Medicine, Radiology, and Obstetrics and Gynecology.

Gaining acceptance as a subspecialty is only one step, however, in bringing palliative care into the mainstream of health care in the United States. The field of geriatric medicine achieved specialization but has had a very difficult time certifying enough physicians to meet the needs of the increasingly aged population. Hospice and palliative medicine will need to find ways to attract young physicians to the field and make it desirable to seek a career. Success may also be found in attracting unneeded specialists who could consider changing areas of practice to specialize in palliation.

Beyond the physician training needed, there is a need for palliative care principles to be part of the basic curriculum of all health care disciplines.

Hospice and palliative care services are by definition interdisciplinary. Each of the health care disciplines needs to incorporate both experiential and didactic learning for disciplines such as nursing, social work, psychology, chaplaincy, and the various therapies. There are no recognized curricula for palliative and end-of-life care in these professional schools. Nursing certification in hospice and palliative care and a certification for social work are available post graduation but no other disciplines have a mechanism for recognition of the unique skills needed to care for people at the end of life.

The effectiveness of clinical work done in hospice and palliative care must continue to be rigorously assessed and variation in the quality of palliative care minimized.

The growing body of literature on care of the dying needs continued expansion. The real outcomes that are important in the care of dying patients have only just begun to be identified. Hospice and palliative care services must understand which outcomes are the most significant in the care of patients and to the health care system. Some promising efforts to identify domains and to put forward conceptual models have begun, but there needs to be widespread agreement on how to measure these outcomes accurately and benchmarks for acceptable care outcomes.

Large-scale collection of accurate patient-level data on the delivery and effectiveness of hospice and palliative care is needed to verify claims for the superiority of services that have to date have been based largely on anecdotes. Although it may be easier to measure the outcomes of physical care, it is also critical that the clinical efficacy of psychosocial and spiritual care be more closely examined. Hospices may believe that their current practices are the best, but this ignores the possibility of even better prevention and management of distress and promotion of growth at the end of life.

There continues to be too much variability in the quality of care delivered by hospice and palliative care programs to a population uninformed about what to expect from caregivers at the end of life. Programs such as NHPCO's Quality Partners Initiative need to be expanded and eventually, meaningful comparative outcome data publically reported.

Providing emotional support is not enough.

In the provision of psychosocial care, there continues to be a lack of specificity to the interventions used in helping patients with their interpersonal and inner distress. Clinicians need to accurately assess the patients' realms of suffering and respond in ways that are focused on their real needs.

Hospices have plans of care, but the psychosocial component is rarely well developed. All team members need to understand the patient's and family's psychosocial and spiritual care needs. Every member of the team should deliver consistent interventions based on a strategy that targets the patient's and family's individuals needs and goals.

If the patient is suffering emotionally because of isolation, the team ought to respond with interventions that bring more human contact into the patient's life. If the patient is anxious about suffocating, team members need to reassure the patient, explain how breathlessness can be managed, and help the patient to learn relaxation and breathing techniques that will reduce symptoms and increase sense of control. If the patient is experiencing existential distress, increasing the morphine dose is not the best intervention.

There is continuing concern about the overmedicalization of hospice and palliative care.
Hospital-based palliative care has developed advanced capability in managing the physical symptoms associated with life-limiting illness. Partly due to limitations in reimbursement in some cases, there has been a relative lack of emphasis on psychosocial and spiritual care including bereavement. Since palliative care patients are not required to have a limited prognosis or to discontinue curative therapies, there may be a tendency to focus on physical symptoms and to avoid dealing emotionally with the knowledge of impending death and thus opportunities to reach some form of life completion.

Some hospice programs claim to be holistic but likewise may succumb to limited provision of psychosocial and spiritual care due also to resource constraints or lack of sophistication. In an effort to grow, patients can be admitted while continuing aggressive therapies and rather than work to help the patient discontinue therapies continue them due to lack of capacity to deal with the emotional difficulties involved. Some hospices provide most of their patients with nursing services only and deprive them of true interdisciplinary care. When looking at hospice records, it is notable how little psychosocial and spiritual care is actually delivered, when this is supposed to be what makes hospice care exemplary.

Hospice and palliative caregivers need to allow for the possibility that the time around dying can include personal growth and an enhanced sense of well-being for the dying person and family.
It is easy to stay too focused on the problems that attend the dying process. After physical symptoms are well managed, some people may be able to continue the human developmental process and use the end of life as a time of resolution, appreciation, and closure. This takes hospice and

palliative care beyond the prevention and treatment of negative outcomes to the promotion of positive outcomes for the people served. This ability to create something good out of adversity is one of the things that distinguishes hospice and palliative care from other forms of care.

Hospices need to be more vocal in bringing the palliative care perspective to the societal debate on euthanasia and PAS.
Too often, this debate is presented as a dichotomy between those who believe assisted dying is a fundamental right and those who believe it is a fundamental wrong. Palliative care occupies the middle ground in this debate and has been largely ignored. The hospice and palliative care perspective needs to be promoted through aggressive advocacy and education efforts at the grassroots level as well as on the national stage. Otherwise, there is danger that we will be caricatured, as in the Terri Schiavo situation, as being complicit in ending lives, rather than helping to honor the wishes of patients and families at the end of life.

Greater support for hospice and palliative care needs to come through government policy and support for research.
In the United States, creation of the Medicare Hospice Benefit has gone a long way toward making hospice care accessible to larger numbers of people. However, there are still a great many with life-limiting illnesses who do not receive the palliative care they need. Hospital-based palliative care is growing, but there is no coordinated national strategy for palliative care development in the United States, and it exists in very few countries around the world.

The SUPPORT Investigators (1995) study documented that most terminally ill people in hospitals are still faced with dying in pain while their treatment wishes are ignored. In spite of the people served by hospices, most are still dying in these hospitals or institutions.

With the exception of a small program through the National Institutes for Nursing Research, there have been few significant government research resources committed to furthering knowledge of palliative care. The NHPCO has published an agenda for research (2004) that stresses improvements in access, quality, and research methods. Enormous sums are provided for research into the treatment of disease, with little success to date. Meanwhile, hundreds of thousands of people die each year with inadequate management of their conditions. The lack of support for palliative care research in the United States ought to be viewed as a disgrace.

In the United Kingdom, those served by hospices remain a fairly small minority of the dying. The National Health Service provides some support to the hospices, but they remain too dependent on philanthropy to reach the great majority of the dying.

Governments concerned for the welfare of citizens ought to promote policies that encourage the use of hospice care. At present, the U.S. health care system is still in many ways motivated by profit to overtreat dying patients. Physicians receive less payments if they refer a patient to hospice, private physicians have billing difficulties if the patient is on the hospice benefit, hospices are penalized by the fiscal intermediaries or the inspector general if they admit a patient too soon and the patient outlives his or her prognosis, and nursing homes are encouraged to provide skilled nursing services to their dying patients rather than allowing hospice to participate in the delivery of care.

Hospital discharge planners are too busy to work up a hospice referral. They have to deal with how informed the patient is and what his or her goals for care are. All these limitations combine to inhibit the growth and development of hospice care. There is considerable room for policy changes that will promote the success of the hospice and palliative care movement.

Hospice care needs to become an integral part of the health care system in every country.

Many of the above problems derive from the difficulties in introducing hospice care into an existing health care system. Each country in the world has unique aspects to its health care delivery system. For palliative care to succeed, it must adapt somewhat to the needs of the existing system. There are few countries where care of the terminally ill is already done well. An assessment of how the existing system cares for people dying will usually reveal many unmet needs for education and caregiving.

Following the assessment of need, it is necessary to achieve a number of significant milestones toward becoming an integral part of a health care system. These milestones include the following: formation of a stakeholders' group of champions for palliative care, the development of country-based national standards for palliative care, the inclusion of palliative care in the legal framework of the country's health care system, achieving ready access to opioids and other essential palliative care medications, the acceptance of palliative care as a form of medical specialization, the creation of a payment system to cover the cost of palliative care, the establishment of curricula and training centers, and the expansion of the number of palliative care providers to meet the population's needs.

Some have criticized the emphasis on building palliative care, referring to it as second class care. This suggests a lack of understanding that palliative care is simply an essential part of the continuum of care in every country.

How Do Hospice and Palliative Care Fit In to the Health Care System?

Hospices developed to redress the reality of insensitive care for dying patients. Hospital-based palliative care developed to meet the needs of the many dying patients that were not being served by hospices. Hospices tended to reject mainstream medicine and to be perceived as outsiders. Although this may have been appropriate 30 years ago, it is counterproductive today. Hospices need to continue to embrace the health care system and work for inclusiveness as palliative care has done generally.

There has been a complaint that hospices are not having much of an impact on end-of-life care in the United States and see too few patients. This is no longer the case. The original goal of putting hospice out of business is not one that will be realized anytime soon. Maybe in another 20 years, generalist palliative care will be so well integrated that the values and practices of hospice care will be built into the system. However, it is also quite likely that there may always be a need for some to specialize in caring for the dying. Human avoidance of death continues to be pervasive.

Conclusion

This book has examined the development of hospice and palliative care primarily in the United States, but with a view toward what the rest of the world has to teach. Hospice began as a revolution against the way the health care system treats those who are dying. It is now a positive force for excellence in the care of those facing life-threatening illnesses. The movement has spread throughout the United States, Europe, parts of Africa, Latin America, and Asia, and is beginning to emerge in the Middle East (Saunders & Kastenbaum, 1997). Palliative care has taken some distinct forms in the different societies it has emerged in, all with the common focus of providing compassionate care directed at relief of physical, psychological, social, and spiritual distress.

In describing hospice and palliative care practice, the focus has been on how the best palliative care is being delivered in the United States. It is important that some of these distinct ways of caring for dying patients are described in detail. Many new organizations and individuals are entering the hospice and end-of-life care area without knowledge of the history of the movement or how to provide effective palliative care.

Beyond the technical aspects of symptom management is a philosophy of caring that is more difficult to convey to new caregivers, who are often hired and thrust into important roles with little more than general orientation to policy and procedures. It is hoped that this book will help some of the thousands of new hospice and palliative care workers and volunteers who are now entering the field.

Also described have been the real problems facing hospices in the current health care system. Until recently, the hospice movement has enjoyed little scrutiny and the halo effect of an industry formed by unselfish, highly principled people, and it has been above reproach. The growth of the movement has brought with it many of the same problems of greed and variable quality seen throughout the rest of the health care system.

The future for hospice care ought to be bright. The U.S. population is aging, as the huge post-World War II "baby boom" generation reaches old age. Current care for most dying patients continues to be fraught with problems, with many patients dying in pain, in institutions, and with their wishes for treatment ignored. Hospice and palliative care offer the most effective system of caring for dying people available today.

Palliative care is an essential part of any health care system. Growth in palliative care generally is essential to achieving the 30-year-old dream of doing away with the need for hospice and palliative care as a separate part of health care.

Impediments to access to palliative care must be removed. Much greater effort must be made to educate the public about options for care at the end of life. Most may want to believe in personal immortality, but without a written plan for how we want to be cared for and competent caregivers, we invite disaster.

Palliative care is at an important juncture. Will it remain on the fringes of the health care system, or will it become part of a fully integrated cradle-to-grave continuum of care? Hospice and palliative care providers themselves have a lot to say about the outcome. If they rise to the challenge of providing expert care based on science and the needs and wishes of the people served, they will have a bright future.

References

Agency for Health Care Policy and Research. (1994). *Management of cancer pain* (AHCPR Publication No. 94-0592). Rockville, MD: U.S. Department of Health and Human Services.

American Medical Association. (2008). *AMA Council on medical and judicial affairs approves policy on sedation to unconsciousness for some terminally ill.* Retrieved September 14, 2008, from http://www.medicalnewsinc.com/news.php?viewStory=177

Autry, J. (1991). *Love and profit: The art of caring leadership.* New York: William Morrow.

Avis, N. E., Brambilla, D. J., Vass, K., & McKinlay, J. B. (1991). The effect of widowhood on health: A prospective analysis from the Massachusetts Women's Health Study. *Social Science Medicine, 33,* 1063–1070.

Barry, K. L., & Fleming, M. F. (1988). Widowhood: A review of the social and medical implication. *Family Medicine, 20,* 413–417.

Becker, E. (1973). *The denial of death.* New York: Free Press.

Beilin, R. (1981). Social functions of denial and death. *Omega, 12*(1), 25–35.

Beissler, A. R. (1979). Denial and affirmation in illness and health. *American Journal of Psychiatry, 136*(8), 1026–1030.

Bengston, V., Ceullar, J., & Ragan, P. (1977). Stratum contrasts and similarities in attitudes toward death. *Journal of Gerontology, 32*(1), 76–78.

Bernheim, J., & Buyse, M. (1984). The anamnestic comparative self assessment for measuring the subjective quality of life of cancer patients. *Journal of Psychosocial Oncology, 7*(4), 25–38.

Birenbaum, H. G., & Kidder, D. (1992). What does hospice cost? *American Journal of Public Health, 74,* 689–697.

Blakney, R. B. (1955). *The way of life.* New York: Mentor.

Bonnano, G., Boerner, K., & Wortman, C. (2008). Trajectories of grieving. In M. Stroebe, R. O. Hansson, H. Schut, & W. Stroebe (Eds.), *Handbook of bereavement research and practice: Advances in theory and intervention.* Washington, DC: American Psychological Association.

Bowlby, J. (1980). *Attachment and loss: Vol. 3. Sadness and depression.* London: Hogarth.

Breitbart, W., & Heller, K. S. (2002). Reframing hope: Meaning-centered care for patients near the end of life: An interview with William Breitbart. *Innovations in End-of-Life Care.* Retrieved October 22, 2008, from http://www.edc.org/lastacts

Breznitz, S. (1983). The seven kinds of denial. In S. Breznitz (Ed.), *The denial of stress* (pp. 257–280). New York: International Universities Press.

Bruera, E., de Stoutz, N., Velasco-Leiva, A., Schoeiler, T., & Hanson, J. (1993, July 3). Effects of oxygen on dyspnoea in hypoxic terminal-cancer patients. *Lancet, 342*(8862), 13–14.

Buckman, R. (1992). *How to break bad news: A guide for health care professionals.* Toronto: University of Toronto Press.

Byock, I. (1997). *Dying well: The prospect for growth at the end of life.* New York: Putnam.

Byock, I., & Merriman, M. (1998). Measuring quality of life for patients with terminal illness: The Missoula Quality of Life Index (MVQOLI). *Palliative Medicine, 12,* 231–244.

Calman, K. (1984). Quality of life in cancer patients: An hypothesis. *Journal of Medical Ethics, 10,* 124–127.

Campbell, D. E., Lyn, J., Louis, T. A., & Shugarman, L. R. (2004). Medicare program expenditures associated with hospice use. *Annals of Internal Medicine, 140*(4), 269–277.

Cappon, D. (1978). Attitudes of the aged toward death. *Essence, 2*(3), 139–147.

Caring Connections. (n.d.). [Home page]. Retrieved October 27, 2008, from http://www.caringinfo.org

Carmichael, E. (2008) William Hewlett and David Packard quotes. Accessed December 5, 2008 at: http://www.evancarmichael.com/Famous-Entrepreneurs/1947/William-Hewlett-and-David-Packard-Quotes.html

Cassell, E. J. (1982). The nature of suffering and the goals of medicine. *New England Journal of Medicine, 306,* 639–645.

Cella, D. (1994). Quality of life: Concepts and definitions. *Journal of Pain and Symptom Management, 9*(3), 186–192.

Cella, D., Lee-Riordan, D., & Siberman, M. (1990). Quality of life in advanced cancer: Three new disease specific measures [Abstract 1225]. *Proceedings of the American Society for Clinical Oncology, 4*(5), 216.

Center to Advance Palliative Care. (2008). *New analysis shows hospitals continue to implement palliative care programs at rapid pace.* CAPC press release dated April 14, 2008. Accessed November 24, 2008 at: http://www.capc.org/news-and-events/releases/news-release-4-14-08

Centers for Medicaid and Medicare Services. (2008). *Medicare conditions of participation for hospice programs.* Washington, DC: Author.

Chochinov, H., Hack, T., Hassard, T., Kristjanson, L., McClement, S., & Harlos, M. (2005). Dignity therapy: A novel psychotherapeutic intervention for patients near the end of life. *Journal of Clinical Oncology, 23*(24), 5520–5525.

Christakis, N. A. (1996). Survival of medicare patients after enrollment in hospice programs. *New England Journal of Medicine, 335,* 172–178.

Christakis, N. A. (1999). *Death foretold: Prophesy and prognosis in medical care.* Chicago: University of Chicago Press.

Christakis, N. A., & Allison, P. D. (2006). Mortality after the hospitalization of a spouse. *New England Journal of Medicine, 354,* 719–730.

Christakis, N. A., & Iwashyna, T. J. (2003). The health impact of health care on families: A matched cohort study of hospice use by decedents and mortality outcomes in surviving, widowed spouses. *Social Science & Medicine, 57*(3), 465–475.

Cicirelli, V. G. (2006). Fear of death in mid-old age. *Journals of Gerontology Series B: Psychological Sciences and Social Sciences, 61,* P75–P81.

Clark, D. (1995). Looking forward: Looking back—a debate. Lecture at International Work Group on Death, Dying, and Bereavement meeting, June 27, 1995. Oxford, England.

Clark, D. (1999, September). "Total pain": Disciplinary power and the body in the work of Cicely Saunders, 1958–1967. *Social Science and Medicine, 49*(6), 727–736.

Collins, J. (2001). *Good to great: Why some companies make the leap … and others don't.* New York: Harper Business.

Connor, S. (1992). Denial in terminal illness: To intervene or not to intervene. *Hospice Journal, 8*(4), 1–15.

Connor, S. (1996a). Hospice, bereavement intervention and use of health care resources by surviving spouses. *HMO Practice, 10*(1), 20–23.

Connor, S. (1996b). [Results of study of patient and caregiver anxiety levels]. Unpublished data, Hospice of Central Kentucky.

Connor, S. (1999). New initiatives transforming hospice care, *Hospice Journal, 14*(3/4), 193–203.

Connor, S., & Adams, J. (2003). Caregiving at the end of life. *Hastings Center Report Special Supplement, 33*(2), S8–S9.

Connor, S., Egan, K., Kwilosz, D., Larson, D., & Reese, D. (2002). Interdisciplinary approaches to assisting with end-of-life care and decision making. *American Behavioral Scientist, 46*(3), 340–356.

Connor, S., Elwert, F., Spence, C., & Christakis, N. (2007). Geographic variation in hospice use in the United States in 2002. *Journal of Pain and Symptom Management, 34*(3), 277–285.

Connor, S., Elwert, F., Spence, C., & Christakis, N. (2008). Racial disparity in hospice use in the United States in 2002. *Palliative Medicine, 22*(3), 205–213.

Connor, S., & Lattanzi-Licht, M. (1995). Trauma response questionnaire results. *NHO Newsline, 21*(5), 4–5.

Connor, S., Lycan, J., & Schumacher, D. (2006). Involvement of psychologists in psychosocial aspects of hospice and end-of-life care. In J. Werth & D. Blevins (Eds.), *Psychosocial issues near the end of life: A resource for professional caregivers* (pp. 203–217). Washington, DC: American Psychological Association.

Connor, S., Pyenson, B., Fitch, K., & Spence, C. (2007). Comparing hospice and non-hospice patient survival among patients who die within a 3-year window. *Journal of Pain and Symptom Management, 33*(3), 238–246.

Connor, S., Teno, J., Spence, C., & Smith, N. (2005). Family evaluation of hospice care: Results from voluntary submission of data via website. *Journal of Pain and Symptom Management, 30*(1), 9–17.

Cranston, J. M., Crockett, A., & Currow, D. (2008). Oxygen therapy for dyspnoea in adults. *Cochrane Database System Review,* (3), CD004769.

Currier, J., Neimeyer, R., & Berman, J. (2008). The effectiveness of psychotherapeutic interventions for the bereaved: A comprehensive quantitative review. *Psychological Bulletin, 134*(5), 648-61.

Dansak, D. A., & Cordes, R. S. (1978–1979). Cancer: Denial or suppression. *International Journal of Psychiatry in Medicine, 9*(3/4), 257–262.

DePree, M. (1989). *Leadership is an art.* New York: Dell.

DePree, M. (1992). *Leadership jazz.* New York: Dell.

Derogatis, L. R., Morrow, G. R., Fetting, J., Penman, D., Piasetsky, S., Schmale, A., et al. (1983). The prevalence of psychiatric disorders among cancer patients. *JAMA, 249*(6), 751–757.

Detwiler, D. A. (1981). The positive functions of denial. *Journal of Pediatrics, 99*(3), 401–402.

Devins, G. (1979). Death anxiety and voluntary passive euthanasia: Influences of proximity to death and experiences with death in important other persons. *Journal of Consulting and Clinical Psychology, 47*, 301–309.

Dickenson, G. E. (2006). Teaching end-of-life issues in US medical schools: 1975 to 2005. *American Journal of Hospice and Palliative Care, 23*(3), 197–204.

Dickenson, G. E. (2007). End-of-life and palliative care issues in medical and nursing schools in the United States. *Death Studies, 31*(8), 713–726.

Douglas, C. (1992). For all the saints. *British Medical Journal, 304*, 579.

Emanuel, E. J., Ash, A., Wei, Y., Gazelle, G., Levinsky, N. G., Saynina, O., et al. (2002). Managed care, hospice use, site of death, and medical expenditures in the last year of life. *Archives of Internal Medicine, 162*(12), 1722–1728.

Falek, A., & Britton, S. (1974). Phases in coping: The hypothesis and its implications. *Social Biology, 21*(1), 1–7.

Feifel, H. (Ed.). (1959). *The meaning of death.* New York: McGraw-Hill.

Feudtner, C., & Connor, S. (2004). Epidemiology of pediatric palliative care. In B. Carter & M. Levetown (Eds.), *Pediatric palliative care for infants, children, and adolescents.* Baltimore: Johns Hopkins University Press.

Foley, K. (1985). Overview of cancer pain and brachial and lumbosacral plexopathy [syllabus from Management of Cancer Pain postgraduate course]. (Available from Memorial Sloan-Kettering Cancer Center, New York)

Fortner, B. V. (1999). *The effectiveness of grief counseling and therapy: A quantitative review.* Memphis, TN: University of Memphis.

Frankl, V. (1963). *Man's search for meaning.* New York: Washington Square Press, Simon & Schuster.

Freud, A. (1948). *The ego and mechanisms of defense.* London: Hogarth Press and the Institute of Psychoanalysis.

Freud, S. (1917). *Mourning and melancholia*. In J. Strachey (Ed. & Trans.), *The standard edition of the complete psychological works of Sigmund Freud* (Vol. 15). London: Hogarth Press and the Institute of Psychoanalysis.

Freud, S. (1924). *The loss of reality in psychosis and neurosis*. In J. Strachey (Ed. & Trans.), *The standard edition of the complete psychological works of Sigmund Freud* (Vol. 22, p. 184). London: Hogarth Press and the Institute of Psychoanalysis.

Freud, S. (1940). *An outline of psychoanalysis*. In J. Strachey (Ed. & Trans.), *Standard edition of the complete psychological works of Sigmund Freud* (Vol. 23, pp. 140–207). London: Hogarth Press and the Institute of Psychoanalysis.

Fulton, R. (1965). *Death and identity*. Bowie, MD: Charles Press.

Gage, B., Miller, S. C., Coppola, K., Harvell, J., Laliberte, L., Mor, V., and Teno, J. (2000). *Important questions for hospice in the next century*. Accessed December 7, 2008 at: http://aspe.hhs.gov/daltcp/reports/impques.htm.

Ganzini, L., Harvath, T. A., Jackson, A., Goy, E. R., Miller, L. L., & Delorit, M. A. (2002). Experiences of Oregon nurses and social workers with hospice patients who requested assistance with suicide. *New England Journal of Medicine, 347*(8), 582–588.

Garfield, C. (1978). Elements of psychosocial oncology: Doctor-patient relationships in terminal illness. In C. Garfield (Ed.), *Psychosocial care of the dying patient*. New York: McGraw-Hill.

Glaser, B. G., & Strauss, A. L. (1965). *Awareness of dying*. Chicago: Aldine.

Gonzales v. Oregon (2006). No. 04-623, 546 U.S. 243

Gough, I., Furnival, C., Schilder, L., & Grove, W. (1983). Assessment of the quality of life of patients with advanced cancer. *European Journal of Cancer and Clinical Oncology, 19*, 1161–1165.

Grossman, S., Sheidler, V. R., Swedeen, K., Mucenski, J., & Piantadosi, S. (1991). Correlation of patient and caregiver ratings of cancer pain. *Journal of Pain and Symptom Management, 6*, 53–57.

Guyatt, G., Feeny, D., & Patrick, D. (1993). Measuring health-related quality of life. *Annals of Internal Medicine, 118*, 622–629.

Haan, N. (1965). Coping and defense mechanisms related to personality inventories. *Journal of Consulting and Clinical Psychology, 29*, 373–378.

Hackett, T. P., & Cassem, N. H. (1970). Psychological reaction to life threatening stress: A study of acute myocardial infarction. In H. S. Abram (Ed.), *Psychological aspects of stress*. Springfield, IL: Charles C Thomas.

Hackett, T. P., & Cassem, N. II. (1974). Development of a quantitative rating scale to assess denial. *Journal of Psychosomatic Research, 18*(2), 93–100.

Hackett, T. P., & Weisman, A. D. (1964). Reactions to the imminence of death. In G. H. Grosser, H. Wechsler, & M. Greenblatt (Eds.), *The threat of impending disaster: Contributions to the psychology of stress* (pp. 300–311). Cambridge, MA: MIT Press.

Hackett, T. P., & Weisman, A. D. (1969). Denial as a factor in patients with heart disease and cancer. *Annals of the New York Academy of Sciences, 164*, 182.

Haine, R. A., Ayers, T. S., Wolchik, S. A., & Sandler, I. N. (2008). Empirically-supported practices for working with parentally bereaved children. *Professional Psychology: Research and Practice, 39*, 113–121.

Hayes, J., & Hendrix, C. (2008). The role of religion in bereavement. In M. Stroebe, R. Hansson, H. Schut, & W. Stroebe (Eds.), *Handbook of bereavement research and practice*. Washington, DC: American Psychological Association.

Hendin, H., Rutenfrancs, C., & Zylich, Z. (1997, June 4). Physician assisted suicide and euthanasia in the Netherlands: Lessons from the Dutch. *Journal of the American Medical Association, 277*(21), 1720–1722.

Hinton, J. (1972). *Dying*. Middlesex, UK: Pelican.

Holland, J. (1989). Clinical course of cancer. In J. Holland & J. Rowland (Eds.), *Handbook of psychooncology* (pp. 75–100). New York: Oxford University Press.

Horowitz, M. (1986). *Stress response syndromes*. Northvale, NJ: Aronson.

Hospice Information Service. (n.d.). [Home page]. Retrieved October 26, 2008, from http://www.hospiceinformation.info

Illinois State Hospice Organization. (1996). *Hospice Medicaid fact sheet [from U.S. Health Care Finance Administration data]*. Chicago: Author.

Institute of Medicine: Committee on Quality Health Care in America. (2000). In L. Kohn, J. Corrigan, & M. Donaldson (Eds.), *To err is human: building a safer health system*. Washington DC: National Academy Press.

International Work Group on Death, Dying, and Bereavement. (1993). A statement of assumptions and principles concerning psychosocial care of dying persons and their families. In *Statements on death, dying and bereavement* (pp. 43–52). Ottawa: International Work Group of the IWG.

Irish, D. P. (1993). *Ethnic variations in dying, death, and grief: Diversity in universality*. Washington, DC: Taylor & Francis.

Jacobs, S., & Leiberman, P. (1987). Bereavement and depression. In O. Cameron (Ed.), *Presentations of depression*. New York: Wiley.

Jacobsen, P. B., Donovan, K.A., Trask, P. C., Fleishman, S. B., Zabora, J., Baker, F., Holland, J. C. (2005). Screening for psychologic distress in ambulatory cancer patients. *Cancer, 103*(7):1494-502.

Joint Commission on Accreditation of Hospitals. (1984). *Hospice standards manual*. Chicago: Author.

Joint Commission on Accreditation of Health Care Organizations. (1994). *1995 accreditation manual for home care*. Chicago: Author.

Kalish, R. (1978). A little myth is a dangerous thing: Research in the service of the dying. In C. Garfield (Ed.), *Psychosocial care of the dying patient* (pp. 219–226). New York: McGraw-Hill.

Kalish, R., & Reynolds, D. (1977). The role of age in death attitudes. *Death Education, 1*(2), 205–230.

Kane, R., Wales, J., Bernstein, L., Leibowitz, A., & Kaplan, S. (1984). A randomized control trial of hospice care. *Lancet, 1*(8232), 890–894.

Karnofsky, D. A. (1949). The clinical evaluation of chemotherapeutic agents in cancer. In C. M. McCleod (Ed.), *Evaluation of chemotherapeutic agents* (pp. 191–205). New York: Columbia University Press.

Kastenbaum, R. (1974). On death and dying: Should we have mixed feelings about our ambivalence toward the aged? *Journal of Geriatric Psychiatry, 7*(1), 94–107.

Kastenbaum, R., & Aisenberg, R. (1972). *The psychology of death*. New York: Springer.

Kastenbaum, R., & Kastenbaum, B. (1989). *Encyclopedia of death*. Phoenix, AZ: Oryx.

Kaye, P. (1993). *Notes on symptom control in hospice and palliative care.* Essex, CT: Hospice Education Institute.

Klass, D., Silverman, P., & Nickman, S. (Eds.). (1996). *Continuing bonds: New understandings of grief.* Washington, DC: Taylor & Francis.

Kübler-Ross, E. (1969). *On death and dying.* New York: Macmillan.

Lang, F. R., Baltes, P. B., & Wagner, G. G. (2007). Desired lifetime and end of life desires across adulthood from 20–90: A dual source information model. *Journals of Gerontology Series B: Psychological Sciences and Social Sciences,* 65(2), P268–P276.

Larson, D. (1993). *The helper's journey: Working with people facing grief, loss, and life threatening illness.* Champaign, IL: Research Press.

Larson, D. & Hoyt, W. (2007). What has become of grief counseling? An evaluation of the empirical foundations of the new pessimism. *Professional Psychology: Research and Practice,* 38(4), 347–355.

Larson, D. G., & Tobin, D. R. (2000). End-of-life conversations: Evolving practice and theory. *JAMA, 284,* 1573–1578.

Lazarus, R. S. (1966). *Psychological stress and the coping process.* New York: McGraw-Hill.

Lazarus, R. S. (1985). The trivialization of distress. In J. D. Rosen & L. J. Solomon (Eds.), *Preventing health risk behaviors and promoting coping with illness* (Vol. 8). Hanover, NH: University Press of New England.

Lazarus, R. S., & Golden, G. (1981). The function of denial in stress, coping, and aging. In E. McGarraugh & S. Kiesler (Eds.), *Biology, behavior and aging* (pp. 283–307). New York: Academic Press.

Lichtenthal, W. G., Cruess, D. G., & Prigerson, H. G. (2004). A case for establishing complicated grief as a distinct mental disorder in *DSM-IV. Clinical Psychology Review, 24,* 637–662.

Lilienfeld, S. O. (2007). Psychological treatments that cause harm. *Perspectives on Psychological Science, 2,* 53–70.

Lorenz, K. A., Lynn, J., Morton, S. C., Dy, S. M., Shugarman, L. M., Wilkinson, A., et al. (2005). Methodological approaches for a systematic review of end-of-life care. *Journal of Palliative Medicine,* 8(Suppl. 1), S4–S11.

Lunney, J. R., Lynn, J., Foley, D. J., Lipson, S., & Guralnik, J. M. (2003). Patterns of functional decline at the end of life. *JAMA, 289,* 2387–2392.

Lynn, J., Tino, J., & Harrell, F. (1995). Accurate prognostication of death: Opportunities and challenges for clinicians. *Western Journal of Medicine, 163,* 1–8.

Maciejewski, P. K., Zhang, B. Block, S. D., & Prigerson, H. G. (2007). An empirical analysis of the stage theory of grief. *JAMA,* 297(7), 716–723.

Maltoni, M., Scarpi, E., Modonesi, C., Passardi, A., Calpona, S., Turriziani, A., et al. (2005). A validation study of the WHO analgesic ladder: A two-step vs three-step strategy. *Supportive Care Cancer, 11,* 888–894.

Maslow, A. H. (1967). A theory of metamotivation: The biological rooting of the value-life. *Journal of Humanistic Psychology, 7,* 93–127.

McCluskey, L., & Houseman, G. (2004). Medicare hospice referral criteria for patients with amyotrophic lateral sclerosis: A need for improvement. *Journal of Palliative Medicine,* 7(1), 47–53.

Minagawa, H., Uchitomi, Y., Yamawaki, S., & Ishitani, K. (1996). Psychiatric morbidity in terminally ill cancer patients: A prospective study. *Cancer, 78*(5), 1131–1137.

Mitchell, S., Kiely, D., Hamel, M. B., Park, P., Morris, J., & Fries, B. (2004). Estimating prognosis for nursing home residents with advanced dementia. *JAMA, 291*(22), 2734–2740.

Mor, V., Greer, D., & Kastenbaum, R. (1988). *The hospice experiment*. Baltimore: Johns Hopkins University Press.

Mount, B., & Cohen, R. (1997, January). Validity of the McGill Quality of Life Questionnaire in the palliative care setting: A multi-centre Canadian study demonstrating the importance of the existential domain. *Palliative Medicine, 11*(1), 3–20.

Murphy, D., Burrows, D., Santilli, S., Kemp, A., Tenner, S., Kreling, B., et al. (1994). Influence of the probability of survival on patient's preference regarding cardiopulmonary resuscitation. *New England Journal of Medicine, 330*(8), 545–549.

National Consensus Project. (2008). *Clinical practice guidelines for quality palliative care*. Retrieved August 11, 2008, from http://www.nationalconsensusproject.org

National Hospice Foundation (1999). *Baby boomers fear talking to parents about death*. Press release on public opinion research dated June 8, 1999.

National Hospice and Palliative Care Organization. (1995). *An analysis of the cost savings of the Medicare Hospice Benefit* (Item No. 712901). Alexandria, VA: Author.

National Hospice and Palliative Care Organization (1996). *Knowledge and attitudes related to hospice care*. Gallop Poll done for NHPCO dated September 1996.

National Hospice and Palliative Care Organization (2000). *Hospice standards of practice*. Alexandria VA: Author.

National Hospice and Palliative Care Organization (2001). *Hospice services: guidelines and definitions*. Item # 711050. Alexandria, VA: Author.

National Hospice and Palliative Care Organization. (2001). *The compendium of pediatric palliative care*. Alexandria, VA: Author.

National Hospice and Palliative Care Organization. (2003). *The education and training curriculum for pediatric palliative care*. Alexandria, VA: Author.

National Hospice and Palliative Care Organization (2004). Development of the NHPCO research agenda. *Journal of Pain and Symptom Management, 28*(5)488-496.

National Hospice and Palliative Care Organization. (2006a). *Caring for kids: How to start a home based care program* Alexandria, VA: Author.

National Hospice and Palliative Care Organization. (2006b). *Standards of practice for a hospice program*. Alexandria VA: Author.

National Hospice and Palliative Care Organization. (2008a, October). *NHPCO facts and figures: Hospice care in America*. Retrieved November 23, 2008, from http://www.nhpco.org/files/public/Statistics_Research/NHPCO_facts-and-figures_2008.pdf

National Hospice and Palliative Care Organization. (2008b). *Mapping levels of palliative care development: A global view*. Retrieved August 11, 2008, from http://www.nhpco.org

National Hospice and Palliative Care Organization. (2008c). *Quality partners self-assessment tools.* Retrieved August 2, 2008, from http://www.nhpco.org/i4a/pages/Index.cfm?pageID=4990

National Hospice and Palliative Care Organization. (2008). *Volunteering for Hospice and Palliative Care...It Must Be Love.* Accessed Dec 3, 2008 at: http://www.nhpco.org/files/public/communications/Volunteer_Statistics_2008.doc

National Hospice and Palliative Care Organization. (n.d.-a). *Association toolkit.* Retrieved October 26, 2008, from http://www.nhpco.org/associationtoolkit

National Hospice and Palliative Care Organization. (n.d.-b). *Statistics.* Retrieved October 25, 2008, from http://www.nhpco.org/statistics

National Hospice and Palliative Care Organization. (manuscript under preparation). Measuring pain in a clinical practice improvement study: Association with length of service.

National Hospice Organization. (1979). *Standards of a hospice program of care.* Alexandria VA: Author.

National Hospice Organization. (1992). Poll says hospice leads. *NHO Newsline, 3*(3), 4.

National Hospice Organization. (1993). *Standards of a hospice program of care.* Arlington, VA: Author.

National Hospice Organization. (1994). *Guidelines for social work in hospice.* Arlington, VA: Author.

National Hospice Organization. (1995a). *Medical guidelines for determining prognosis in selected non-cancer diseases.* Arlington, VA: Author.

National Hospice Organization. (1995b). [Results of pain control study]. Unpublished data.

National Hospice Organization. (1996a). *Medical guidelines for determining prognosis in selected non-cancer diseases* (2nd ed., Item No. 713008). Arlington, VA: Author.

National Hospice Organization. (1996b). *Results of NHO provider member census.* Arlington, VA: Author.

National Hospice Organization. (1997a). *A pathway for patients and families facing terminal illness.* Arlington, VA: Author.

National Hospice Organization. (1997b). [Results of survey on research interests of hospices]. Unpublished data.

National Quality Forum. (2006). *A national framework and preferred practices for palliative and hospice care quality.* Washington, DC: Author. Retrieved October 23, 2008, from http://www.qualityforum.org

Neimeyer, R. (2001). *Meaning reconstruction and the experience of loss.* Washington, DC: American Psychological Association.

Neimeyer, R., Hogan, N., & Laurie, A. (2008). The measurement of grief: Psychometric considerations in the assessment of reactions to bereavement. In M. Stroebe, R. O. Hansson, H. Schut, & W. Stroebe (Eds.), *Handbook of bereavement research, and practice: Advances in theory and intervention* (pp. 133–162). Washington, DC: American Psychological Association.

Neimeyer, R. A., & Mahoney, M. (1999). *Constructivism in psychotherapy.* Washington, DC: American Psychological Association.

Osterweis, M., Solomon, F., & Green, M. (Eds.). (1984). *Bereavement: Reactions, consequences, and care.* Washington, DC: National Academy Press.

Padilla, G. (1992). Validity of health related quality of life subscales. *Progress in Cardiovascular Nursing, 7*(2), 13–20.

Pang, W. S. (1994). Dyspnoea in advanced malignancies: A palliative care approach. *Annals of the Academy of Medicine Singapore, 23*(2), 183–185.

Pantilat, S. Z., & Steimle, A. E. (2004). Palliative care for patients with heart failure. *JAMA, 291*(20), 2476–2482.

Pattison, E. M. (1978). The living-dying process. In C. Garfield (Ed.), *Psychosocial care of the dying patient* (pp. 133–167). New York: McGraw-Hill.

Pijnenborg, L., van der Maas, P., van Delden, J., & Looman, C. (1993). Life terminating acts without explicit request of patient. *Lancet, 341*, 1196–1199.

Pyenson, B., Connor, S., Fitch, K., & Kinzbrunner, B. (2004). Medicare cost in matched hospice and non-hospice cohorts. *Journal of Pain Symptom Management, 28*(3), 200–210.

Rando, T. (1993). *Treatment of complicated mourning.* Champaign, IL: Research Press.

Rando, T. (2000). *Clinical dimensions of anticipatory mourning: Theory and practice in working with the dying, their loved ones, and their caregivers.* Champaign, IL: Research Press.

Robert Wood Johnson Foundation. (1996). *Chronic care in America.* Princeton, NJ: Author.

Robert Wood Johnson Foundation. (n.d.). *Promoting excellence in end-of-life care.* Retrieved October 27, 2008, from http://www.promotingexcellence.org

Rosen, E. (1990). *Families facing death: Family dynamics of terminal illness.* Lexington, MA: Lexington Books.

Sanders, C. (1993). Risk factors in bereavement outcome. In M. Stroebe, W. Stroebe, & R. O. Hansson (Eds.), *Handbook of bereavement: Theory, research, & intervention* (pp. 255–270). New York: Cambridge University Press.

Saunders, C., & Kastenbaum, R. (1997). *Hospice care on the international scene.* New York: Springer.

Schonwetter, R. S., Han, B., Small, B. J., Martin, B., Tope, K., & Haley, W. E. (2003). Predictors of six-month survival among patients with dementia: An evaluation of hospice Medicare guidelines. *American Journal of Hospice and Palliative Care, 20*(2), 105–113.

Schulz, R., Boerner, K., & Hebert, R. (2008). Caregiving and bereavement, In M. Stroebe, R. O. Hansson, H. Schut, & W. Stroebe (Eds.), *Handbook of bereavement research, and practice: Advances in theory and intervention* (pp. 265–286). Washington, DC: American Psychological Association.

Silverman, P. R. (2004) *Widow to widow: How the bereaved help one another.* New York: Routledge.

Sjoback, H. (1973). *The psychoanalytic theory of defensive processes.* New York: Wiley.

Stjernwärd J., Clark, D. (2003) Palliative medicine—a global perspective. In D Doyle, GWC Hanks, N Cherny, KC Calman (Eds) *Oxford Textbook of Palliative Medicine, third edition.* Oxford: Oxford University Press.

Strasser, S., & Davis, R. M. (1991). *Measuring patient satisfaction for improved patient services.* Ann Arbor, MI: Health Administration Press.

Stroebe, M. S., Hansson, R. O., Stroebe, W., & Schut, H. (Eds.). (2001). *Handbook of bereavement research: Consequences, coping, and caring.* New York: American Psychological Association.

Stroebe, M., Hansson, R. O., Schut, H., & Stroebe, W. (Eds.). (2008). *Handbook of bereavement research, and practice: Advances in theory and intervention.* Washington, DC: American Psychological Association.

Stroebe, M., & Schut, H. (1999). The dual process model of coping with bereavement: Rationale and description. *Death Studies, 23*, 197–224.

Stroebe, W., & Stroebe, M. (1987). *Bereavement and health.* New York: Cambridge University Press.

SUPPORT Investigators. (1995). A controlled trial to improve care for seriously ill patients. *JAMA, 274*(20), 1591–1598.

Taylor, D. H., Ostermann, J., Van Houtven, C. H., Tulsky, J. A., & Steinhauser, K. (2007). What length of hospice use maximizes reduction in medical expenditures near death in the US Medicare program? *Social Science and Medicine, 65*(7), 1466–1478.

Taylor, S. (1989). *Positive illusions: Creative self deceptions and the healthy mind.* New York: Basic Books.

Teno, J., Clarridge, B. R., Casey, V., Welch, L., Wetle, T., Shield, R., et al. (2004). Family perspective on end-of-life care at the last place of care. *JAMA, 291*(1), 88–93.

Teno, J., & Connor, S. R. (2009). Referring a patient and family to high quality palliative care at the close of life: "We met a new personality ..., with this level of compassion and empathy." *Journal of the American Medical Association, 301*(6), 649–657.

Teno, J., Shu, J. E., Casarett, D., Spence, C., Rhodes, R., & Connor, S. (2007). Timing of referral to hospice and quality of care: Length of stay and bereaved family members perceptions of the timing of hospice referral. *Journal of Pain and Symptom Management, 34*(2), 120–125.

Teske, K., Dant, R., & Cleeland, C. (1983). Relationships between nurses' observations and self-report of pain. *Pain, 16*, 289–296.

Vacco v. Quill. 1997 WL 348037, 65 USLW 4695.

Washington v. Glucksberg. 1997 WL 348094, 65 USLW 4669.

Wass, H. (1977). Views and opinions of elderly persons concerning death. *Educational Gerontology, 2*(1), 15–26.

Weil, A. (2005). *Health aging: A lifelong guide to your physical and spiritual well-being.* Missasauga, ON: Random House.

Weisman, A. D. (1972). *On dying and denying: A psychiatric study of terminality.* New York: Behavioral Publications.

Wilkie, D. J., Kampbell, J., Cutshall, S., Halabisky, H., Harmon, H., Johnson, L. P., Weinacht, L., & Rake-Marona, M. (2000). Effects of massage on pain intensity, analgesics and quality of life in patients with cancer pain: a pilot study of a randomized clinical trial conducted within hospice care delivery. *Hospice Journal*, 2000; 15(3):31-53.

Wolinsky, F. D., & Johnson, R. J. (1992). Widowhood, health status, and use of health services by older adults: A cross sectional and perspective approach. *Journal of Gerontology, 47*, S8–S16.

Worden, W. J. (2009). *Grief counseling and grief therapy: A handbook for the mental health practitioner* (4th ed.). New York: Springer.

World Health Organization. (1990). *Cancer pain relief and palliative care* (WHO Technical Report Series 804). Geneva: Author.

Wortman, C., & Silver, R. C. (1989). The myths of coping with loss. *Journal of Consulting and Clinical Psychology, 57,* 349–357.

Zerwekh, J. (1993). Transcending life: The practical wisdom of nursing hospice experts. *American Journal of Hospice and Palliative Care, 10*(5), 26–31.

Zubrod, C. G., Schneidermann, M., Frei, E., III, Brinkley, C., Gold, G. L. Shnider, B., et al. (1960). Appraisal of methods for the study of chemotherapy of cancer in man: Comparative therapeutic trial of nitrogen mustard and triethylene thiophosophoramide. *Journal of Chronic Disease, 11,* 7–33.

Appendix 1: Discussion Questions and Activities by Chapter

Chapter 1: What Are Hospice and Palliative Care?

1. Who is the founder of the modern hospice movement?
2. What is the difference between hospice and palliative care?
3. List at least three of the characteristics found in all hospices.
4. Give the name of the largest national organization that advocates for hospice care.
5. Give one major psychosocial issue facing a dying person.

Activity: Visit a hospice or palliative care program in your community.

Chapter 2: The Interdisciplinary Team

1. What is the preferred type of hospice team functioning?
   A. Unidisciplinary
   B. Multidisciplinary
   C. Interdisciplinary
   D. Transdisciplinary
2. Is the administration part of the hospice team?
3. What is the primary function of the home health aide?
4. Volunteers are primarily used in a professional capacity. Yes or No
5. Counseling is provided by a variety of disciplines. Yes or No

Activity: Interview a hospice team member in your community.

242 • Appendix 1: Discussion Questions and Activities by Chapter

Chapter 3: Symptom Management and Physical Care

1. What are the two major types of pain?
2. Name three other symptoms commonly dealt with in hospice care.
3. The World Health Organization analgesic ladder is divided into what three steps?
4. Pain is what the patient says pain is. True or False
5. Pain medication should be given whenever the patient requests it. True or False

Activity: Interview a hospice patient or family member.

Chapter 4: Psychosocial and Spiritual Care

1. Were Elisabeth Kübler-Ross's five stages of dying an empirically valid description of how people face death?
2. Is it normal for a dying patient to choose not to acknowledge impending death?
3. When told of their terminal illness, do some patients experience relief?
4. Is acceptance the same thing as resignation?
5. When giving bad news, is it important to ask the patients how much they want to know?

Activity: Arrange to have a grief counselor do a death personal awareness exercise with the group.

Chapter 5: Grief and Bereavement

1. What is the minimum amount of time a hospice provides bereavement support to a family?
2. Do most hospices provide bereavement support to the community at large?
3. List two examples of pathological or complicated grief.
4. Give two red flags for complicated grief.
5. Has hospice bereavement follow-up been found to help reduce health care use?

Activity: Visit a funeral home or have the group discuss their reactions to the deaths of relatives.

Chapter 6: Community and Public Engagement

1. Are the advanced health care directives of most dying patients honored when they are in the hospital?
2. Are some hospices involved in responding to trauma in the community?
3. Is there an accepted medical specialty for palliative care?
4. Do many hospices run support groups for cancer patients?
5. Give two topics often found in hospice volunteer training.

Activity: Find out if there are any classes on death and dying offered in the community. Volunteer for a local hospice.

Chapter 7: Managing Hospice and Palliative Care

1. Name at least 2 of the 11 chapters in the NHPCO *Standards of Practice for a Hospice Program*.
2. Can Medicare hospice patients receive curative treatments while in hospice?
3. Name one of the national programs that accredits hospices.
4. What is a per diem payment?
5. What is the difference between a palliative and a prolongative treatment?

Activity: Discuss with your group whether you would want to seek aggressive or palliative treatment if you had an advanced cancer.

Chapter 8: Hospice and Palliative Care in the U.S. Health Care System

1. Name the four levels of care covered under the Hospice Medicare Benefit.
2. Is it difficult for hospices to determine a patient's prognosis?
3. Is hospice care of better quality than traditional care?
4. Are all hospices nonprofit corporations?
5. Is there a medical specialty for hospice and palliative medicine?

Activity: Visit a local hospital to see where cancer patients are cared for. Ask about the hospital's relationship with any hospices.

Chapter 9: Society and Denial

Activity: Discuss with the group how you would want to be told if you had a terminal illness. How would you respond to this news? Would you want to put it out of your mind, or would you want to face it?

Chapter 10: A Right to Die?

Activity: Discuss the issue of physician-assisted suicide with your group. Explore the arguments in favor of it and those against it. Discuss hospice's role in the assisted-suicide debate.

Chapter 11: How Palliative Care Is Unique in the Health Care System

Activity: Discuss with the group whether they see the time before death as a time for personal growth and development. Review some of the unique aspects of hospice care such as prevention of distress, deinstitutionalization, and teamwork.

Chapter 12: How Good Are Hospice and Palliative Care?

Activity: Discuss with the group possible outcomes for hospice care, including measures of symptom distress, quality of life, and satisfaction. See if the group can come up with additional outcomes.

Chapter 13: Hospice and Palliative Care Around the World

Activity: Review the map of palliative care development worldwide. Discuss countries of origin and the ethics of universal provision of relief for suffering around the world. Discuss how countries that lack palliative care might develop care.

Chapter 14: The Future of Hospice and Palliative Care

Activity: Discuss the future of hospice with your group, using the 13 issues for the future of hospice care given in this chapter.

Appendix 2: Organizational Resources

African Palliative Care Association
Kampala, Uganda
http://www.apca.co.ug
APCA's mission is to promote and support affordable and culturally
   appropriate palliative care throughout Africa.

Alliance for Care at the End of Life
1731 King Street, Suite 400
Alexandria, VA 22314
703-647-8505
http://www.afceol.org
The alliance is a 501(c)4 organization created by NHPCO to provide
   a more aggressive and comprehensive advocacy voice for those
   near the end of life.

American Academy of Hospice and Palliative Medicine
4700 W. Lake Avenue
Glenview, IL 60025-1485
847-375-4712
http://www.aahpm.org
This is the professional organization for physicians specializing in
   hospice and palliative medicine.

American Hospice Foundation
2120 L. Street NW, Suite 200
Washington, DC 20037

800-347-1413

http://www.americanhospice.org

The American Hospice Foundation supports programs that serve the needs of terminally ill and grieving individuals of all ages.

Asia Pacific Hospice Palliative Care Network

Singapore

http://www.aphn.org

The Asia Pacific Hospice Palliative Care Network was established to empower and support individuals and organizations committed to alleviating suffering from life-threatening illness in the Asia Pacific region.

Association for Death Education and Counseling

111 Deer Lake Road, Suite 100

Deerfield, IL 60015

847-509-0403

http://www.adec.org

The Association for Death Education and Counseling is a professional organization dedicated to promoting excellence and recognizing diversity in death education, care of the dying, grief counseling, and research in thanatology.

Canadian Hospice Palliative Care Association

http://www.chpca.net

The Canadian Hospice Palliative Care Association is the national association that provides leadership in hospice palliative care in Canada.

Candlelighters Childhood Cancer Foundation

National Office

P.O. Box 498

Kensington, MD 20895-0498

800-366-CCCF (2223)

http://www.candlelighters.org

The Candlelighters Childhood Cancer Foundation National Office was founded in 1970 by concerned parents of children with cancer.

Caring Connections

800-658-8898

http://www.caringinfo.org

Caring Connections is a national consumer and community engagement initiative to improve care at the end of life.

Center for Death Education and Bioethics
University of Minnesota
435 Wimberly Hall
1725 State Street
La Crosse, WI 54601-3742
http://www.uwlax.edu/Sociology/cde&b
The Center for Death Education and Bioethics (CDEB) is a resource
center for academic materials concerned with the issues of death,
dying, and bereavement in contemporary society.

Center for Thanatology Research and Education
391 Atlantic Avenue
Brooklyn, NY 11217-1701
718-858-3026
http://www.thanatology.org
A nonprofit small press, library, museum, resource center, and mail
order bookseller that handles books, media, and periodicals on
one major subject: the study of mortality.

Centers for Disease Control AIDS Information
http://www.cdc.gov/hiv/
As a part of its overall public health mission, the CDC provides leadership in helping control the HIV/AIDS epidemic by working
with communities.

Center to Advance Palliative Care
1255 Fifth Avenue, Suite C-2
New York, NY 10029
212-201-2670
http://www.capc.org
The Center to Advance Palliative Care (CAPC) provides health care
professionals with the tools, training, and technical assistance
necessary to start and sustain successful palliative care programs
in hospitals and other health care settings.

Cicely Saunders International
http://www.cicelysaundersfoundation.org
Cicely Saunders International focuses on carrying out quality
research to improve the care and treatment of all patients with

progressive illness and to make high-quality palliative care available to everyone who needs it.

Compassion and Choices
P.O. Box 101810
Denver, CO 80250-1810
800-247-7421
http://www.compassionandchoices.org
Compassion and Choices is an information center for death-related information; it also provides copies of model durable power of attorney and living will forms.

Compassionate Friends
P.O. Box 3696
Oak Brook, IL 60522-3696
877-969-0010
http://www.compassionatefriends.org
Headquarters for local chapters that provide support and education for parents and siblings on childhood loss.

Cruse Bereavement Care
P.O. Box 800
Richmond, Surrey
TW9 1RG United Kingdom
0844 477 9400
http://www.crusebereavementcare.org.uk
Cruse Bereavement Care exists to promote the well-being of bereaved people and to enable anyone bereaved by death to understand their grief and cope with their loss.

Dougy Center
3909 SE 52nd Avenue
Portland, OR 97206
503-775-5683
http://www.dougy.org
The Dougy Center provides support in a safe place where children, teens, young adults, and their families grieving a death can share their experience.

European Association for Palliative Care
http://www.eapcnet.org
The aim of the European Association for Palliative Care (EAPC) is to promote palliative care in Europe and to act as a focus for all of

those who work, or have an interest, in the field of palliative care at the scientific, clinical, and social levels.

Foundation for Hospices in Sub-Saharan Africa
1731 King Street
Alexandria, VA 22314
703-647-5176
http://www.fhssa.org
The Foundation for Hospices in Sub-Saharan Africa (FHSSA), an affiliate of the National Hospice and Palliative Care Organization (NHPCO; see below), helps to generate resources and technical support for hospice organizations in sub-Saharan Africa, primarily through developing partnerships between U.S. and African hospice and palliative care programs.

Hospice and Palliative Nurses Association
One Penn Center West, Suite 229
Pittsburgh, PA 15276-0100
412-787-9301
http://www.hpna.org
The Hospice and Palliative Nurses Association is a membership association for nurses working in hospice and palliative care; it offers national boards for the certification of hospice nurses.

Hospice Association of America
228 7th Street SE
Washington, DC 20003
202-547-7424
http://www.nahc.org/haa
A membership organization within the National Association for Home Care that advocates for hospice care.

Hospice Education Institute
3 Unity Square
P.O. Box 98
Machiasport, ME 04655-0098
800-331-1620
http://www.hospiceworld.org
The Hospice Education Institute provides members of the public and health care professionals with information and education about the many facets of caring for the dying and the bereaved.

Hospice Foundation of America
1621 Connecticut Ave. NW, Suite 300
Washington, DC 20009
800-854-3402
http://www.hospicefoundation.org
Promotes education on death, dying, and bereavement through publications and teleconferences.

Hospice Information Service
http://www.hospiceinformation.info
A world-class information service for health professionals and members of the public on UK and international palliative care.

International Association for Hospice and Palliative Care
http://www.hospicecare.com
The International Association for Hospice and Palliative Care's mission is to collaborate with, and work to improve the quality of life of, patients with advanced life-threatening conditions and their families by advancing hospice and palliative care programs, education, research, and favorable policies around the world.

International Observatory on End-of-Life Care
http://www.eolc-observatory.net
The IOEOLC website contains vital information on country-level palliative care development.

Latin American Association for Palliative Care
http://www.cuidadospaliativos.org
The Latin American Association for Palliative Care's mission is to promote the development of palliative care in Latin America and the Caribbean through its communication and the integration of all stakeholders in improving the quality of life of patients with progressive incurable diseases and their families.

National Cancer Institute, Cancer Information Service
1-800-422-6237 (1-800-4CANCER)
http://cis.nci.nih.gov
Offers information about conventional and experimental cancer treatments, trials, and protocols and referral to specialized cancer centers.

National Center for Death Education
Mount Ida College

777 Dedham Street
Newton Center, MA 02159
617-928-4500
http://www.mountida.edu/sp.cfm?pageid=307
Offers educational materials and online learning programs.

National Funeral Directors Association
13625 Bishop's Drive
Brookfield, WI 53005
800-228-6332
http://www.nfda.org
Helps to educate about all aspects of care of the deceased.

National Hospice and Palliative Care Organization
1731 King Street, Suite 100
Alexandria, VA 22314
703-837-1500
http://www.nhpco.org
The National Hospice and Palliative Care Organization (NHPCO)
    is the largest nonprofit membership organization representing
    hospice and palliative care programs and professionals in the
    United States.

National Hospice Foundation
1731 King Street, Suite 100
Alexandria, VA 22314
703-516-4928
http://www.nationalhospicefoundation.org
The national charity for end-of-life care in the United States.

National Organization for Victim Assistance
510 King Street, Suite 424
Alexandria, VA 22314
703-535-5500
http://www.trynova.org
An organization that advocates for the rights of victims of crime and
    disaster and provides services to local programs.

National Palliative Care Research Center
Brookdale Department of Geriatrics and Adult Development
P.O. Box 1070
Mount Sinai School of Medicine
One Gustave L. Levy Place

New York, NY 10029
212-241-7447
http://www.npcrc.org
The National Palliative Care Research Center (NPCRC) is committed to stimulating, developing, and funding research directed at improving care for seriously ill patients and their families.

Open Society Institute
International Palliative Care Initiative
400 West 59th Street
New York, NY 10019
212-548-0600
http://www.soros.org/initiatives/health/focus/ipci
The goal of the Open Society Institute's (OSI) International Palliative Care Initiative is to improve end-of-life care for patients and their families, with a special focus on vulnerable populations including the elderly, children, and patients with cancer or HIV/AIDS.

St. Christopher's Hospice
51-59 Lawrie Park Road
Sydenham, London
SE26 6DZ United Kingdom
020 8768 4500
http://www.stchristophers.org.uk
The first modern hospice, St. Christopher's exists to promote and provide skilled and compassionate palliative care of the highest quality.

Widowed Persons Services
American Association of Retired Persons
601 E Street NW
Washington, DC 20049
800-687-2277
http://www.aarp.org/families/grief_loss
Information on grief, loss, and end-of-life issues.

Worldwide Palliative Care Alliance
http://www.thewpca.org
The Worldwide Palliative Care Alliance (WPCA) is the network of national and regional hospice and palliative care organizations around the world. The WPCA works to support efforts to develop hospice and palliative care services globally.

JOURNALS

American Journal of Hospice and Palliative Medicine
Thousand Oaks, CA: Sage
http://ajh.sagepub.com

Death Studies
New York: Routledge
http://www.tandf.co.uk/journals/titles/07481187.asp

European Journal of Palliative Care
Newmarket, UK
http://www.ejpc.eu.com

Illness, Crisis, and Loss
Amityville, NY: Baywood
http://www.baywood.com/journals/PreviewJournals.
   asp?Id=1054-1373

Journal of Pain and Symptom Management
New York: Elsevier
http://www.elsevier.com/wps/find/journaldescription.
   cws_home/505775/description#description

Journal of Palliative Care
Montreal: Center for Bioethics—IRCM
http://www.ircm.qc.ca/bioethique/english/publications/journal_of_
   palliative_care.html

Journal of Palliative Medicine
New Rochelle, NY: Mary Ann Liebert
http://www.liebertpub.com/publication.aspx?pub_id=41

Journal of Pharmaceutical Care in Pain and Symptom Control
Philadelphia: Taylor & Francis Group, Haworth Press
http://www.haworthpress.com/store/product.asp?sku=J088

Mortality
London: Routledge
http://www.tandt.co.uk/Journals/titles/13576275.asp

OMEGA: The Journal of Death & Dying
Amityville, NY: Baywood

http://www.baywood.com/journals/PreviewJournals.
asp?Id=0030-2228

Palliative and Supportive Care
New York: Cambridge University Press
http://journals.cambridge.org/action/displayJournal?jid=PAX

Palliative Medicine
London: Sage
http://www.sagepub.co.uk/journalsProdDesc.nav?prodId=
Journal201823

Supportive Care in Cancer
Berlin: Springer
http://www.springer.com/content/101182

Index